W9-ATM-697

American Contract Bridge League

Introduction to Bridge
Play of the Hand
"Diamond Series"

By Audrey Grant

Copyright © 1988 by American Contract Bridge League
All rights reserved. No part of this book may be reproduced or transmitted in any
form or by any means, electronic or mechanical, including photocopying, recording,
or by any information storage or retrieval system, without permission in writing from
American Contract Bridge League.

Revised 1992
Library of Congress No.: 88-82580
ISBN 0-943855-11-X

American Contract Bridge League

presents

 The ACBL Diamond Series

"The Play of the Hand"

This is the second book in the four–book series that forms the basis of the ACBL teaching program. The other books:

♣ *The ACBL Club Series* — "Bridge: An Introduction"

♥ *The ACBL Heart Series* — "Defense"

♠ *The ACBL Spade Series* — "Introduction to Duplicate Bridge"

American Contract Bridge League
2990 Airways Boulevard
Memphis, TN   38116–3847

(901) 332-5586

American Contract Bridge League

American Contract Bridge League (ACBL) is dedicated to the playing, teaching and advancement of contract bridge.

The current membership of 190,000 includes a wide range — from the thousands who are just learning the joys of bridge to the most proficient players in North America.

ACBL offers a variety of services. These include:

• Tournament play. Thousands of tournaments — North American Bridge Championships (three a year), as well as tournaments at the regional, sectional, local and club levels — are sanctioned annually.

• A monthly magazine. *The BULLETIN* offers articles on tournaments, card play, the Laws, personalities, special ACBL activities, etc.

• A ranking plan. Each time a member does well in any ACBL event, whether it be at the club level or at a North American Bridge Championships, that member receives a masterpoint award. Players achieve rankings and prestige as a result of their cumulative masterpoint holdings.

• A teaching program. This book is one in a series of volumes being used in the ACBL Teaching Program.

• A novice program. ACBL offers special games and programs for players new to bridge and duplicate.

• A charity program. Each year the ACBL Charity Foundation selects a "Charity of the Year," which is the main beneficiary of ACBL charity games and general donations by the membership. All ACBL clubs participate to raise money for the charity.

• An education program. The ACBL Educational Foundation is dedicated to bringing the enjoyment of bridge to people of all ages and firmly believes this can be accomplished through bridge education. Grants are provided for special bridge projects.

• A college program. ACBL cooperates with the nation's colleges in making bridge instruction and play available to college students.

• A youth program (for players age 19 and under). ACBL offers a funded teaching program, youth membership, special events and a quarterly youth newsletter.

• Products. ACBL offers a wide variety of bridge supplies, books, clothing and other bridge-related items through its Customer Service Department.

• Membership in the World Bridge Federation. Each year ACBL sends premiere players to compete in the world championships. In alternate years, ACBL's Junior Team is entered in the World Competition.

• Membership benefits. Credit card programs, member discounts on product purchases, special hotel rates at tournaments, airline discounts for NABCs and supplemental insurances are offered.

ACBL has long been the center of North American bridge activity — in 1987 ACBL celebrated its 50th anniversary. We invite you to enjoy our second half-century with us.

TABLE OF CONTENTS

INTRODUCTION

The American Contract Bridge League's *Diamond Series* Student Text is the second in a four-part series of bridge books for beginning players. It focuses on the play of the hand.

This series of books is unusual in the field of bridge writing for several reasons. First, they were written by a professional educator, Audrey Grant, who also happens to be a bridge player. Accordingly these books encompass all of the sound principles that facilitate learning any subject, and are built on the firm foundation of a basic understanding of the game of bridge.

Next, the technical approach to these books was determined by surveying a cross section of North American bridge teachers. This means that whether a student learns bridge from this book in Vancouver, British Columbia; St. Louis, Missouri; or Orlando, Florida, he'll be able to play bridge with virtually any other bridge player.

Third, the effectiveness of the teaching principles was field-tested in five cities prior to the publication of the first book in this series (*The Club Series Text, 1987*), with more than 800 actual bridge students and at least 25 bridge teachers involved. To the best of ACBL's knowledge, this has never been done before.

Finally, it is the first time in the 50-year history of ACBL that the sanctioning body for bridge in North America has collaborated on basic bridge texts. The end result of the joint effort between Audrey Grant and ACBL is a four-book series that enables the reader to learn bridge (or update his game) in a logical and progressive fashion. More importantly, the reader will have fun while learning the fundamental concepts of good bridge bidding and play.

LESSON 1
Making a Plan

Workshop Material
Group Activities

◆ THE PLAN ◆

For most players, the play of the hand is the most exciting part of the game. You and your partner have exchanged information through the bidding and have decided on what you both think is the best contract. Now one member of the partnership, the declarer, must try to take the required number of tricks. When you are declarer, you will often have to depend on lady luck to help *bring home the contract*. The more you learn about the play of the hand, the more frequently she will be on your side.

As declarer, it's tempting to start to play without making a plan. You usually can see a couple of tricks you can take right away and may feel that everyone's eyes are on you, waiting for you to do something. If you do start with no plan in mind, however, halfway through the play you often will find yourself looking longingly at winners in one hand with no way to reach them. Or you may realize after the hand is finished how you could have made your contract. Learn to take a few moments at the beginning of each hand to make a plan; it is well worth the effort.

The Planning Steps

There are four basic steps when making a plan, whether you are trying to put a man on the moon or play a bridge hand:

1. *Determine your objective.* Start by deciding exactly what you want to do. To put someone on the moon, your objective is to land a man on the moon and return him safely to earth. When playing a bridge hand, your objective is to fulfill your contract.

2. *Determine how close you are to your objective.* By assessing your current situation, see how far you must go to reach your goal. If you're standing on earth, you must travel 240,000 miles to reach the moon. If you're playing a contract that requires nine tricks and you have only seven, you'll need to find two more tricks to make the contract.

3. *Determine the resources you have available.* Once you know what you must do to meet your objective, look at the various resources at your disposal that may help you meet it. Several alternatives may be available. You may have a manned satellite already in orbit, the materials to build a spaceship or the technology to build a transporter ("Beam me up, Scottie"). At the bridge table you may be able to promote an extra trick, take a finesse or trump a loser in dummy.

4. *Decide how to put it all together.* Finally, select the best option from among the various choices. Plan to do things in the right order and prepare for any contingency. Should you build the spaceship first or train the astronaut first? When playing a hand, the best play in an individual suit may not be best when you take the whole deal into consideration.

The PLAN for Playing a Bridge Hand

To help remember the four steps, use the following PLAN:

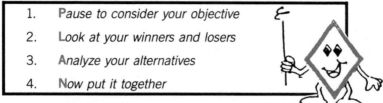

1.	**P**ause to consider your objective
2.	**L**ook at your winners and losers
3.	**A**nalyze your alternatives
4.	**N**ow put it together

Let's take a closer look at each of the steps in the PLAN.

STEP ONE — THE OBJECTIVE

The first step in the PLAN is to *Pause to consider your objective*. Whether you are playing your first hand of bridge or are a world champion, consider your goal. A seasoned player does this automatically, but nevertheless does it. Considering your objective is as simple as reminding yourself of how many tricks you need to make the contract. However, there is a different focus depending on whether you, as declarer, are playing in a suit contract or in notrump.

The Objective in a Notrump Contract

In notrump consider your objective from the point of view of how many tricks, or *winners*, you need. In 1 NT, you need seven winners: the book of six tricks plus one. In 7 NT, you need all 13 tricks: six plus seven.

The Objective in a Suit Contract

In a suit contract consider your objective from the point of view of *losers*, the number of tricks you can afford to lose. In a contract of 4♠ you can afford three losers. The opponents can take three tricks of the 13 tricks available and you will still end up with 10. In a 6♡ contract you can afford only one loser. If you lose one trick, you can still take the remaining 12 to make your contract.

Winners or Losers?

It may seem simpler to count either winners or losers and not worry about whether the contract is in notrump or a suit. In a notrump contract, however, you can predict your winners more easily because the opponents cannot trump them. It is not as easy to determine your losers since you have no trump suit to stop the opponents, and the number of tricks they take may depend on how long a suit they have.

In a suit contract the effect of the trump suit generally makes it easier to focus on losers. The trump suit allows you to avoid losing tricks that you might have to lose at notrump. You can get rid of losers by trumping them in dummy or discarding them on extra winners.

Remember, counting winners or losers is only a matter of perspective. There are times when you need to consider your potential losers in a notrump contract, if you must give up the lead to the opponents. In a suit contract you need to look at the source of your winners. When you are starting to use the PLAN, though, count winners in notrump and losers in a suit contract.

STEP TWO — COUNTING WINNERS

The second step in the PLAN is to *Look at your winners and losers*. By doing this and comparing the result to the objective determined in the first step, you can see how much work you must do to reach your goal.

In a notrump contract start by counting winners or sure tricks — those you can take without giving up the lead. If your objective is to take nine tricks and you can count seven winners, you need to find two additional tricks to make your contract.

Counting Winners in a Suit

How do you count winners? Start by looking at your combined (declarer's hand and dummy's hand) holding in each suit to decide how many winners, or sure tricks, you have. Then add up the total for all four suits. Consider these examples:

DUMMY:	A K Q J	Four sure tricks: the ace, king, queen and jack can be taken without giving up the lead.
DECLARER:	5 4 3 2	

DUMMY:	K Q J 10	This suit has a lot of potential, but before you can take any tricks, the opponents will get the lead with the ace. Therefore, count no sure tricks.
DECLARER:	5 4 3	

Winners don't have to be all in the same hand. Compare this holding with the first example:

DUMMY:	A K 5 4	You have four winners. Since both hands have the same number of cards, taking four tricks in any order won't be difficult.
DECLARER:	Q J 3 2	

The maximum number of winners you can count is the number of cards in the longer hand (i.e., the hand that has more cards in the suit than the other hand):

DUMMY:	A K	Although there are four high cards, you can take only two tricks because that's the number of cards in the longer hand.
DECLARER:	Q J	

DUMMY:	A K 3	Now there are three winners because the longer side is three cards in length. Only one high card will be wasted.
DECLARER:	Q J	

DUMMY:	A K Q 3 2	You have five top cards: the ace, king, queen, jack and 10. The longer side has five cards, so five winners are available in this suit.
DECLARER:	J 10	

You do not need all the high cards if the opponents will have no cards left in the suit after you play your high cards:

DUMMY:	A K Q J 2	Since you have nine cards in the combined hands, the opponents can hold only four. After you play the ace, king, queen and jack, the opponents will have no cards left in the suit and your 2 will be a winner. Count five winners in the suit.
DECLARER:	6 5 4 3	

DUMMY:	A K 3 2	Similarly, this suit combination will produce six winners.
DECLARER:	Q 8 7 6 5 4	

DUMMY:	A K 3	This suit probably will produce six tricks, but one of the opponents may hold all four of the missing cards: J-10-9-2. Count it as three winners, but it will be one of the first places you look for extra tricks if you need them.
DECLARER:	Q 8 7 6 5 4	

Counting Winners in a Hand

Let's count the number of sure tricks in an entire hand. The contract is 3 NT. The objective is to take nine tricks. How many winners do you have?

DUMMY
♠ 9 8 7
♡ A K Q
◇ Q J 6 4 2
♣ 9 8

DECLARER
♠ K Q J 10
♡ 7 6 3
◇ A K 5 3
♣ A 7

In spades there are no sure tricks, although there is potential for extra tricks after the ace is played. You can't count sure tricks yet since you can't take them without giving the lead to the opponents. There are three heart winners: the ♡A, ♡K and ♡Q; five diamond winners: the ◇A, ◇K, ◇Q, ◇J and either the ◇2, ◇4 or ◇6 (the opponents have only four diamonds, so the ◇2, ◇4 or ◇6 will be a winner); one club winner: the ♣A. The total is nine tricks. You have what you need to make your contract.

 COUNTING LOSERS ◆

In a trump contract, start by counting your losers — the tricks you may have to lose to the opponents. If your objective is to make 4♠ and you can count four losers, you must find a way to get rid of one of your losers in order to make your contract.

Counting Losers in a Suit

How do you count losers? Counting losers is usually more challenging than counting winners. Start by looking at each suit in turn, focusing on your (declarer's) holding in the suit but looking across at dummy to see if any high cards can help out. Then, add up the losers in all four suits. Consider the following examples, remembering to focus on declarer's holding:

DUMMY:	Q 4	In declarer's hand there is one loser, the 3. Does dummy have any high-card help? Yes, the queen will take care of the 3, so count no losers in this suit.
DECLARER:	A K 3	

DUMMY:	7 5 4	There are no winners in declarer's hand and dummy can provide no help. Count three losers in this suit. The opponents can take only three tricks in the suit because you will use your trump suit to win the trick if they lead this suit a fourth time.
DECLARER:	J 6 3	

The number of losers in *a side suit* (a suit other than the trump suit) is never counted as more than the number of cards in declarer's hand. This is because it is assumed that declarer will play a trump if the suit is led again. Declarer eventually may run out of trumps, but this is not usually a concern when initially planning the play. This problem will be discussed further in Lesson 7.

The situation is different if declarer has more cards than dummy. Compare these examples:

DUMMY:	8 7 5 4	Declarer has only two cards in the suit — with no high cards to help in dummy, he counts two losers in the suit.
DECLARER:	3 2	

DUMMY:	3 2	Here there are four losers. Even though dummy has only two cards, the focus is on declarer's hand.
DECLARER:	8 7 5 4	

Sequences

When you have a sequence of cards in the combined hands and are missing one or more higher ranking cards, count your losers as the number of missing high cards. For example:

DUMMY:	K Q J	Missing only the ace, count only one loser.
DECLARER:	9 4 2	

DUMMY:	Q 10 4	This time, the ace and king of the suit are missing, so you have two losers.
DECLARER:	J 6 3	

DUMMY:	J 8 4 3	You are missing the ace, king and queen, so count three losers.
DECLARER:	10 9 7 2	

It is interesting to note the difference between counting winners and losers when you have a sequence of cards in a suit. You count only one loser when you have the king, queen and jack, and yet you count no winners for the suit. *A winner, by definition, is a sure trick — one you can take without giving up the lead.* Keep in mind that the actual cards in the suit are the same in both cases. The change in perspective is only to make problem solving easier. It is easier to view the sequence of king, queen and jack as having only one loser in a trump contract, even though, until the ace is played, they are technically all losers.

Unsupported High Cards

If you have only one high card by itself, and the opponents have one or more higher cards, count it as a loser. Your high card may win a trick, but when making your initial plan count it as a loser. For example:

DUMMY:	K 3	There are two losers in declarer's hand. Dummy has the king, which may be a trick, depending on which opponent has the ace. For now, count this suit as two losers.
DECLARER:	8 6	

DUMMY:	8 7 3	Count this suit as three losers. True, the queen might win a trick, but that depends on where the king and ace are. It is best to be cautious.
DECLARER:	Q 6 2	

Broken Sequences

Sometimes the high cards are in broken sequences — you are missing one or more high cards. Look carefully at these suits to determine the number of losers. Consider these examples:

DUMMY:	9 7 2	This time, you have one loser, the king. You may be able to eliminate this loser by trapping it, as you will see later. For now, count one loser.
DECLARER:	A Q J	

DUMMY:	K J 10	You are missing two of the five top cards — the ace and queen. Count two losers.
DECLARER:	8 7 5	

DUMMY:	K J 4	This time you are missing three of the top five cards — the ace, queen and 10. It is possible to lose all three tricks, so count three losers.
DECLARER:	6 3 2	

DUMMY:	A Q 10	The ace will take a trick, but you are missing the king and jack. Count two losers in this suit.
DECLARER:	7 4 2	

Other Combinations

Sometimes you need to consider both the high cards and the length of the suit. Look at this example:.

DUMMY:	K Q 7 6	You are missing the ace, jack, 10, 9 and 8. How many losers you actually have depends on which opponent has the ace and how the missing cards are divided. If they are divided *3-2* (three in one
DECLARER:	5 4 3 2	

opponent's hand, two in the other), you will lose at most two tricks and may lose only one. If they are divided 4-1, you lose two or three tricks. A conservative view would be two losers, and you plan in later steps to eliminate one of them.

Such combinations may be difficult to estimate when you are just starting to play bridge.

7

As you become more familiar with the various techniques for handling such card combinations, you will find it easier to estimate your losers.

Counting Losers in a Hand

Let's count the losers in an entire hand. The contract is 4 ♠, so you can afford only three losers. How many losers do you have?

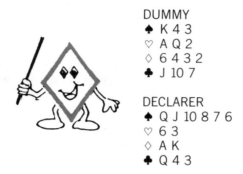

DUMMY
♠ K 4 3
♡ A Q 2
◇ 6 4 3 2
♣ J 10 7

DECLARER
♠ Q J 10 8 7 6
♡ 6 3
◇ A K
♣ Q 4 3

There is one loser in spades, the ♣ A. There are two low hearts in declarer's hand, but dummy has the ♡ A to take care of one of them. Dummy also has the ♡ Q, but that may not prevent the loss of a trick to the ♡ K — count one loser in this suit. There are no losers in diamonds since declarer has only two cards in the suit, the ◇ A and ◇ K. After they have been played, declarer will be able to trump diamonds if they are led. There are two losers in clubs since the ♣ A and ♣ K are missing. The total is four losers — one more than you can afford.

Quick and Slow Losers

As you develop your PLAN, it will become important to distinguish between two types of losers — quick and slow. *A quick loser* is one that the opponents can take as soon as they get the lead. *A slow loser* is one that they could take eventually but not immediately since you have one or more winners still left in the suit.

In the above hand, for example, the spade and club losers are quick losers. The opponents get to make the opening lead and are in a position to take the ♠ A, ♣ A and ♣ K right away. The heart loser is slow. Since you have the ♡ A, the opponents cannot take their ♡ K right away.

If you have too many quick losers, you do not want to give up the lead, since the opponents will be in a position to defeat your contract. If the losers are slow, you can afford to give up the lead if necessary since you will regain it before the opponents take too many tricks. As you will see in later lessons, differentiating between quick and slow losers often will affect how you plan to play the hand. Here are more examples:

DUMMY: K Q J

DECLARER: 4 3 2

This suit has only one loser, but it is a quick loser. As soon as the opponents get the lead, they can take the ace.

DUMMY: A 4 3

DECLARER: 8 7 2

The two losers in this suit are both slow, because if the opponents lead the suit, you can win the first trick with the ace. In Lesson 4 we'll look at how you might get rid of such losers before the opponents have a chance to take them.

STEP THREE — THE ALTERNATIVES

After completing the first two steps of your PLAN, you will know what your objective is and how far you are from it. Sometimes, you will have the winners you need or no more losers than you can afford. In that case, you can skip over the third step and go right to putting it together. More frequently, you will need to develop some extra winners or get rid of some losers to make your contract. The third step of the PLAN tells you to **A**nalyze *your alternatives*.

The Alternatives in Notrump

You can use a variety of techniques to develop the extra winners you need when playing in a notrump contract:

- Promoting high cards

- Developing long suits

- Finessing (leading toward the high card).

When analyzing your alternatives, look at the combined holding in each suit to see which technique may produce one or more of the extra tricks you need. In future lessons you will see how each method can be used to develop extra winners.

The Alternatives in a Suit Contract

The techniques used in notrump also can be applied to suit contracts to help you get rid of extra losers. Because of the effect of the trump suit, two additional methods are commonly used to eliminate losers:

- Trumping losers in dummy

- Discarding losers

In later lessons we will see how to use these alternatives.

STEP FOUR — THE OVERALL STRATEGY

The last step of the PLAN reminds you to **N**ow *put it together*. You may have more than one alternative for developing the extra tricks you need or getting rid of extra losers. Select the best alternative or combine your chances whenever possible. Even if you have the tricks you need, there are some pitfalls to watch out for. In later lessons you will learn to be careful with entries between the two hands and to keep an eye on what the opponents are doing.

Even if you have all the tricks you need, you should keep some things in mind when putting it together.

Avoiding Temptation

Sometimes, you may find yourself trying to get more tricks than you need to make your contract. Look at this example. The contract is 3 NT, and the opening lead is the ♣5.

DUMMY
♠ K Q 4
♡ 7 5 2
◇ K J 10
♣ A Q 7 6

DECLARER
♠ A 3 2
♡ K 8 6
◇ A Q 7 5 3
♣ 3 2

You may be tempted to try to win the first trick with dummy's ♣Q. It seems like a good opportunity to get an extra trick. How are you to know whether this play is a good idea?

Before deciding on the play in a particular suit, make your PLAN. The first step tells you to **Pause to consider your objective**. You need nine tricks to make the contract of 3 NT. The second step reminds you to **Look at your winners and losers**. Count your sure tricks: three spades, five diamonds and one club — a total of nine winners. On this hand the third step, **Analyze your alternatives**, is unnecessary since you already have enough tricks to meet your objective. Move to the fourth step, **Now put it together**, and concentrate your energy on taking your nine winners.

Your PLAN tells you that you can make the contract without playing the ♣Q on the first trick. What could go wrong if you forgot to PLAN and yielded to the temptation to play the ♣Q? If the ♣Q were taken by your right-hand opponent's ♣K, he might lead a heart, perhaps the ♡Q, and your ♡K could be trapped. You might lose four heart tricks along with the club trick and be defeated in a contract you could have made.

Always make your PLAN. If you have all of the tricks you need, take them before something goes wrong.

Avoid Stranding a Suit

Sometimes you have to be careful of the order in which you take your tricks. Take a look at the following suit combination:

DUMMY: A Q J 2

DECLARER: K 3

Counting winners, you, as declarer, have four sure tricks: the ace, king, queen and jack. When a suit is unevenly divided between your hand and dummy, you need to plan the order in which you will play your winners. Suppose you start by winning a trick with dummy's ace, playing the 3 from your hand. Next you lead dummy's 2 to your king. You have taken two tricks but now you have a problem. The queen and jack are left in dummy, but you must lead from your hand and have no cards left in the suit. You may have a winner in another suit that will let you get to dummy, but you won't always be so fortunate.

The secret is to start by winning the first trick with the *high card from the short side*. Win the first trick with the king in your hand and then play the 3 to dummy's ace. Now you are in the right hand at the right time and can take your queen and jack.

Examples:

DUMMY:	J 10 2	To take your five winners, start by winning the first two tricks with dummy's jack and 10. Then play
DECLARER:	A K Q 4 3	dummy's 2 to your ace, king and queen.

DUMMY:	A K 3	Win the first trick with the high card in the short hand, the queen. Then play the 2 to dummy's ace
DECLARER:	Q 2	and king.

Avoid Letting the Opponents Trump Your Winners

If you are in a trump contract, you may lose an extra trick if an opponent plays a trump on one of your winners in a side suit. You can prevent this by playing the trump suit before taking your winners in the side suit. *Draw the opponents' trumps* until they have none left.

When to draw trumps will be discussed further in later lessons. For now, start by drawing the opponents' trumps if you have no more losers than you can afford.

 GUIDELINES FOR DEFENSE

While these lessons concentrate on play of the hand, more frequently you will find yourself defending. One of the most important aspects of defense is the opening lead, since you must decide what to lead before you get to look at dummy. Here are a few guidelines to help you get started when leading against notrump contracts.

Choosing the Suit to Lead Against a Notrump Contract

Because there is no trump suit in a notrump contract, once you get the lead as a defender and have established winners in a suit, you can take them. Declarer is powerless to stop you. The defender's objective, therefore, is to establish enough tricks to defeat the contract and then get the lead and take them. While your high cards are a potential source of tricks, an equally important source is the small cards in long suits. You generally won't have enough high cards to defeat the contract right away, so you must work at establishing low cards as winners, using high cards to help you get the lead back.

With the advantage of the opening lead, you normally want to start your defense by establishing tricks in the longest suit in the combined defenders' hands — the longer the suit, the more potential for establishing your low cards as winners. Unfortunately, you cannot see your partner's hand when making the opening lead, so you must try to determine which is your side's longest suit.

If your partner has bid a suit, he has provided you with some information. With nothing clearly better to do, lead your partner's suit. If the opponents have bid a suit, showing some length in the suit, avoid leading that suit. With no other clues, choose the longest suit in your hand. If you have a choice of long suits, pick the stronger suit.

Suppose you are leading against a contract of 3 NT with the following hand:

♠ J 10 9 8 7
♡ A K
◇ J 10 9
♣ 8 4 2

Left to your own devices, you would choose your longest suit and lead a spade, hoping to establish some of your spades as winners and keeping your high cards in the other suits to help you regain the lead. If your partner had bid diamonds, you would lead a diamond instead.

Always keep your objective in mind. If the contract were 6 NT, rather than 3 NT, you would need only two tricks to defeat it and would start by taking the ♡A and ♡K.

Choosing the Card to Lead Against a Notrump Contract

Once you have selected the suit, decide which card in the suit to lead. If you have three or more high cards (A, K, Q, J or 10) that are touching, lead the top card, e.g., *K-Q-J-7-4, Q-J-10-7*. Leading the top card of an *honor sequence* helps your partner. He knows you have the next-lower card but do not have the next-higher card.

If, as is more common, you do not have a sequence of touching high cards, lead a low card. For reasons we will not go into here, you lead your *fourth-highest* card if you have a suit of four or more cards, e.g., *K-J-7-5, Q-10-8-6-3*. Since you usually lead your longest suit against a notrump contract (picking the stronger suit if you have a choice), you might hear bridge players use the adage, *"Lead the fourth highest of your longest and strongest suit against notrump."* This is good advice if you have nothing better to guide you.

Here are some examples of choosing the opening lead against a contract of 3 NT with nothing to guide you:

♠ A 3
♡ **Q** J 10 6 3
◇ 9 5 3
♣ J 6 3

Pick your longest suit, hearts. With three touching high cards, lead the top card, the ♡Q.

♠ K J 6 **3**
♡ 7 3
◇ J 9 4 2
♣ Q 6 5

With a choice of long suits, pick the stronger, spades. With no honor sequence, lead low, the ♠3.

♠ 2
♡ Q 4
◇ K 10 8 **7** 4 2
♣ A J 6 3

Pick your long suit, diamonds. Traditionally, you would select the fourth-highest card, the ◇7. At this stage in your bridge career, it would not make much difference if you chose the ◇4 or ◇2 instead.

◆ *BIDDING REVIEW* ◆

To refresh your memory, here is a review of some of the bidding concepts covered in the *Club Series* that may prove useful when bidding the practice hands.

HAND VALUATION

High-card Points		Distribution Points	
Ace	4 points	Five-card suit	1 point
King	3 points	Six-card suit	2 points
Queen	2 points	Seven-card suit	3 points
Jack	1 point	Eight-card suit	4 points

OPEN THE BIDDING 1NT OR ONE OF A SUIT

- With fewer than 13 total points, pass.

- With 16 to 18 points and a balanced hand bid 1 NT.

- With 13 to 21 points:
  - With a five-card or longer suit:
    - Bid your longest suit.
    - Bid the higher ranking of two four-card or two six-card suits.

  - With no five-card or longer suit:
    - Bid your longer *minor* suit.
    - Bid the higher ranking of two four-card minor suits or the lower ranking of two three-card minor suits.

RESPONSES TO OPENING BIDS OF 1 NT

0–7
- Bid 2♢, 2♡ or 2♠ with a five-card or longer suit (2♣ is reserved for the Stayman convention*).
- Otherwise, pass.

8–9
- Bid 2 NT (the Stayman convention* can be used to uncover an eight-card major suit fit).

10–14
- Bid 4♡ or 4♠ with a six-card or longer suit.
- Bid 3♡ or 3♠ with a five-card suit.
- Otherwise, bid 3 NT (the Stayman convention* can be used to uncover an eight-card major suit fit).

The Stayman convention will be discussed in Lesson 5.

RESPONSES TO OPENING BIDS OF ONE OF A SUIT

0–5	• Pass

6–10   *Responding to a major suit*
- Raise to the two level with three-card support.
- Bid a new suit at the one level.
- Bid 1 NT.

Responding to a minor suit
- Bid a new suit at the one level.
- Raise to the two level with five-card support.
- Bid 1 NT.

11–12   *Responding to a major suit*
- Raise to the three level with three-card or longer support.
- Bid a new suit.

Responding to a minor suit
- Bid a new suit.
- Raise to the three level with five-card or longer support.

---

13 or more   *Responding to a major suit*
- Jump to 2 NT with a balanced hand.
- Bid a new suit.

Responding to a minor suit
- Bid a new suit.
- Jump to 2 NT with a balanced hand.

◆ SUMMARY ◆

When you are declarer, take the time to make a PLAN before you start to play the hand:

1. **P**ause to consider your objective
2. **L**ook at your winners and losers
3. **A**nalyze your alternatives
4. **N**ow put it together

Consider your objective in terms of the number of winners you must take or losers you can afford to make your contract. In notrump contracts count your winners. In trump contracts count your losers. If you need to develop extra winners or get rid of extra losers, look at each suit to see what alternatives are available. When putting it together, take your tricks if you have enough to make the contract, remembering to *play the high card from the short hand first* and to *draw trumps* if playing in a suit contract.

When defending against a notrump contract, use the adage *fourth highest from your longest and strongest* to guide you when selecting an opening lead.

◆ *GROUP ACTIVITIES* ◆

Exercise One — The Objective

In a contract of 3 NT, the objective is to take nine tricks. In a contract of 2 ♣, the objective is to lose no more than five tricks. Look at the following contracts and decide your objective, counting winners in notrump and losers in a trump contract.

   1) 3 ♣   2) 6 NT   3) 4 ♠   4) 1 NT   5) 2 ◇

_____   _____   _____   _____   _____

Exercise Two — Counting Winners

Count the number of sure winners in each suit — the tricks that you can take without giving up the lead.

	1)	2)	3)	4)	5)
DUMMY:	A K Q	A J	Q J 7 5	A 8 3 2	K Q
DECLARER:	4 2	K Q	A K 4 3 2	K 9 5	4 2
	_____	_____	_____	_____	_____

Exercise Three — Counting Losers

Count the number of losers that declarer has in each suit — the tricks that could be lost to the opponents. Are the losers quick or slow?

	1)	2)	3)	4)	5)
DUMMY:	K Q J 4	J 10 9 8	9 8 6 2	A 5	K 6 4
DECLARER:	9 8	5 4 3 2	A 5	9 8 6 2	8 5
Losers:	_____	_____	_____	_____	_____
Quick/Slow:	_____	_____	_____	_____	_____

	6)	7)	8)	9)	10)
DUMMY:	Q 4 2	K 7 6	7 4 3 2	K Q 5	A J 10
DECLARER:	9 8 3	J 10 9 3	A K J	7 4 2	8 4 2
Losers:	_____	_____	_____	_____	_____
Quick/Slow:	_____	_____	_____	_____	_____

Exercise Four — High Card from the Short Side

With what card would you win the first trick in each of the following suits?

	1)	2)	3)	4)	5)
DUMMY:	A Q J 10 3	A 4	A J 4	Q 5	K Q 6
DECLARER:	K 2	K Q 5	K Q 7 3	A K J 7	A J 9
	_____	_____	_____	_____	_____

Exercise Five — Leading Against a Notrump Contract

Which card would you lead from each of the following hands against a contract of 3 NT?

1) ♠ J 6 3
   ♡ Q 7
   ◇ K Q J 8 5
   ♣ 10 8 4

2) ♠ 9 4
   ♡ J 10 8 6
   ◇ Q J 10 8
   ♣ A 7 3

3) ♠ 10 8 6 5 2
   ♡ A J 7
   ◇ K 5
   ♣ Q 5 2

_____

_____

_____

Exercise Six — Review of Opening Bids

You are the dealer. What would you say with each of the following hands?

1) ♠ K 9 7
   ♡ J 4
   ◇ Q J 9 8 4
   ♣ K 7 3

2) ♠ A Q
   ♡ K 10 5
   ◇ K J 4
   ♣ Q J 10 8 4

3) ♠ A K J 5
   ♡ 3
   ◇ Q 10 7 5 3
   ♣ Q 9 4

_____

_____

_____

4) ♠ Q 10 8 7 4
   ♡ A K
   ◇ A K 10 7 3
   ♣ 6

5) ♠ A J 5 3
   ♡ Q J 6
   ◇ A 4
   ♣ Q 9 6 2

6) ♠ K 8 4 2
   ♡ 7
   ◇ A Q J 5
   ♣ A K Q 4

_____

_____

_____

Exercise Seven — Review of Responses to 1 NT Opening Bids

Your partner opens the bidding 1 NT. What would you respond with each of the following hands?

1) ♠ J 8 4
   ♡ Q 6 2
   ◇ 10 8 5 3
   ♣ J 9 3

2) ♠ 10 8 6 4 3 2
   ♡ J 5
   ◇ 9 6
   ♣ J 10 9

3) ♠ K 9
   ♡ Q J 8
   ◇ J 10 8 3
   ♣ Q 8 6 3

_____

_____

_____

4) ♠ A 5
   ♡ J 10 8 6 4 3
   ◇ K Q 6
   ♣ 5 2

5) ♠ K J 9 8 3
   ♡ A 4 2
   ◇ 7 2
   ♣ Q 10 3

6) ♠ 7 2
   ♡ K 5
   ◇ Q 10 9 7 5 2
   ♣ A 4 2

_____

_____

_____

Exercise Eight — Review of Responses to Opening Bids in a Suit

Your partner opens the bidding 1♡. What would you respond with each of the following hands?

1) ♠ J 7 3
   ♡ 9 4
   ◇ Q 4 3
   ♣ 10 8 7 6 2

2) ♠ 8 2
   ♡ Q J 5
   ◇ J 9 6 4 2
   ♣ K 8 3

3) ♠ Q 9 6 4
   ♡ A 2
   ◇ 7 4 3
   ♣ Q 9 5 2

4) ♠ Q J 10
   ♡ 6 2
   ◇ K 9 7 6 3
   ♣ J 10 5

5) ♠ 8 4
   ♡ Q 6
   ◇ A 8 3 2
   ♣ K Q 10 6 2

6) ♠ A K 4
   ♡ K J 6 5
   ◇ 10 9 6 3
   ♣ 8 7

Bid: _____   _____   _____

Exercise Nine — Counting Winners

Turn up all the cards on the first pre-dealt hand. Put each hand dummy style at the edge of the table in front of each player.

Dealer: North

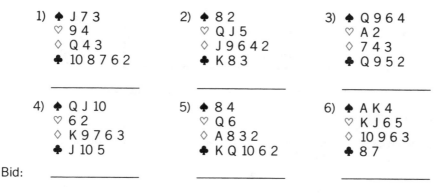

```
                    ♠ 7 5
                    ♡ 7 3 2
                    ◇ A Q 10 6 3
                    ♣ A 9 2
   ♠ K Q J 10 6                       ♠ 9 4 3
   ♡ A 10 6                           ♡ Q J 9 8 4
   ◇ 9 7                              ◇ 2
   ♣ 10 6 5                           ♣ J 8 7 4
                    ♠ A 8 2
                    ♡ K 5
                    ◇ K J 8 5 4
                    ♣ K Q 3
```

The Bidding

Neither North nor East has enough to open the bidding. With a balanced hand and 17 total points, what opening bid best describes South's hand?

West passes. North is the captain and decides the level and denomination of the contract. With 11 total points and no interest in the major suits, what should North's decision be?

How will the auction proceed from there?

What will be the contract? Who will be declarer?

The Play

Which player makes the opening lead? What will the opening lead be?

Declarer starts by making a PLAN:

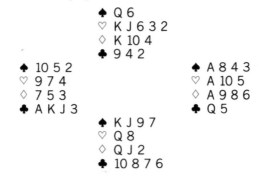

1. **P**ause to consider your objective
2. **L**ook at your winners and losers
3. **A**nalyze your alternatives
4. **N**ow put it together

After going through the four steps, how will declarer play the hand?

Exercise Ten — Taking Winners

Turn up all the cards on the second pre-dealt hand. Put each hand dummy style at the edge of the table in front of each player.

Dealer: East

```
                          ♠ Q 6
                          ♡ K J 6 3 2
                          ◇ K 10 4
                          ♣ 9 4 2
         ♠ 10 5 2                          ♠ A 8 4 3
         ♡ 9 7 4                           ♡ A 10 5
         ◇ 7 5 3                           ◇ A 9 8 6
         ♣ A K J 3                         ♣ Q 5
                          ♠ K J 9 7
                          ♡ Q 8
                          ◇ Q J 2
                          ♣ 10 8 7 6
```

The Bidding

East has a balanced hand. Why can it not be opened 1 NT? What would East open?

South passes. Does West have a suit he can bid at the one level? Why can West not bid a new suit at the two level? What will West respond?

How will the auction proceed from there?

What will be the contract? Who will be declarer?

The Play

Which player makes the opening lead? What will the opening lead be?

Declarer starts by making a PLAN. After going through the four steps, how will declarer play the hand? In putting it together, why must declarer be careful about how he plays the club suit?

Exercise Eleven — Counting Losers

Turn up all the cards on the third pre-dealt hand. Put each hand dummy style at the edge of the table in front of each player.

Dealer: South

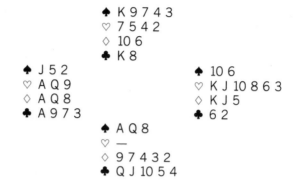

```
                  ♠ K 9 7 4 3
                  ♡ 7 5 4 2
                  ◇ 10 6
                  ♣ K 8
 ♠ J 5 2                          ♠ 10 6
 ♡ A Q 9                          ♡ K J 10 8 6 3
 ◇ A Q 8                          ◇ K J 5
 ♣ A 9 7 3                        ♣ 6 2
                  ♠ A Q 8
                  ♡ —
                  ◇ 9 7 4 3 2
                  ♣ Q J 10 5 4
```

The Bidding

South does not have enough to open the bidding. With 17 points and a balanced hand, what will West open?

North passes. East is the captain. At what level does the partnership belong? What should be the denomination of the contract? What will East respond?

How will the auction proceed from there?

What will be the contract? Who will be declarer?

The Play

Which player makes the opening lead? What will the opening lead be?

Declarer starts by making a PLAN. After going through the four steps, how will declarer play the hand? In putting it together, what precaution must declarer take?

Exercise Twelve — Drawing Trumps

Turn up all the cards on the fourth pre–dealt hand. Put each hand dummy style at the edge of the table in front of each player.

Dealer: West

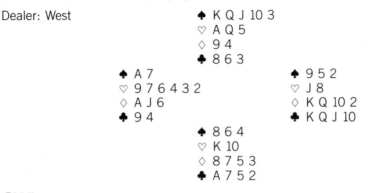

The Bidding

West does not have enough to open the bidding. What will be North's opening bid?

East passes. Does South have support for partner's major suit? What will South respond?

How will the auction proceed from there?

What will be the contract? Who will be declarer?

The Play

Which player makes the opening lead? What will the opening lead be?

Declarer starts by making a PLAN. Why can declarer skip to the fourth question in the plan after answering the first two questions? Why may declarer be tempted to delay drawing trumps and play another suit? Why is this not a good idea?

LESSON 2
Developing Tricks — Promotion and Length

Promoting High Cards
Developing Long Suits
Promotion and Length Combined
Guidelines for Defense
Bidding Review — Rebids by Opener
Summary

Workshop Material
Group Activities

The first step of the PLAN tells you to **P**ause to consider your objective. Once you have determined your goal, the second step of the PLAN reminds you to **L**ook at your winners and losers. After you have completed these two steps, you will find yourself in one of two situations: either you have enough winners (or few enough losers) to make your contract or you don't. As you saw in the first lesson, if you have enough tricks, you can skip over the third step and concentrate on putting it together. This may require some care — taking your tricks in the right order or getting rid of the opponents' trumps first. You do not have to worry about developing additional tricks or getting rid of extra losers.

Usually, however, when you compare the number of tricks you need to make your contract with the number of tricks you have, you will find that you have too few winners or too many losers. This is where the third step in the PLAN, **A**nalyze your alternatives, comes into use. In this lesson we'll look at two ways to develop the extra tricks you need — through promotion and length. These methods are useful in both notrump and suit contracts.

◆ *PROMOTING HIGH CARDS* ◆

The most common, and certain, method of developing tricks is through the force of your own high cards to drive out the opponents' higher cards. Let's see how this works.

The Value of High Cards

The more high cards you have in a suit, the more potential the suit has for taking tricks, even when the opponents have one or more higher cards. Here is an example:

DUMMY:	K Q J 10	There are no sure winners in this suit, but you can use the king to drive out the opponents' ace and promote your queen, jack and 10 into three winners.
DECLARER:	5 4 3 2	

With a suit such as this, it does not matter whether you lead the king, queen, jack or 10. They all have equal power since the ace is the only higher card the opponents have. To keep discussions simple, we will assume that you lead your highest card in such situations. Note, also, that the opponents are not forced to win the first trick with their ace. However, it will make no difference, since you can continue by leading the queen or jack to make them take the ace. You will still end up with three winners.

In a suit contract you would view the above holding a little differently. Count it as one loser. However, you still need to do the work of promoting three winners by driving out the opponents' ace.

The idea of promotion is very straightforward. You are making a trade-off. You are willing to give the opponents one or more tricks in return for developing one or more tricks of your own. Consider this combination:

DUMMY:	4 3 2	You are missing the ace and king but you have the next three highest cards in the suit. Use the queen to drive out the opponents' king, and the jack to drive out their ace. Your 10 then will be promoted into a winner.
DECLARER:	Q J 10	

Sometimes a lot of patience is required to develop tricks through promoting high cards.

DUMMY: J 10 9 8

DECLARER: 5 4 3 2

A trick is still available in this suit after the opponents' ace, king and queen have been played. This may seem like a lot of work to take one trick since you have to give up the lead three times, but a trick that is won by a low card is as worthwhile as a trick won by an ace. You're taking a little time to turn a low card into an *ace*.

When the Suit Is Unevenly Divided

Cards are winners only if you can reach them once they have been promoted. If both dummy and declarer have the same number of cards in a suit, there is no problem since you will always have a low card left on one side of the table to get to the winners on the other side. If the cards are unevenly divided, with more on one side of the table than the other, you must be more careful. Look at this layout of the diamond and club suits in a hand:

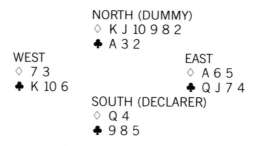

NORTH (DUMMY)
◇ K J 10 9 8 2
♣ A 3 2

WEST
◇ 7 3
♣ K 10 6

EAST
◇ A 6 5
♣ Q J 7 4

SOUTH (DECLARER)
◇ Q 4
♣ 9 8 5

The diamond suit has no sure tricks, but with all the high cards except the ace, you plan to promote five winners by driving out the opponents' ◇ A. Even though the diamond suit is divided unevenly between the two hands, there does not appear to be a problem — you have the ♣A in the dummy as a way to reach your winners once they are established. You still must be careful, however, of the order in which you play your cards.

Suppose you start by playing the ◇ 4 from your hand to dummy's ◇ K. East can make things difficult in one of two ways. If East wins this trick and leads back a club, your ♣A will be driven out. You can lead dummy's ◇ 2 back to your established ◇ Q, but now you will be in your hand with no way back to dummy! You have no small diamonds left and the ♣A is gone. Alternatively, East could refuse to win the first trick. You would now lead the ◇ 2 back to your ◇ Q, and East again may refuse to take the ace. You have won two tricks but are in your hand and have no diamonds left. You can play a club to dummy's ♣A, lead another diamond and force East to take the ◇ A, but now you are in the same position as before. Dummy's remaining diamonds are established but you have no way to get to them.

The solution is to use the same principle we came across in Lesson 1 when taking winners: *Play the high card from the short side first*. Look at the difference this makes. Start by playing the ◇ Q from your hand. If East wins the ace, you will have no problem taking your remaining winners. If East does not win the ace, continue by leading your ◇ 4 to dummy's ◇ K. If East wins the ace, you still have the ♣A in dummy to get to your established winners. If East refuses to take the ace, you are in dummy and can continue by leading the ◇ J to force East to take the ace. Once again, the ♣A remains in dummy as a way to get to the established winners.

A small change in the order of play, but what a difference! Here are some more examples:

DUMMY:	J 3	To establish three winners, start by playing the high card from the short side first. If you are in the dummy, lead the jack. If you are in your hand, lead the 4 to dummy's jack.
DECLARER:	K Q 10 4	

DUMMY:	Q 10 8 3 2	Start by leading the king from your hand. If the opponents do not take their ace, continue by leading your remaining high card from the short side, the jack.
DECLARER:	K J 5	

Losing Tricks to the Opponents

When you have all of the tricks you need, you generally take your winners and get on with the next hand. The situation is different when you have to develop extra tricks. As you have seen with the idea of promotion, the development of tricks may involve giving up the lead to the opponents.

At first glance this may appear dangerous. Every time you give up the lead, the opponents have a chance to take their tricks — they may be able to defeat your contract. Losing tricks is a normal part of the game. If you are in a contract of 3 NT, you do not need to take 12 or 13 tricks, only nine. You can afford to lose four tricks. You also do not need to take the first nine. The idea is to lose tricks when you gain the most by doing so.

Most of the time, it is best to *take your losses early*. If you need to promote tricks in a suit, go to work on that suit, giving up tricks as necessary while you still have winners left in the other suits. Your other winners will prevent the opponents from taking tricks and also will help you to regain the lead and take your newly-established winners.

The concept of *taking your losses early* is easier to understand by looking at a full hand. The contract is 3 NT, and the opening lead is the ♡ Q.

```
                         NORTH (DUMMY)
                         ♠ A 6 4
                         ♡ K 9 6
                         ◇ K 8 2
                         ♣ 9 7 6 3
         WEST                              EAST
         ♠ J 9 7                           ♠ Q 10 3 2
         ♡ Q J 10 7 4                      ♡ 8 5
         ◇ 9 5 3                           ◇ Q J 7 6
         ♣ A 4                             ♣ 8 5 2
                         SOUTH (DECLARER)
                         ♠ K 8 5
                         ♡ A 3 2
                         ◇ A 10 4
                         ♣ K Q J 10
```

Since the contract is 3 NT, you need nine tricks to fulfill the contract. You have two sure tricks in spades, two in hearts and two in diamonds, a total of six. Three more tricks need to be developed. It's time to **A**nalyze your alternatives and look at each suit to consider the potential for developing extra tricks. The club suit jumps out at you. By driving out the opponents' ace, you can promote the remaining three clubs into the winners you need.

When putting it together, remember to *take your losses early* and immediately lead clubs when you win the first trick. After the opponents win their ace, you will have high cards left in all the other suits and can win whichever suit they lead. Now that you have your nine winners, you can *take your tricks and run*.

Look at what would happen if you did not lose the club trick early. Suppose you start by taking your winners: the ♡A and ♡K, the ♠A and ♠K, and the ◇A and ◇K. You have six tricks in the bag, but when you belatedly lead the ♣K to get your extra winners, the opponents are in control. By taking your ♡A and ♡K, you promote all of West's remaining hearts into winners. Similarly, you set up winning spade and club tricks in the opponents' hands. When they get in with the ♣A, they will take enough of their winners to defeat your contract.

Think of it from the defenders' point of view. When West leads the ♡Q, he is hoping to promote his lower-ranking hearts into winners — just as you intend to promote your clubs into winners. If you take both the ♡A and ♡K right away, you are doing West's work for him!

◆ *DEVELOPING LONG SUITS* ◆

Tricks can be developed not only from high cards but also through length. A long suit contains a lot of trick-taking potential. The more cards your side holds in a suit, the fewer the opponents hold. After the suit has been played a few times, the opponents will have no cards left in the suit, and all your remaining cards will be winners, whether they are high cards or low cards.

The Division of a Suit

When you first start playing bridge, keeping track of the cards you hold in a suit is enough to keep you busy. What the opponents hold remains a mystery. As your experience and confidence grow, it becomes increasingly important to consider the opponents' *holding* in each suit. The key is to recognize that each suit has only 13 cards. If you and your partner have eight of them, the opponents have five; if you have nine cards in the combined hands, the opponents have only four.

When you are declarer, you know the exact number of cards the opponents hold in each suit but not how they are divided between the opponents' hands. For example, if you have seven cards in a suit, their six cards could be divided 3-3 (three in one opponent's hand and three in the other) or 4-2 or even 5-1 or 6-0.

Sometimes, the opponents' bidding will suggest how the missing cards are divided. More often, you will have to guess (and find out for sure as the hand is played out). Since it is important to know what to expect, here are some useful guidelines:

- An even number of missing cards usually will divide slightly unevenly. For example, if the opponents have four cards, they are likely to be divided 3-1 rather than 2-2; if the opponents have six cards, they are likely to be divided 4-2 rather than 3-3; if the opponents have eight cards, they are likely to be divided 5-3 rather than 4-4.

- *An odd number of missing cards usually will divide as evenly as possible.* For example, if the opponents have three cards, they are likely to be divided 2-1; if the opponents have five cards, they are likely to be divided 3-2; if the opponents have seven cards, they are likely to be divided 4-3.

Here is the same information on the likely division of the opponents' cards shown in tabular form:

NUMBER OF MISSING CARDS	MOST LIKELY DISTRIBUTION
3	2–1
4	3–1
5	3–2
6	4–2
7	4–3
8	5–3

Let's see how to make use of this information when looking for extra winners or trying to eliminate losers.

Developing Long Suits

Some suits will develop extra tricks through length no matter how the missing cards are divided. For example:

DUMMY: A K Q J 3 2

DECLARER: 6 5 4

You have nine cards, the opponents have four. Even if one opponent has all four of the missing cards, he will have none left by the time you have played the ace, king, queen and jack. Your 3 and 2 will be winners.

In some cases, you will just have to hope for a favorable division of the opponents cards:

DUMMY: A K Q 2

DECLARER: 6 5 4 3

You have eight cards, the opponents have five. If one opponent has all five of the missing cards or four of the five, he will have a high card left after you have played your ace, king and queen. The most likely distribution of the missing cards, however, is 3-2. If this is the case, you will get four tricks from the suit instead of three. A typical layout of the missing cards might be:

                              NORTH (DUMMY)
                              A K Q 2
            WEST   EAST
            J 9 7   10 8
                              SOUTH (DECLARER)
                              6 5 4 3

In the following example you would have to be lucky to get an extra trick:

DUMMY: K Q 3 2   You have seven cards, leaving the opponents with
                                 six. You will get an extra trick if the missing cards
DECLARER: A 5 4   are divided 3-3. After you have played the ace,
                                 king and queen, neither opponent will have
any left, so your remaining low card will be a winner. However, it is more likely that the
missing cards will divide 4-2 than 3-3, and they could be divided 5-1 or 6-0.

Frequently, you must let the opponents win one or more tricks to establish a long suit.
Look at this example:

DUMMY: A K 3 2   You have eight cards, the opponents have five.
                                 Hopefully, the missing cards are divided 3-2, but
DECLARER: 7 6 5 4   even so, you cannot win all the tricks. To develop
                                 an extra trick in this suit, you must give up a trick.

The complete layout of the suit could be:

                              NORTH (DUMMY)
                              A K 3 2
            WEST   EAST
            J 9   Q 10 8
                              SOUTH (DECLARER)
                              7 6 5 4

After you play your ace and king, East still has the queen left. Play the suit again, letting
East win a trick. When you next get the lead, you will have the only cards left in the suit
and will take a trick with them. You get three of the four tricks by *sacrificing* a trick to
the opponents.

Here are more examples where you must give up tricks in order to establish long suits:

DUMMY: A 4 3 2   You have eight cards, the opponents have five. If
                                 the missing cards are divided 3-2, you can develop
DECLARER: 8 7 6 5   a second trick in the suit by giving up *two* tricks.

DUMMY: A 9 7 6 5   You have nine cards, the opponents have four. If
                                 the opponents' cards are divided 2-2, you can get
DECLARER: 8 4 3 2   four tricks in the suit by taking your ace and then
                                 giving up a trick. If the opponents' cards are divid-
ed 3-1, you still can get three tricks but will have to give up two tricks first. If one opponent
had all four of the missing cards, you eventually could establish one trick but would have
to give up three tricks.

DUMMY: K 6 5 4 3

DECLARER: A 2

You have seven cards, the opponents have six. You can try playing the ace and king and then leading the suit again from dummy. If the missing cards are divided 3-3, you will establish two extra win-

ners in dummy. If the suit is divided 4-2, you will have to get back to dummy and give up another trick to finally set one up for yourself. If the suit breaks 5-0, you get only the two tricks you started with — the ace and king.

DUMMY: A K Q 3 2

DECLARER: 6 5 4

With this suit you won't have to lose any tricks if the opponents' cards divide 3-2, as is most likely. If they divide 4-1, you will have to give up a trick to set up your remaining low card as a winner.

DUMMY: 10 8 7 4 3

DECLARER: 9 6 5 2

The more cards you have in the suit, the more potential for developing tricks. Lead the suit, giv- ing up a trick. When you next get the lead, play the suit again, giving up another trick. If the miss-

ing cards are divided 2-2, your remaining cards are winners. If not, lead the suit again at your next opportunity and you still can establish two tricks.

A Complete Hand

Let's take a look at the development of a long suit in a complete hand. You are in 3 NT, and the opening lead is the ♠ 3.

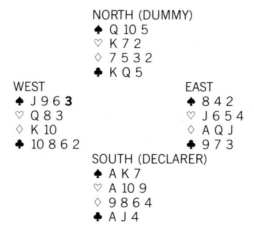

```
                    NORTH (DUMMY)
                    ♠ Q 10 5
                    ♡ K 7 2
                    ◇ 7 5 3 2
                    ♣ K Q 5
WEST                                    EAST
♠ J 9 6 3                               ♠ 8 4 2
♡ Q 8 3                                 ♡ J 6 5 4
◇ K 10                                  ◇ A Q J
♣ 10 8 6 2                              ♣ 9 7 3
                    SOUTH (DECLARER)
                    ♠ A K 7
                    ♡ A 10 9
                    ◇ 9 8 6 4
                    ♣ A J 4
```

Your objective is to take nine tricks, and you start with eight winners: three sure tricks in spades, two in hearts and three in clubs. You need to find one more trick. When you analyze your alternatives, the only suit that presents some potential is diamonds. Even though you have no high cards in the suit, you do have eight cards in the combined hands. The opponents have only five, and hopefully they are divided 3-2.

As you put it together, remember the earlier advice to *take your losses early*. After win- ning the first spade trick, play a diamond immediately, giving up a trick. Whatever the opponents lead back, you can win and lead another diamond, giving up a second trick in the suit. Since you still have winners left in all the other suits, you can win whatever the opponents lead and play a diamond once again. Although you also lose this trick, you finally have established the extra trick you need and can take your remaining winners when you get the lead back.

This seems like a lot of work, but making your PLAN and knowing about developing long suits really pays off when you make a contract like this one.

When the Suit Is Unevenly Divided

When a suit is unevenly divided between your hand and dummy, be careful not to strand the winners in the long hand after you establish them. Look at this layout of a suit:

```
                    NORTH (DUMMY)
                    A K 4 3 2
        WEST                        EAST
        Q J 9                       10 8
                    SOUTH (DECLARER)
                    7 6 5
```

You have eight cards in the suit. If the missing cards are divided 3-2, you plan to develop two more tricks by giving up one trick. If dummy had no other high cards, deciding which trick to give up to the opponents would be crucial. Suppose you try taking the ace and king and then leading the suit again, giving West a trick with the queen. The remaining cards in the suit are:

```
                    NORTH (DUMMY)
                    4 3
        WEST                        EAST

                    SOUTH (DECLARER)
```

You have two winners in dummy but no way to reach them! Instead, remember the advice to *take your losses early* and give up the first trick by playing a low card from both hands Now the suit looks like this:

```
                    NORTH (DUMMY)
                    A K 4 3
        WEST                        EAST
        Q J                         10
                    SOUTH (DECLARER)
                    7 6
```

You have lost one trick, but when you regain the lead, take the ace and king. You will be in dummy to take your remaining two winners. In fact, you could achieve the same result by winning the first trick and giving up the *second* trick.

Here is a similar case:

```
                    NORTH (DUMMY)
                    A 9 7 6 3
      WEST                          EAST
      K J                           Q 10 5
                    SOUTH (DECLARER)
                    8 4 2
```

To establish extra winners in this suit, you must give up two tricks. If dummy has no other high cards, keep the ace until the suit is established. Give up a trick by playing a low card from both hands. This is called *ducking* a trick. When you next get the lead, *duck* another trick by playing low from both hands. The remaining cards are:

```
                    NORTH (DUMMY)
                    A 9 7
      WEST                          EAST
                                    Q
                    SOUTH (DECLARER)
                    8
```

Now you are in business. When you next get the lead, play your 8 to dummy's ace and take your two established winners.

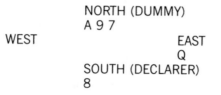

PROMOTION AND LENGTH COMBINED

It is often possible to combine the idea of promotion with that of length when developing tricks in a suit.

Promotion and Long Suits Working Together

Take a look at this suit layout:

```
                    NORTH (DUMMY)
                    K Q J 3
      WEST                          EAST
      10 5                          A 9 2
                    SOUTH (DECLARER)
                    8 7 6 4
```

You start with no sure tricks in this suit but plan to promote the queen and jack into winners by playing the king to drive out the opponents' ace. Since you have eight cards in the combined hand, you will get another trick if the suit divides 3-2. After the king, queen and jack have been played, the opponents will have no cards left in the suit.

DUMMY:	7 5 3	You can lead the queen to drive out the king, and the jack to drive out the ace, promoting your 10 into a winner. If the opponents' cards are divided 3-2, your 4 and 2 also will be winners.
DECLARER:	Q J 10 4 2	

30

DUMMY: 6 5 3 2

DECLARER: K Q J

In this suit you plan to promote two tricks by using your king to drive out the opponents' ace. In addition, you may end up with a third trick if the missing cards are divided exactly 3-3. You will have to be lucky, since the missing cards are more likely to be divided 4-2. Even if they are 3-3, you will need a high card in another suit in dummy so you can reach your winner.

Another Look at Winners and Losers

Knowing about promotion and the development of long suits helps you decide whether you need to develop extra winners or get rid of losers. Take a look at your holding in this suit:

```
                    NORTH (DUMMY)
                    A 6 4 3
     WEST                            EAST
     ?                               ?
                    SOUTH (DECLARER)
                    9 7 5 2
```

When counting winners, you would count one sure trick in this suit. When counting losers, you would count three losers. When analyzing your alternatives, you would look at this suit and see that you are missing only five cards and they are probably divided 3-2. You hope the actual layout is something like this:

```
                    NORTH (DUMMY)
                    A 6 4 3
     WEST                            EAST
     K J 10                          Q 8
                    SOUTH (DECLARER)
                    9 7 5 2
```

In a notrump contract you could plan to develop an extra winner by giving up two tricks. Alternatively, in a suit contract you could plan to eliminate one of your losers by giving up two tricks. Two sides of the same coin.

Of course, developing an extra winner or eliminating an extra loser is not guaranteed. The actual layout could be:

```
                    NORTH (DUMMY)
                    A 6 4 3
     WEST                            EAST
     K J 10 8                        Q
                    SOUTH (DECLARER)
                    9 7 5 2
```

You cannot get more than your one sure trick and you still have three losers in the suit. That is why you count one sure trick or three losers in the second step of your PLAN. Hoping that the missing cards are divided 3-2 is one of your alternatives in the third step. You may have better prospects elsewhere.

Choosing the Suit to Develop

Sometimes you will have a choice of suits to develop. In general, pick the suit that will give you the most tricks. This is usually the suit in which you have the most cards. Compare these two suits:

1)   DUMMY: A K 6 5 2   2)   DUMMY: A K 6 5 2

      DECLARER: 4 3   DECLARER: 7 4 3

If you need to develop two more tricks to make your contract, the second suit has much more potential than the first. In the first case you have only seven cards, so the opponents have six. You can hope that the missing cards are divided 3-3 and plan to give up one trick while developing two more. However, it is more likely that the missing cards are divided 4-2 and they could be 5-1 or 6-0.

In the second case you have eight cards and are missing five. It is quite likely that the missing cards are divided 3-2. By giving up a trick in the suit, you can develop the two extra winners you need.

If you have the same number of cards in both suits, the suit that is more unevenly divided has the more potential for extra tricks. Compare these two suits:

1)   DUMMY: A K 6 5   2)   DUMMY: A K 6 5 2

      DECLARER: 7 4 3 2   DECLARER: 7 4 3

In both cases you have eight cards and the opponents have five. If the missing cards are divided 3-2, you can develop one extra trick in the first example by giving up a trick. In the second example, however, you will get *two* extra tricks if the suit divides 3-2.

◆ *GUIDELINES FOR DEFENSE* ◆

In the previous lesson you saw that you generally lead your longest suit against a notrump contract, hoping to establish enough winners to defeat declarer. When you lead against a suit contract, there are some other considerations.

Choosing the Suit to Lead Against a Trump Contract

When defending against a notrump contract, you often are willing to give up one or two tricks to establish your long suit. If you can regain the lead, you can take all your winners. When defending against a suit contract, it may not do you much good to develop your long suit — by the time you get to lead your winners, declarer usually will be able to trump them. If you must give up a trick while establishing your winners, you may never get it back.

Instead of automatically leading your longest suit, you often look for a *safe* suit to lead — one that is unlikely to present declarer with a trick he could not get himself. A suit with an honor sequence is usually safe (e.g., K-Q-J or Q-J-10) or a suit with no high cards (e.g., 8-7-4-2). A suit with only one high card is usually more dangerous (e.g., K-7-5-2). If you have two touching high cards, it is somewhere in between (e.g., Q-J-4-2). At least leading the king from K-Q-3-2 is likely to set up one trick for the defense and maybe more if partner has the ace or jack.

A different approach is to use declarer's trump suit against him. You might try leading a short suit of one or two cards. You hope to win a trick by ruffing (trumping) when the suit is led again.

It usually is not a good idea to lead a trump because you are helping declarer draw trumps. However, if you think that declarer may be planning to trump some losers with dummy's trumps, leading a trump might work out well.

If partner has bid a suit, you should lead his suit unless you have a clearly better alternative. If partner has not bid and you do not have a clear-cut choice, you still must pick a suit. Choose one that the opponents did not bid, if possible.

Let's see how you would choose a lead against a contract of 4♠ with the following hand:

♠ 7 4 3
♡ K 8 6 2
◇ 3 2
♣ Q J 10 2

The safest suit to lead is clubs since you have an honor sequence. Even if declarer has the ace and king, you will start to drive them out and eventually may establish a club trick for your side. If partner has the ace or king, you may get two or three tricks. If one of the opponents has bid clubs, you can try leading your short suit, diamonds. You may get to use one of your trumps to ruff (trump) one of declarer's winning diamond tricks.

Leading a heart from your king is dangerous. It would be fine if partner had bid hearts or the opponents had bid all the other suits. If the opponents' bidding has suggested that dummy may have only one or two hearts, you could lead a trump, hoping to stop declarer from ruffing (trumping) his heart losers in dummy. Perhaps dummy has bid spades, diamonds and clubs, indicating that not much room is left in his hand for hearts.

Choosing the Card to Lead Against a Suit Contract

Once you have selected the suit, decide which card in the suit to lead. If you have two or more high cards that are touching, lead the top card, e.g., **K**-Q-3 or **Q**-J-8-7. As when leading the top card of an honor sequence against a notrump contract, you are telling partner that you have the next-lower card but not the next-higher card.

If you are leading a short suit, lead the top card, e.g., **7**-2 or **5**-4. Otherwise, lead a low card, e.g., Q-7-**4** or K-J-6-**3**. As against notrump contracts, you traditionally lead your *fourth-highest* card if you have a suit of four or more cards, e.g., Q-9-5-**4**-2.

Here are some examples of choosing the opening lead against a contract of 4♡ with nothing else to guide you:

♠ K Q J
♡ J 5
◇ J 8 4 2
♣ A 6 5 3

Leading a spade is safe and offers a good opportunity to develop a couple of tricks in the suit. With touching high cards lead the top card, the ♠**K**.

♠ Q 7 5 2
♡ 8 4 3
◇ 5
♣ 10 9 7 3 2

This time you can try leading your short suit, the ◇ **5**. Perhaps partner can win the trick with the ace and lead another diamond to let you ruff (trump) one of declarer's winners. If partner has another ace, he may be able to win another trick and again lead a diamond for you to ruff — four tricks from only two aces!

♠ K 10 7
♡ 6 4 2
◇ Q 9 6 2
♣ J 10 3

On this hand no lead is really attractive. Anything could be right. You could try the ♣**J** since you also have the ♣10. You also could lead a trump if you think declarer may be planning to use dummy's trumps to ruff some losers. Even a low diamond or spade could prove to be the best lead.

◆ *BIDDING REVIEW* ◆

Rebids by Opener

Opener's bid of one in a suit describes a hand with 13 to 21 points. That is too wide a range for responder to determine the level at which the partnership belongs. When opener makes his rebid, he tries to narrow the description of the strength of the hand into one of three categories:

Minimum Hand	13–16 points
Medium Hand	17–18 points
Maximum Hand	19–21 points

At the same time, opener tries to further describe his distribution so that responder can determine the appropriate denomination for the contract. The rebid opener chooses depends on his partner's initial response as shown in the following summaries:

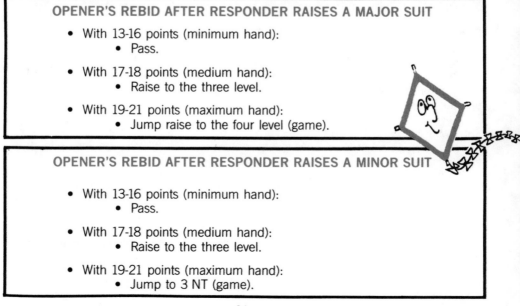

OPENER'S REBID AFTER RESPONDER RAISES A MAJOR SUIT

- With 13-16 points (minimum hand):
  - Pass.

- With 17-18 points (medium hand):
  - Raise to the three level.

- With 19-21 points (maximum hand):
  - Jump raise to the four level (game).

OPENER'S REBID AFTER RESPONDER RAISES A MINOR SUIT

- With 13-16 points (minimum hand):
  - Pass.

- With 17-18 points (medium hand):
  - Raise to the three level.

- With 19-21 points (maximum hand):
  - Jump to 3 NT (game).

OPENER'S REBID AFTER RESPONDER BIDS 1 NT

- With 13-16 points (minimum hand):
    - Pass with a balanced hand.
    - Bid a second suit of four cards or longer if it is lower-ranking than the original suit.
    - Rebid the original suit at the two level.

- With 17-18 points (medium hand):
    - Bid a second suit of four cards or longer, even if it is higher-ranking than the original suit.
    - Rebid the original suit at the three level.

- With 19-21 points (maximum hand):
    - Bid 3 NT with a balanced hand.
    - Bid a second suit of four cards or longer, jumping a level (jump shift) if it is lower-ranking than the original suit.
    - Rebid the original suit, jumping to game.

OPENER'S REBID AFTER RESPONDER BIDS A NEW SUIT

- With 13-16 points (minimum hand):
    - Raise partner's major to the cheapest available level with four-card support (count dummy points).
    - Bid a second suit of four cards or longer if it can be bid at the one level. A suit that ranks below the original one can be bid at the two level.
    - Bid notrump with a balanced hand at the cheapest available level.
    - Rebid the original suit at the cheapest available level.

- With 17-18 points (medium hand):
    - Raise partner's major, jumping one level, with four-card support (count dummy points).
    - Bid a second suit of four cards or longer (even if it is higher-ranking than the original and must be bid at the two level).
    - Rebid the original suit, jumping one level.

- With 19-21 points (maximum hand):
    - Raise partner's major, jumping two levels, with four-card support (count dummy points).
    - Bid a second suit of four cards or longer, jumping one level (jump shift).
    - Bid notrump with a balanced hand, jumping one level.
    - Rebid the original suit, jumping to game.

OPENER'S REBID AFTER RESPONDER JUMP RAISES OPENER'S SUIT

- With 13–16 points (minimum hand):
    - With 13–14 pass.
    - With 15–16 raise to game.
- With 17–18 points (medium hand):
    - Bid a new suit (usually one containing an ace), inviting responder to bid a slam.
- With 19–21 points (maximum hand):
    - Jump to the six level (slam).

OPENER'S REBID AFTER RESPONDER BIDS 2NT

- With 13–16 points (minimum hand):
    - With a balanced hand raise to 3NT.
    - With an unbalanced hand bid a second suit of four cards or longer or rebid the original suit.
- With 17–18 points (medium hand):
    - With a balanced hand raise to 4NT, inviting opener to bid a slam with a maximum.
    - With an unbalanced hand bid a second suit of four cards or longer or rebid the original suit.
- With 19–21 points (maximum hand):
    - With a balanced hand bid 6NT.
    - With an unbalanced hand bid a second suit of four cards or longer or rebid the original suit.

Rebids by Responder

When you make your rebid as responder, you put your hand into one of the following categories according to the point count (using dummy points if planning to support opener's major suit):

Minimum Hand		6–10 points
Medium Hand		11–12 points
Maximum Hand		13 or more points

By combining this information with the strength and distribution shown by opener's rebid, you try to decide the level and denomination of the contract. When you have enough information, sign off in the appropriate contract. If you need more information, make an invitational or forcing bid. The bid you choose depends on whether opener has shown a minimum, medium or maximum hand.

RESPONDER'S REBID

OPENER'S RANGE	RESPONDER'S RANGE	FINAL LEVEL	RESPONDER'S OPTIONS
13–16 (Minimum)	6–10	Partscore	• Pass • 1 NT • Two–level bid of a suit already mentioned by the partnership
	11–12	Partscore or Game	• 2 NT • Three-level bid of a suit already mentioned by the partnership
	13 or more	Game	• Bid a Golden Game • Bid a new suit at the three level
17–18 (Medium)	6–8	Partscore	• Pass • Cheapest bid of a suit already mentioned by the partnership
	9–10	Game	• Bid a Golden Game • Bid a new suit
	11–12	Game	• Bid a Golden Game
	13 or more	Game or Slam	• Bid a Golden Game • Bid a Slam
19–21 (Maximum)	6–10	Game	• Pass • Bid a Golden Game • Bid a new suit
	11–12	Game	• Bid a Golden Game • Pass in game • Bid a new suit
	13 or more	Slam	• Bid a slam

◆ *SUMMARY* ◆

When you come to the third step in your PLAN, A*nalyze your alternatives*, there are a number of ways to develop extra winners or eliminate losers. Extra tricks can be developed by *promotion,* driving out the opponents' higher cards so your high cards can take tricks. Tricks also can be developed by playing a *long suit* so the small cards are good after the opponents run out of the suit.

You can expect the missing cards to divide in the following manner:

- *An even number of missing cards usually will divide slightly unevenly.*

- *An odd number of missing cards usually will divide as evenly as possible.*

Don't be afraid to give up tricks to the opponents to develop tricks for yourself. If you do need to give up tricks, remember the advice: *Take your losses early*. Make sure you can reach your winners once they are established. You want to retain a high card in the hand that contains the winners you are establishing.

When you have a choice of suits to develop, pick the longer suit. With equal-length suits, pick the suit that is more unevenly divided between declarer's hand and dummy.

GROUP ACTIVITIES ◆

Exercise One — Promotion

How many tricks do you expect to take from each of the following suits? How many times would you have to give up the lead before you could enjoy your winners?

DUMMY: 1) K Q J 10   2) J 10 9 8   3) Q 10 3   4) K 3   5) J 8 7

DECLARER: 7 6 4 2   5 4 3 2   J 7 4   Q 7   10 9 4

_____ _____ _____ _____ _____

Exercise Two — High Card from the Short Side

In each of the following examples, assume that an ace in another suit is in dummy. How many tricks do you expect to get from the suit? How would you play these suit combinations? What could happen if you were not careful?

DUMMY: 1) K J 10 9 4 2) Q J 3   3) K Q 10 3   4) J 10 5   5) Q 10 9 8 3

DECLARER: Q 7   K 4   J 4   Q 7   K J

_____ _____ _____ _____ _____

Exercise Three — The Division of the Opponents' Cards

If the opponents hold the following number of cards in a suit, how would you expect them to be divided between the two hands?

  1) 3   2) 4   3) 5   4) 6   5) 7   6) 8   7) 9

_____ _____ _____ _____ _____ _____ _____

Exercise Four — Developing Tricks Through Length

If the opponents' cards are divided as you would expect, how many tricks are you likely to get from each of the following suits? How many tricks would you get if the suits are divided as favorably as possible?

DUMMY: 1) A K 6 3   2) A 5 4 2   3) A 8 7 4 2   4) K 8 7 5 3 2 5) A K 8 6 2

DECLARER: 7 5 4 2   K Q 3   K 6 3   A 4   7 5 4 3

_____ _____ _____ _____ _____

Exercise Five — Stranding a Suit

Assuming that dummy has no high cards other than those in this suit, how would you play the suit to avoid stranding your established winners in dummy? How many tricks would you expect to take? How would you expect the opponents' cards to be divided?

DUMMY: 1) A K 7 6 3   2) A 8 6 4 2   3) A K 8 7 4 2   4) A 8 6 3 2   5) A 7 6 2

DECLARER: 8 5 2   K 9 3   6 3   7 5 4   K 4 3

_____   _____   _____   _____   _____

Exercise Six — Leading Against a Suit Contract

Which card would you lead from each of the following hands against a contract of 4♠?

1) ♠ J 6 3   2) ♠ 10 9 4   3) ♠ J 5 2
   ♡ A 6 3   ♡ Q 10 6 5 3   ♡ K 8 7
   ◊ K Q J   ◊ 10 9 7 3   ◊ Q 5 2
   ♣ J 9 5 4   ♣ 3   ♣ K Q 10 9

_____   _____   _____

Exercise Seven — Review of Rebids by Opener

You open the bidding 1♡, and your partner responds 1♠. What do you rebid with each of the following hands?

1) ♠ 7 6 4 2   2) ♠ Q 5   3) ♠ 5
   ♡ A Q J 4 3   ♡ K 10 5 3 2   ♡ K Q 10 7 3
   ◊ A 2   ◊ K J 4   ◊ A J 2
   ♣ Q 3   ♣ A J 10   ♣ Q J 9 4

_____   _____   _____

4) ♠ 7 4   5) ♠ A J   6) ♠ K 8 4 2
   ♡ A K J 7 6 2   ♡ Q J 7 6 2   ♡ A Q J 6 2
   ◊ K 7 3   ◊ A Q 4   ◊ 5
   ♣ J 4   ♣ K Q 9   ♣ K Q 4

_____   _____   _____

7) ♠ 7 4   8) ♠ A K 7 4   9) ♠ A 8
   ♡ A K Q 7 6 2   ♡ K Q J 6 2   ♡ A K Q 6 2
   ◊ A K 3   ◊ 4 2   ◊ 5 3
   ♣ 10 4   ♣ A J   ♣ K Q J 4

_____   _____   _____

Exercise Eight — Review of Rebids by Responder

Your partner opens the bidding 1◊, you respond 1♡ and your partner rebids 1 NT. What do you rebid with each of the following hands?

1) ♠ 7 6 4 2   2) ♠ 3   3) ♠ A 5
   ♡ K Q 4 2   ♡ K 10 5 3   ♡ J 9 8 7 4 3
   ◊ A 4   ◊ K J 5 4   ◊ J 8 2
   ♣ 8 6 2   ♣ 8 6 4 2   ♣ 9 4

_____   _____   _____

4) ♠ K 6 3
   ♡ A Q J 6
   ◊ J 7 3
   ♣ J 5 4

5) ♠ 10 8
   ♡ K Q J 7 6 2
   ◊ K 9 2
   ♣ 10 5

6) ♠ 6 2
   ♡ K J 6 2
   ◊ A J 5 3 2
   ♣ Q 4

7) ♠ A 8 7 4
   ♡ K Q 6 3
   ◊ K 3
   ♣ J 10 4

8) ♠ 4
   ♡ Q J 9 8 6 2
   ◊ A J 2
   ♣ K 10 3

9) ♠ Q 8
   ♡ A J 5 4
   ◊ K Q 7 5 3
   ♣ Q 3

Exercise Nine — Promotion in a Notrump Contract

Turn up all the cards on the first pre-dealt hand. Put each hand dummy style at the edge of the table in front of each player.

Dealer: North

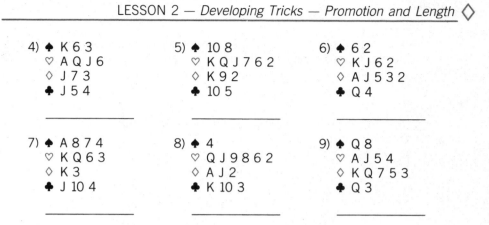

```
                    ♠ A 6 5
                    ♡ J 4
                    ◊ A 7 6 4
                    ♣ A 9 8 3
   ♠ 9 4                          ♠ Q J 10 7 3
   ♡ A 7 6                        ♡ 9 8 5 2
   ◊ Q J 9 8                      ◊ K 3
   ♣ K J 10 5                     ♣ Q 7
                    ♠ K 8 2
                    ♡ K Q 10 3
                    ◊ 10 5 2
                    ♣ 6 4 2
```

The Bidding

Does North have enough to open the bidding? With a choice of suits, which suit does North choose?

East passes. Can South bid a suit at the one level? What does South respond?

West passes. Can North support partner's suit? Can North bid a new suit at the *one level*? What rebid describes North's hand?

East passes. South asks himself what level and what denomination is best for the partnership. What will South's rebid be? What will be the contract? Who will be declarer?

The Play

Which player makes the opening lead? What will the opening lead be?

Declarer starts by making a PLAN:
1. **P**ause to consider your objective
2. **L**ook at your winners and losers
3. **A**nalyze your alternatives
4. **N**ow put it together

How many extra winners does declarer need? Which suit can provide them? How does declarer plan to play the suit? Should declarer win the first trick in his hand or in dummy? Why?

Exercise Ten — Promotion in a Suit Contract

Turn up all the cards on the second pre-dealt hand. Put each hand dummy style at the edge of the table in front of each player.

Dealer: East

```
                        ♠ 9 2
                        ♡ K Q 6 5 2
                        ◇ 10 6
                        ♣ 10 8 4 3
      ♠ A K J 4 3                      ♠ Q 10 6 5
      ♡ 10 3                           ♡ J 8 4
      ◇ Q 9 7                          ◇ K J 3
      ♣ K 7 2                          ♣ A Q 6
                        ♠ 8 7
                        ♡ A 9 7
                        ◇ A 8 5 4 2
                        ♣ J 9 5
```

The Bidding

East has a balanced hand. Why can it not be opened 1 NT? Why can East not open his longest suit? What will East open?

South passes. What does West respond?

North passes. What does East rebid?

South passes. West asks himself what level the partnership belongs in and what denomination. What rebid does West make? What will be the contract? Who will be declarer?

The Play

Which player makes the opening lead? What will the opening lead be?

How many losers can declarer afford in a 4♠ contract? How many losers are there?

Declarer starts by making a PLAN. After going through the four steps, how will declarer play the hand? What could interfere with declarer making the contract? When should West draw trumps? What cards can be promoted into winners?

Exercise Eleven — Using Length in a Notrump Contract

Turn up all the cards on the third pre-dealt hand. Put each hand dummy style at the edge of the table in front of each player.

Dealer: South

```
                        ♠ J 8 2
                        ♡ A 6 3 2
                        ◇ K 4 2
                        ♣ A 8 4
        ♠ Q 10 4                        ♠ K 7 6 3
        ♡ Q 10 8                        ♡ J 9 7 5
        ◇ J 8                           ◇ Q 10 9
        ♣ Q 10 7 5 2                    ♣ J 9
                        ♠ A 9 5
                        ♡ K 4
                        ◇ A 7 6 5 3
                        ♣ K 6 3
```

The Bidding

What is South's opening bid?

West passes. Does North have a suit he can bid at the one level? What would North respond?

East passes. Can South support his partner's suit? Does he have another suit he can bid at the one level? Does he have a balanced hand? What does South rebid to finish describing his hand?

West passes. At what level does the partnership belong: partscore, game or maybe game? In what denomination should the partnership play? What rebid can North make to invite his partner to bid game?

East passes. Should South accept North's invitation? What will be the contract? Who will be declarer?

The Play

Which player makes the opening lead? What will the opening lead be?

Declarer starts by making a PLAN. How many additional tricks does declarer need? Which suit offers the potential for developing the extra winners? How does declarer plan to make the contract?

Exercise Twelve — Using Length in a Suit Contract

Turn up all the cards on the fourth pre-dealt hand. Put each hand dummy style at the edge of the table in front of each player.

Dealer: West

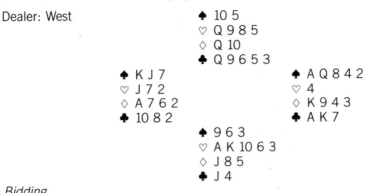

```
                        ♠ 10 5
                        ♡ Q 9 8 5
                        ◇ Q 10
                        ♣ Q 9 6 5 3
        ♠ K J 7                         ♠ A Q 8 4 2
        ♡ J 7 2                         ♡ 4
        ◇ A 7 6 2                       ◇ K 9 4 3
        ♣ 10 8 2                        ♣ A K 7
                        ♠ 9 6 3
                        ♡ A K 10 6 3
                        ◇ J 8 5
                        ♣ J 4
```

The Bidding

Neither West nor North has enough to open the bidding. What will be East's opening bid?

South passes. Does West have support for partner's major suit? What will West respond?

North passes. Does East have a minimum, medium or maximum hand? How will East show the strength of his hand?

South passes. What does West do now? What will be the contract? Who will be declarer?

The Play

Which player makes the opening lead? What will the opening lead be?

Declarer starts by making a PLAN. How many losers does declarer have? How can one of the losers be eliminated? What must declarer hope for? What is declarer's first play?

LESSON 3

Developing Tricks — The Finesse

Leading Toward a High Card
Repeating a Finesse
Finessing Against Two Cards
Leading a High Card
Guidelines for Defense
Bidding Review — Making and
Responding to an Overcall
Summary

Workshop Material
Group Activities

In the last lesson extra tricks were developed by promoting high cards that were in a sequence or by developing low cards that were in long suits. Another popular way of getting extra tricks is by finessing. This is an attempt to win a trick with a high card when the opponents have a higher card to play. This may seem like an impossible task, but it is all a matter of the position of the cards.

◆ LEADING TOWARD A HIGH CARD ◆

Finessing Against the Ace

Look at this layout of a suit:

```
                    NORTH (DUMMY)
                    K 4
        WEST                      EAST
        ?                         ?
                    SOUTH (DECLARER)
                    3 2
```

You do not have a sure trick in the suit since the opponents have the ace, but you do have the second- highest card, the king. Is there any way to get a trick with it? If you had the queen, it would be easy to get a trick, as you saw in the last lesson. You could lead the king and promote your queen into a winner. In this case, you have nothing to promote. If you lead the king, the opponents will win their ace and you have nothing but low cards left.

Suppose you lead your 4 instead of the king. The opponents can win the trick with one of their other high cards and then take your king with their ace. Again, no trick.

Since leading the king or the 4 from dummy doesn't work, consider leading a low card from your hand toward the high card in the dummy. This gives you a chance to win a trick with your king. Why? West must play before you choose the card to play from dummy. If West has the ace, you are sure to get a trick. Suppose this is the layout:

```
                    NORTH (DUMMY)
                    K 4
        WEST                      EAST
        A J 10 8 6                 Q 9 7 5
                    SOUTH (DECLARER)
                    3 2
```

If West plays the ace, you play the 4 from dummy and later win a trick with the king. If West does not play the ace, you play the king. Either way, you get a trick with your king because East does not hold the ace.

What if East has the ace? The layout could be:

```
                    NORTH (DUMMY)
                    K 4
        WEST                      EAST
        Q 9 7 5                    A J 10 8 6
                    SOUTH (DECLARER)
                    3 2
```

You lead a low card from your hand and West also plays a low card. If you play your king, East wins the ace. If you do not play your king, East wins a lower card and then plays the ace to take your king. Notice, however, that you cannot get a trick in any other fashion if this is the layout and *you* have to play the suit.

By leading toward your king, you give yourself a chance. If West has the ace, you get a trick with your king. If East has it, you do not get a trick. This is the concept of a *finesse*. You hope that one or more missing high cards lie in a particular opponent's hand.

How often will West have the ace rather than East? Unless you are unluckier than the average bridge player, half the time. It's a 50–50 proposition.

A finesse is similar to the idea of developing long suits in the previous lesson. There, you hoped the opponents' cards were *divided* in a friendly fashion. Here, you hope some of the opponents' cards are *located* in a friendly fashion. By leading *toward* your king, you at least give yourself the chance that the ace lies where you want it to be.

Finessing Against the King

In the previous example you finessed against the *ace*, the higher card held by the opponents. You also can finesse against a missing king.

```
                        NORTH (DUMMY)
                        A Q 4
        WEST                              EAST
        ?                                 ?
                        SOUTH (DECLARER)
                        5 3 2
```

Here you have one sure trick, the ace, and would like to get a second trick with your queen. To lead the queen would do no good. The opponents will win their king, and since they have the jack, you have not promoted another winner. How do you go about getting a trick with your queen? Follow the same principle of leading toward the card you hope will win a trick. Hope West has the king and the complete layout is something like this:

```
                        NORTH (DUMMY)
                        A Q 4
        WEST                              EAST
        K J 8 6                           10 9 7
                        SOUTH (DECLARER)
                        5 3 2
```

If you lead a low card from your hand toward dummy, West must play before you choose dummy's card. If he plays the king, win your ace and then your queen will be a second trick. If West plays a low card, *finesse* the queen. It wins the trick when East has no higher card to play. Of course your finesse will lose if East has the king and you will be back to the one sure trick you already had.

Here is a different layout in which you are missing the king:

                    NORTH (DUMMY)
                    A 5 4
    WEST   EAST
    ?   ?
                    SOUTH (DECLARER)
                    Q 3 2

The principle is the same. Try to win a trick with your queen by leading a low card from dummy toward the queen. This time you are hoping East has the king and the complete layout is:

                    NORTH (DUMMY)
                    A 5 4
    WEST   EAST
    9 8 7   K J 10 6
                    SOUTH (DECLARER)
                    Q 3 2

Whether or not East plays the king, you will get a trick with your queen. But suppose the layout is:

                    NORTH (DUMMY)
                    A 5 4
    WEST   EAST
    K J 10 6   9 8 7
                    SOUTH (DECLARER)
                    Q 3 2

When you lead a low card from dummy toward your queen, West wins the king and you are back to one trick in the suit. Could you do better by leading the queen instead of leading toward it? No, West would play the king, making you use dummy's ace to win the trick. Since you do not have the jack or 10, none of your remaining cards would be promoted into a winner. Instead, the opponents' jack and 10 would be promoted. Leading the queen gains you nothing — you will not get an extra trick whether West or East has the king.

Finessing Against the Queen

When you hope to take a trick with the jack and the opponents have the queen, you are finessing against the queen. Consider this layout:

                    NORTH (DUMMY)
                    A K J
    WEST   EAST
    ?   ?
                    SOUTH (DECLARER)
                    5 3 2

You have two sure tricks, the ace and king. The jack could be a winner, so lead toward the jack from your hand. If West plays a low card, play (finesse) the jack. If West has the queen, your jack will win the trick and you end up with three tricks. If East has the queen, you don't win a trick with the jack and you are left with the two sure tricks you already had.

The ace and king do not have to be in the same hand. In the following example you are still looking for the queen:

NORTH (DUMMY)
A J 4

WEST   EAST
?   ?

SOUTH (DECLARER)
K 6 2

The king is played first and then a low card is led toward dummy's ace and jack. If West has the queen, you can finesse the jack and take three tricks.

In the previous examples you did not have to lose a trick if the queen was favorably located. When the jack is in the hand opposite the ace and king, you may have to lose a trick to get a trick with your jack.

NORTH (DUMMY)
J 4

WEST   EAST
?   ?

SOUTH (DECLARER)
A K 6 2

The ace and king are two sure tricks. If you need a third trick, you must use the idea of leading toward the card you hope will win a trick. Lead a low card from your hand toward dummy's jack. You are hoping West has the queen and the complete layout looks something like this:

NORTH (DUMMY)
J 4

WEST   EAST
Q 10 8 3   9 7 5

SOUTH (DECLARER)
A K 6 2

If West plays the queen, you play the 4 from dummy and later get a trick with your jack as well as your ace and king. If West does not play the queen, play dummy's jack. It will win the trick while you still have the ace and king left.

Finessing for Lower Cards

You sometimes must finesse for cards lower than the queen. Consider this layout:

NORTH (DUMMY)
A K Q 10 2

WEST   EAST
J 9 8 5   7

SOUTH (DECLARER)
6 4 3

With eight cards in the suit you normally would play the ace, king and queen, hoping the missing cards were divided 3-2. However, in this situation, when you play the ace and king, East *shows out* (discards) on the second round. It becomes apparent that West started with four cards including the jack.

To avoid losing a trick, return to your hand with a high card in another suit and then lead your remaining low card toward dummy. If West plays a low card, you finesse dummy's 10 and end up taking all the tricks in the suit.

Using the Finesse

Now that you have an understanding of the principle of the finesse, let's see how you would use it in a complete hand. The contract is 3 NT and the opening lead is the ◇ Q.

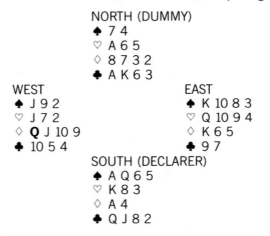

NORTH (DUMMY)
♠ 7 4
♡ A 6 5
◇ 8 7 3 2
♣ A K 6 3

WEST
♠ J 9 2
♡ J 7 2
◇ Q J 10 9
♣ 10 5 4

EAST
♠ K 10 8 3
♡ Q 10 9 4
◇ K 6 5
♣ 9 7

SOUTH (DECLARER)
♠ A Q 6 5
♡ K 8 3
◇ A 4
♣ Q J 8 2

The objective in 3 NT is nine tricks. You have one sure trick in spades, two in hearts, one in diamonds and four in clubs, for a total of eight. When analyzing your alternatives, you can see the opportunity for a finesse in spades. You have the ace and queen, but are missing the king. None of the other suits offer any hope for an extra trick.

When you put your PLAN together, take into consideration that you need to be in the dummy to lead toward the spades in your hand. Therefore, after winning the ◇ A, plan to use one of your high cards in another suit to get to dummy. Then lead a low spade toward your hand, finessing the ♠ Q if East plays a low spade. Since East has the ♠ K, you will make the contract.

Here is another opportunity for a finesse. This time, you are playing in a trump contract of 3◇. West leads the ♠J.

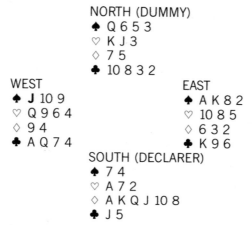

NORTH (DUMMY)
♠ Q 6 5 3
♡ K J 3
◇ 7 5
♣ 10 8 3 2

WEST
♠ J 10 9
♡ Q 9 6 4
◇ 9 4
♣ A Q 7 4

EAST
♠ A K 8 2
♡ 10 8 5
◇ 6 3 2
♣ K 9 6

SOUTH (DECLARER)
♠ 7 4
♡ A 7 2
◇ A K Q J 10 8
♣ J 5

You can afford four losers and you have two spade losers, a heart loser and two club losers. You can't do much about the spade and club losers, but the ♡J offers you an opportunity in the heart suit. When you get the lead, you plan to draw trumps, then play the ♡A and lead a low heart toward dummy's ♡K and ♡J. When West plays a low heart, you finesse the ♡J, making the contract when East does not have the ♡Q.

◆ *REPEATING A FINESSE* ◆

Sometimes, you can finesse more than once in the same suit. This is called a *repeating finesse*.

Repeating a Finesse Against the Ace

Look at the following combination of cards:

NORTH (DUMMY)
K Q 5

WEST
?

EAST
?

SOUTH (DECLARER)
7 4 3

As we saw in the previous lesson, you can get one trick from this combination of cards using promotion. Lead the king to drive out the opponents' ace and establish your queen as a trick. However, by using the principle of the finesse, you can get two tricks if West has the ace. You hope the complete layout is something like this:

NORTH (DUMMY)
K Q 5

WEST
A J 9 2

EAST
10 8 6

SOUTH (DECLARER)
7 4 3

Following the idea of leading toward the high card, lead a low card from your hand toward dummy. If West plays the ace, play the 5 from dummy — later you will get two tricks with your king and queen. If West plays a low card, play the queen (or king) from dummy. Since East does not have the ace, the queen will win the trick. The situation is now similar to one we have seen before:

                    NORTH (DUMMY)
                    K 5
    WEST   EAST
    A J 9   10 8
                    SOUTH (DECLARER)
                    7 4

You want to lead toward the high card again to take a trick with the king. Of course, you must return to your hand in another suit to do this, but then you can *repeat the finesse* by leading toward the king. Whether or not West takes the ace, you will end up with two tricks in the suit.

If East started with the ace, he will take your king or queen — you will win only one trick. The repeated finesse is not a sure thing. It lets you take two tricks when the ace is favorably placed.

Repeating a Finesse Against the King

Here is another example of a repeated finesse. This time, you are missing the king.

                    NORTH (DUMMY)
                    A Q J
    WEST   EAST
    ?   ?
                    SOUTH (DECLARER)
                    6 5 3

Start by leading a low card from your hand toward dummy. If West plays a low card, play the jack (or queen). If East does not have the king, your finesse will work and the jack will win the trick. Now, get back to your hand in another suit and repeat the finesse by leading another low card toward dummy. When West plays a low card, finesse the queen. You will end up with three tricks when West started with the king.

The Repeated Finesse in Action

Let's take a look at the use of the repeated finesse in a critical situation. You are in a 4♠ contract with a rather precarious holding in the trump suit. West leads the ♣K.

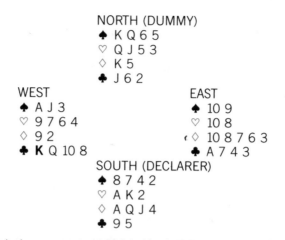

NORTH (DUMMY)
♠ K Q 6 5
♡ Q J 5 3
◇ K 5
♣ J 6 2

WEST
♠ A J 3
♡ 9 7 6 4
◇ 9 2
♣ K Q 10 8

EAST
♠ 10 9
♡ 10 8
◇ 10 8 7 6 3
♣ A 7 4 3

SOUTH (DECLARER)
♠ 8 7 4 2
♡ A K 2
◇ A Q J 4
♣ 9 5

You can lose three tricks in your contract of 4♠. You have no losers in hearts or diamonds but you will lose the first two tricks in clubs. You can afford to lose only one spade trick. You are missing the ace, as well as the jack, 10 and 9. You could lead the king to drive out the ace, promoting your queen, but then, even if the missing cards divided 3-2, you would lose a second spade trick.

Instead, use the art of the finesse. Suppose the opponents take the ♣K and ♣Q and lead another club, which you trump with the ♠2. Lead the ♠4 toward dummy. If West takes the ♠A, life is a bit easier. Whatever West leads back, you can win and play the ♠K and ♠Q. When the suit divides 3-2, you end up with only three losers.

If West plays a low spade, play dummy's ♠Q (or ♠K), which wins the trick. Now come back to your hand by leading the ♡3 to your ♡K (for example). Lead another low spade toward dummy. No matter when West takes the ♠A, you end up losing only one spade trick and making the contract.

◆ *FINESSING AGAINST TWO CARDS* ◆

Sometimes, you must finesse against more than one missing card. The general guideline is to lead toward the *lower* of your high cards first. Let's see how this works:

Missing the King and Jack

Suppose you have these cards:

NORTH (DUMMY)
A Q 10

WEST
?

EAST
?

SOUTH (DECLARER)
7 4 2

If dummy did not have the 10, this would be the situation for a simple finesse against West's king. However, the 10 provides an additional possibility since you can consider finessing against the jack as well as the king. Following the general principle of leading toward the high card, you would start by leading a low card from your hand toward dummy. But if West plays low, should you play the queen or the 10?

Playing the 10, the *lower* of your high cards, gives you an opportunity to make the maximum number of tricks. Suppose this is the complete layout:

```
                    NORTH (DUMMY)
                    A Q 10
        WEST                      EAST
        K J 8 5                   9 6 3
                    SOUTH (DECLARER)
                    7 4 2
```

If you play the 10, it will win the trick because West has both the king and jack. You now can come back to your hand and lead another low card toward dummy's remaining ace and queen. This time you can finesse the queen and end up winning all three tricks.

Suppose you had played dummy's queen the first time. It would win the trick, but the remaining cards would be:

```
                    NORTH (DUMMY)
                    A 10
        WEST                      EAST
        K J 8                     9 6
                    SOUTH (DECLARER)
                    7 4
```

If you led another low card toward dummy, West would play the jack, forcing dummy's ace. West could win the next trick with the king, and you would take only two tricks.

If West does not have both the king and the jack, your play of the 10 will not lose anything. Suppose the complete layout is:

```
                    NORTH (DUMMY)
                    A Q 10
        WEST                      EAST
        J 8 5                     K 9 6 3
                    SOUTH (DECLARER)
                    7 4 2
```

You play the 2, West plays the 5 and you play dummy's 10. East wins the king. Now your ace and queen are established as two sure tricks.

What would happen if this were the layout?

```
                    NORTH (DUMMY)
                    A Q 10
        WEST                      EAST
        K 8 5                     J 9 6 3
                    SOUTH (DECLARER)
                    7 4 2
```

You play the 2, West plays the 5 and you play dummy's 10. East wins the jack, but later you can repeat the finesse by playing a low card to dummy's queen. This time, your finesse will work and you end up with two tricks.

Of course, the complete layout may be:

NORTH (DUMMY)
A Q 10

WEST   EAST
8 5 3   K J 9 6

SOUTH (DECLARER)
7 4 2

Your first finesse of the 10 will lose to East's jack and your second finesse of the queen will lose to East's king. You end up with only one trick, but there was nothing else you could have done. The two missing cards were both unfavorably located.

Missing the King and Queen

Take a look at this layout:

NORTH (DUMMY)
A J 10

WEST   EAST
?   ?

SOUTH (DECLARER)
8 5 3

This time, the king and queen are missing. You have a sure trick with the ace, but it would be nice to get a second trick since you also have the jack and the 10.

Start by leading a low card from your hand. If West plays low, follow the principle of playing the lower of your high cards first and play dummy's 10. This will win the trick if the complete layout is:

NORTH (DUMMY)
A J 10

WEST   EAST
K Q 9 6   7 4 2

SOUTH (DECLARER)
8 5 3

Since East has neither the king nor the queen with which to win the trick, you end up winning two tricks.

When you lead a low card toward dummy, West may play the queen (or the king) rather than a low card. You can win this with the ace and use the jack to drive out West's remaining high card, again establishing the 10 as a second trick.

Most of the time, West will not have both the missing high cards. Leading low to the 10, however, will work out even if East has either the king or the queen. Suppose the complete layout is:

```
                        NORTH (DUMMY)
                        A J 10
        WEST                          EAST
        Q 9 6                         K 7 4 2
                        SOUTH (DECLARER)
                        8 5 3
```

You play the 3, West the 6 and dummy the 10. East can win the king. The remaining cards will be:

```
                        NORTH (DUMMY)
                        A J
        WEST                          EAST
        Q 9                           7 4 2
                        SOUTH (DECLARER)
                        8 5
```

When you regain the lead, you can play another low card toward dummy. If West contributes the 9, you play dummy's jack — this time your finesse is successful. You again end up winning two tricks.

You also would win two tricks if East had the queen and West had the king. Only if East held both the king *and* the queen would both of your finesses lose and you would end up with one trick. At least you would have given it your best try.

Missing the Ace and the Queen

Look at this combination of cards:

```
                        NORTH (DUMMY)
                        K J 10
        WEST                          EAST
        ?                             ?
                        SOUTH (DECLARER)
                        6 4 3
```

Missing the ace and the queen, start by leading a low card toward dummy, playing the 10 if West plays low. If West started with both the ace and the queen, the 10 will win the trick:

```
                        NORTH (DUMMY)
                        K J 10
        WEST                          EAST
        A Q 7 5                       9 8 2
                        SOUTH (DECLARER)
                        6 4 3
```

You then can come back to your hand and repeat the finesse, ending up with two tricks.

Even if East has the ace, playing the 10 will be successful:

```
                        NORTH (DUMMY)
                        K J 10
        WEST                          EAST
        Q 7 5                         A 9 8 2
                        SOUTH (DECLARER)
                        6 4 3
```

East must win the ace and you later can take another finesse against West's queen to end up with two tricks.

If East has the queen, you will win only one trick:

```
                        NORTH (DUMMY)
                        K J 10
        WEST                          EAST
        A 7 5                         Q 9 8 2
                        SOUTH (DECLARER)
                        6 4 3
```

When you lead low to the 10, East will win the queen. You later can use the king to drive out West's ace, establishing your jack. It would not have helped to lead low to the king the first time. You would win the trick but the opponents would win the next two with their queen and ace.

Playing the lower card first, the 10, gains when West has the queen and costs nothing if East has the queen.

Example of Finessing Against Two Cards

Suppose you are playing in a contract of 3 NT on the following hand. West leads the ♡ Q.

```
                        NORTH (DUMMY)
                        ♠ 8 4 2
                        ♡ 9 4 2
                        ◇ A Q 3 2
                        ♣ 7 4 2
        WEST                          EAST
        ♠ Q 6 3                       ♠ K 9 7 5
        ♡ Q J 10 7                    ♡ 6 5 3
        ◇ 9 6                         ◇ 10 5 4
        ♣ Q 10 6 3                    ♣ K J 8
                        SOUTH (DECLARER)
                        ♠ A J 10
                        ♡ A K 8
                        ◇ K J 8 7
                        ♣ A 9 5
```

You need nine tricks. You have one sure spade trick, two heart tricks, four diamond tricks and a club trick, for a total of eight. When you analyze your alternatives, the spade suit offers the only chance to develop the extra trick you need.

When you come to the fourth step of the PLAN, **N**ow put it together, you must be careful of the order in which you play the cards. Since you lack both the ♠K and the ♠Q, you will have to lead twice from dummy toward your hand. The ◇A and ◇Q are the only high cards in dummy, so you must use them appropriately.

After winning the first heart trick, lead a diamond to dummy's ace (or queen) so you can lead a spade toward your hand. When East plays a low spade, play the ♠10, the lower of your high cards. West will win the ♠Q and probably lead another heart. You win this and lead a diamond to dummy's queen. Now lead another spade toward your hand. When East plays a low spade, play your ♠J. This finesse is successful, and you have the ninth trick you needed to make the contract.

◆ LEADING A HIGH CARD ◆

So far, the focus has been on leading toward the card you hope will take a trick. Sometimes, you can afford to lead a high card.

When You Can Afford to Lead a High Card

Earlier, we looked at this holding in a suit:

```
                    NORTH (DUMMY)
                    A 5 4
    WEST                            EAST
    ?                               ?
                    SOUTH (DECLARER)
                    Q 3 2
```

Starting with one sure trick, the ace, you can try to get a second trick by leading *toward* the queen, hoping that East has the king. But if West has the king, leading toward your queen will not work.

If West has the king, it might seem reasonable to lead the queen from your hand, since the ace is in dummy. However, this will do you no good. Suppose the complete layout is:

```
                    NORTH (DUMMY)
                    A 5 4
    WEST                            EAST
    K J 9 6                         10 8 7
                    SOUTH (DECLARER)
                    Q 3 2
```

When you lead the queen, West will *cover* (play a higher card) with the king, making you use the ace to win the trick. The opponents will win the next two tricks since they have the jack and 10.

The situation is different if you have the jack and 10:

```
                    NORTH (DUMMY)
                    A 5 4
    WEST                            EAST
    K 9 6 3                         8 7 2
                    SOUTH (DECLARER)
                    Q J 10
```

Here, you can afford to lead the queen. If West covers with the king, you can win the ace, and *your* jack and 10 are promoted into winners. If West does not cover with the king, play low from dummy — your queen will win the trick since East does not have the king. You then can repeat the finesse by leading the jack (or 10) from your hand.

If East has the king instead of West, you will lose the finesse but still win two tricks since you have the ace and jack left.

How can you tell when to *lead* a high card and when to lead *toward* a high card? The secret is to look at the other cards you hold in the suit. You can lead a high card if you can afford to have an opponent cover it with a higher card. Otherwise, you should lead toward the high card.

In the above example, you can afford to lead the queen — if West covers with the king, your jack and 10 will be promoted into winners. In the earlier example, you could not afford to lead the queen — if West covers with the king, the opponents' jack and 10 will be promoted into winners.

Take a look at this layout:

```
                    NORTH (DUMMY)
                    A K 3
         WEST                      EAST
         Q 8 7 5                   9 4 2
                    SOUTH (DECLARER)
                    J 10 6
```

You have two sure tricks with the ace and king. If you lead the ace and king, you will get only two tricks in the suit unless one of the opponents holds a singleton or doubleton queen. Holding the jack and 10 gives you an opportunity to trap the queen if West has it. Can you afford to lead the jack? Yes. If West covers with the queen, you can win the trick, and your 10 is promoted into a winner.

Contrast that layout with the following:

```
                    NORTH (DUMMY)
                    A K 3 2
         WEST                      EAST
         ?                         ?
                    SOUTH (DECLARER)
                    J 6 5 4
```

Again, you are missing the queen. Can you afford to lead the jack to trap the queen in West's hand? This time, you do not have the 10. If you lead the jack, West can cover with the queen and the opponents' 10 will be promoted into a trick. Leading the ace and king is better — you hope that one of the opponents started with a singleton or doubleton queen. For example the complete layout may be:

```
                              NORTH (DUMMY)
                              A K 3 2
        WEST                                  EAST
        Q 9                                   10 8 7
                              SOUTH (DECLARER)
                              J 6 5 4
```

By playing the ace and king, you can take all the tricks in the suit. If you lead the jack and West covers with the queen, East eventually will win a trick with the 10.

Leading a High Card

Leading a high card often allows you to repeat a finesse. Take a look at the following hand.

```
                              NORTH (DUMMY)
 Contract: 3◇                 ♠ A 7 5 3 2
 Lead: ♠K                      ♡ 9 4 3
                              ◇ J 5
                              ♣ 8 7 5
           WEST                                  EAST
           ♠ K Q J 10                            ♠ 9 6
           ♡ K J 7 6                             ♡ A 10 8 2
           ◇ 7 2                                 ◇ K 8 3
           ♣ 10 6 3                              ♣ Q J 4 2
                              SOUTH (DECLARER)
                              ♠ 8 4
                              ♡ Q 5
                              ◇ A Q 10 9 6 4
                              ♣ A K 9
```

You can afford four losers in a contract of 3◇. You have a spade loser, two heart losers and a club loser, and you are missing the ◇ K. You plan to eliminate your diamond loser by taking a finesse against East's (hoped-for) king.

After winning dummy's ♠A, you lead the ◇ J. If East covers with the ◇ K, you win the ◇ A and take the rest of the diamond tricks. If East does not cover with the ◇ K, you play a low diamond from your hand — dummy's jack will win the trick. Now you lead dummy's ◇ 5 and repeat the finesse, trapping East's king.

Suppose you had led dummy's ◇ 5 first, rather than the ◇ J. When East played a low diamond, you could win your 9 (or 10 or queen). But now you would be in your hand with no way to return to dummy to repeat the finesse. East eventually would win a trick with the ◇ K. Knowing that you can afford to lead the ◇ J is the key to making the contract.

◆ GUIDELINES FOR DEFENSE ◆

If your partner has bid a suit, and you must make the opening lead, it is a good idea to *lead your partner's suit unless you clearly have a better alternative*. You and your partner must cooperate on defense. If your partner has opened the bidding or overcalled in a suit, you have a strong indication of which suit is most likely to produce tricks for the defense. You can begin immediately to help partner develop tricks in that suit.

Leading Partner's Suit

If you have a singleton in partner's suit, you have no choice of cards to lead. If you have a doubleton, lead the top card, e.g., K-3 or 7-5. With three or more cards, lead the top of two or more touching high cards, otherwise lead low (fourth best if you have four or more). For example, **Q**-J-5, K-8-**2**, Q-9-8-**4**-3.

In general, avoid leading a low card when you have the ace and are defending against a trump contract. If you lead the suit, lead the ace. This is an exception to leading low when you do not have touching high cards.

Here are some examples of choosing the opening lead against a 3 NT contract when your partner has opened the bidding 1♡:

♠ Q 9 4 2 ♡ J 5 ◇ J 7 6 2 ♣ 10 8 3	You have no good reason for leading anything other than partner's suit. With a doubleton, lead the top card, the ♡ **J**.
♠ 6 4 ♡ Q 6 2 ◇ 10 8 6 3 ♣ Q 9 6 4	Again, you should lead partner's suit. With three cards but without touching high cards, lead a low card, the ♡ **2**.
♠ K 7 2 ♡ Q J 8 3 ◇ 9 6 2 ♣ J 10 3	With touching high cards, lead the top card, the ♡ **Q**, rather than fourth best. This tells partner that you have the next-lower card, the ♡ J, but not the next-higher card, the ♡ K. Of course, you also would lead the ♡ Q if you had a doubleton. Partner often will be able to tell from the auction and the number of cards in dummy and his own hand how many cards you have.

Returning Partner's Suit

In addition to leading your partner's suit, it is also a good idea to *return partner's suit* unless you have something clearly better to do. This means that when you get the lead, you should lead the suit that partner led originally. Again, you are working as a partnership — if partner chose a suit to lead, in most cases you should work with him to develop tricks in that suit.

The card you lead back in partner's suit is the same card you normally would lead from your *remaining holding* . For example, suppose you originally had K-7-3 in a suit. Partner leads the 4, and you play the king on the first trick. If you get a chance to lead the suit back, lead the 7, the top of your remaining doubleton. If you started with K-7-3-2, you would lead back the 2 — low from your three remaining cards.

◆ *BIDDING REVIEW* ◆

Making an Overcall

When the opponents open the bidding, you can consider whether to overcall using the following guidelines:

REQUIREMENTS FOR AN OVERCALL IN A SUIT

- A five-card or longer suit (for both majors and minors)
- 13 or more points (occasionally fewer with a good suit if not vulnerable and at the one level)

REQUIREMENTS FOR A 1 NT OVERCALL

- 16-18 points
- Balanced hand
- Some strength in the opponent's suit

Responding to an Overcall

If partner overcalls 1 NT, you can use the same responses as when partner opens the bidding 1 NT. If partner overcalls in a suit, use the following guidelines:

- With a minimum hand (6-10 points):
    - Pass if already at the two level.
    - Raise partner's suit to the two level with three-card or longer support.
    - Bid a new suit at the one level.
    - Bid 1 NT with some strength in the opponent's suit and a balanced hand.

- With a medium hand (11-12 points):
    - Raise partner's suit to the three level with three-card or longer support.
    - Bid a new suit (even if it is at the two level).
    - Bid 2 NT with some strength in the opponent's suit and a balanced hand.

- With a maximum hand (13 or more points):
    - Raise partner's suit to game with three-card or longer support.
    - Bid a new suit.
    - Bid 3 NT with some strength in the opponent's suit and a balanced hand.

◆ *SUMMARY* ◆

When you come to the third step in your PLAN, *Analyze your alternatives*, one of the methods that can help you establish extra winners or eliminate losers is the *finesse*. The principle of the finesse is to *lead toward the high card* that you are hoping will win a trick.

If you are finessing for more than one missing card, lead toward the *lower* of your high cards first. Sometimes, you can afford to lead a high card to trap a missing card in an opponent's hand. You should lead a high card only *if you can afford to have an opponent cover it with a higher card*.

When partner has bid a suit and you are defending, you should lead partner's suit unless you have a clearly better alternative. Also, if your partner has led a suit, you should return partner's suit when you get an opportunity, unless you have something clearly better to do.

GROUP ACTIVITIES

Exercise One — The Finesse

In the following examples, how many sure tricks are there? How could you get an extra trick?

DUMMY: 1) A Q 3   2) 4 3   3) A K J   4) Q 4 2   5) K J 3

DECLARER: 7 6 5   K 5   7 5 3   A 7 3   A 5

_____   _____   _____   _____   _____

Exercise Two — Repeated Finesses

How would you play each of the following suits to get the maximum number of tricks? For you to succeed, where would the missing high card have to be?

DUMMY: 1) 7 4 3   2) A Q J   3) 8 7

DECLARER: K Q 5   5 3 2   A K J 10

_____   _____   _____

Exercise Three — Suit Development

Combine the ideas of the finesse and the development of long suits and determine how many tricks you could take with each of the following combinations if the location and division of the missing cards is as favorable as possible.

DUMMY: 1) Q 4 3   2) K Q 3 2   3) K 9 7 5 2 4) A Q J 3 2 5) 9 7 4

DECLARER: A 8 7 6 5   7 6 5 4   8 6 3   7 6 5   A K J 3

_____   _____   _____   _____   _____

Exercise Four — Leading the High Card

How would you play each of the following suits to get the maximum number of tricks?

DUMMY: 1) A 7 3   2) J 10 9   3) Q 7   4) Q J 5 2   5) J 4

DECLARER: Q J 10   A K 3 2   A 9 3   A 6 3   A Q 10 9

_____   _____   _____   _____   _____

Exercise Five — Leading Toward the Lower High Card First

How can you take the maximum number of tricks with each of the following combinations? How must the missing cards be located?

DUMMY: 1) A Q 10   2) 5 4 3   3) A J 10

DECLARER: 7 5 3   K J 10   8 6 4

_____   _____   _____

Exercise Six — Leading Partner's Suit

Which card would you lead from the following combinations if your partner has bid the suit?

    1) Q J 3   2) J 3   3) K 7 4   4) 10 8 6 2 5) A J 3

_____   _____   _____   _____   _____

Exercise Seven — Review of Overcalls

What would you bid with each of the following hands if the opponent on your right opened the bidding 1 ◇?

1) ♠ A Q J 10 7	2) ♠ K Q J	3) ♠ J 8 5 3
♡ K 3	♡ A Q J	♡ A Q
◇ 6 4 2	◇ K J 10	◇ Q J 6 2
♣ A 6 3	♣ 10 9 6 3	♣ Q J 7

4) ♠ K J 10 6 3	5) ♠ J 5 3	6) ♠ J 10
♡ A Q 8 6 5	♡ 4 2	♡ A 8 4
◇ 6	◇ A K J 8 4	◇ Q 9 2
♣ Q 4	♣ A 7 5	♣ Q 10 8 6 3

Exercise Eight — Review of Responses to Overcalls

What would you respond with each of the following hands if the opponent on your left opened the bidding 1 ◇, your partner overcalled 1 ♡ and your right-hand opponent passed?

1) ♠ A J 10 7	2) ♠ J 9 8 6 2	3) ♠ J 8 5
♡ Q 8 3	♡ 3	♡ 5 4
◇ 6 2	◇ Q 5 3	◇ A Q 10 3
♣ J 10 6 3	♣ 10 9 6 2	♣ Q 9 7 4

4) ♠ A K 10 6 3	5) ♠ A 5 3	6) ♠ K J 10
♡ 8 5	♡ Q J 4 2	♡ J 4
◇ J 7 4	◇ 6	◇ Q J 9 2
♣ K 7 3	♣ K J 8 7 5	♣ A K 3 2

Exercise Nine — Taking a Finesse

Turn up all the cards on the first pre-dealt hand. Put each hand dummy style at the edge of the table in front of each player.

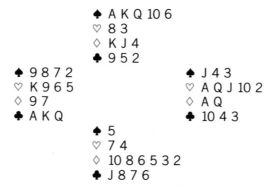

Dealer: North

```
                    ♠ A K Q 10 6
                    ♡ 8 3
                    ◇ K J 4
                    ♣ 9 5 2
    ♠ 9 8 7 2                          ♠ J 4 3
    ♡ K 9 6 5                          ♡ A Q J 10 2
    ◇ 9 7                              ◇ A Q
    ♣ A K Q                            ♣ 10 4 3
                    ♠ 5
                    ♡ 7 4
                    ◇ 10 8 6 5 3 2
                    ♣ J 8 7 6
```

The Bidding

What opening bid best describes North's hand?

East has an opening bid and a good five-card suit. What bid can East make to compete?

South passes. With support for partner's suit West can use dummy points to evaluate his hand. At what level does the partnership belong? In what denomination? What will West bid?

How will the auction proceed from there? What will be the contract? Who will be declarer?

The Play

Which player makes the opening lead? What will the opening lead be? Why?

Declarer starts by making a PLAN:

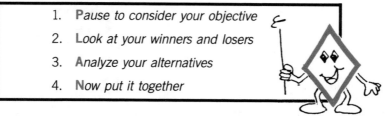

1. **P**ause to consider your objective
2. **L**ook at your winners and losers
3. **A**nalyze your alternatives
4. **N**ow put it together

After going through the four steps, how does declarer plan to get rid of his extra loser? What precaution must declarer take after the opening lead if North continues to lead spades?

Exercise Ten — A Repeated Finesse

Turn up all the cards on the second pre-dealt hand. Put each hand dummy style at the edge of the table in front of each player.

Dealer: East

```
              ♠ 10 8 4
              ♡ A J 3
              ◇ 9 4 2
              ♣ K Q 9 2
♠ 7 6 3 2                    ♠ K 9 5
♡ Q 7 6                      ♡ K 10 8 4
◇ 8 6                        ◇ K Q J 10 5
♣ 10 8 5 3                   ♣ 7
              ♠ A Q J
              ♡ 9 5 2
              ◇ A 7 3
              ♣ A J 6 4
```

The Bidding

East has 13 points. What is East's opening bid?

South has a balanced hand with 16 points. What bid best describes South's hand?

West passes. North is the captain. At what level does the partnership belong? In what denomination should the partnership play? What does North respond?

How will the auction proceed from there? What will be the contract? Who will be declarer?

The Play

Which player makes the opening lead? What will the opening lead be? Why?

Declarer starts by making a PLAN. After going through the four steps, how will declarer play the hand? In putting it together, what precaution must declarer take?

Exercise Eleven — Finessing Against Two Cards

Turn up all the cards on the third pre-dealt hand. Put each hand dummy style at the edge of the table in front of each player.

Dealer: South

```
              ♠ 9 6 2
              ♡ 10 7 6 2
              ◇ Q J 6
              ♣ Q 7 5
♠ A K J 10 8                 ♠ Q 4 3
♡ 8 5 4                      ♡ A 9 3
◇ 7 2                        ◇ K 5 4 3
♣ A J 10                     ♣ 8 6 2
              ♠ 7 5
              ♡ K Q J
              ◇ A 10 9 8
              ♣ K 9 4 3
```

67

The Bidding

What is South's opening bid?

What bid does West make to compete?

North passes. What does East respond to West's overcall?

South passes. How many points is East showing? Does West bid again? What will be the contract? Who will be declarer?

The Play

Which player makes the opening lead? What will the opening lead be? Why?

Declarer starts by making a PLAN. After going through the four steps, how does declarer plan to eliminate one of the club losers? To do this, what precaution must declarer take?

Exercise Twelve — Leading a High Card

Turn up all the cards on the fourth pre-dealt hand. Put each hand dummy style at the edge of the table in front of each player.

Dealer: West

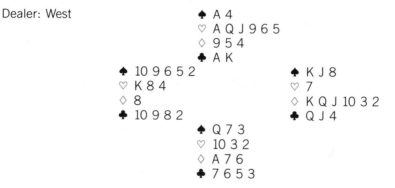

```
                    ♠ A 4
                    ♡ A Q J 9 6 5
                    ♢ 9 5 4
                    ♣ A K
   ♠ 10 9 6 5 2                      ♠ K J 8
   ♡ K 8 4                           ♡ 7
   ♢ 8                               ♢ K Q J 10 3 2
   ♣ 10 9 8 2                        ♣ Q J 4
                    ♠ Q 7 3
                    ♡ 10 3 2
                    ♢ A 7 6
                    ♣ 7 6 5 3
```

The Bidding

West does not have enough to open the bidding. What will North bid?

East has a good suit and an opening bid. What will East bid?

Does South have support for partner's major suit? What will South respond?

West passes. Does North have a minimum, medium or maximum hand? What will be North's rebid?

How will the auction proceed from there? What will be the contract? Who will be declarer?

The Play

Which player makes the opening lead? What will the opening lead be?

Declarer starts by making a PLAN. After going through the four steps, how will declarer play the hand? How does declarer plan to avoid losing a trump trick? Which card must declarer be careful to lead from dummy? Why?

LESSON 4

Eliminating Losers —
Trumping and Discarding

Trumping Losers in Dummy
Discarding Losers
Guidelines for Defense
Bidding Review — The Takeout Double
Summary

Workshop Material
Group Activities

As you saw in the previous two lessons, a number of techniques are available to help create extra winners in notrump contracts or eliminate extra losers in trump contracts: promotion of high cards, development of long suits and leading toward high cards (the finesse). In this lesson we will look at two techniques that are useful only in trump contracts: trumping losers in dummy and discarding losers on extra winners in dummy. Both methods take advantage of the unique power of the trump suit.

◆ *TRUMPING LOSERS IN DUMMY* ◆

An advantage of playing a trump contract is the tremendous power of the trump suit. Even an ace in another suit can fall to the lowliest trump. The ability to trump (ruff) the opponents' winners is the key to one of the most common techniques for eliminating losers.

Trumping in Dummy

Having played in some trump contracts, you are familiar with using the trump suit to stop the opponents from taking tricks in other suits. However, trumping in declarer's hand does not eliminate any of the losers you started with. To see this, suppose that hearts is the trump suit and look at the following layout of your heart and club suits:

DUMMY
♡ 4 3 2
♣ 4 3 2

DECLARER (YOU)
♡ A K Q J 10
♣ 5

When counting your losers, concentrate on declarer's hand — count none in hearts and one in clubs. If the opponents try to take tricks in clubs, you will lose the first trick but trump the next trick. You have gained nothing since you still have the one loser you originally counted.

Nothing is gained by trumping dummy's clubs in your hand other than to prevent losing a trick. You still end up with the same five heart tricks that you started with. You should not go out of your way to trump dummy's clubs, since you eventually may run out of trumps in your hand and be unable to draw the opponents' trumps or stop the opponents from taking their winners in other suits.

Suppose we change the layout of the club suit:

DUMMY
♡ 4 3 2
♣ 5

DECLARER (YOU)
♡ A K Q J 10
♣ 4 3 2

This time, you have three club losers in your hand. If the opponents try to take tricks in clubs, you will lose the first trick but you can trump the next trick with one of dummy's trumps. In this case you have gained something since you have eliminated one of your losers by trumping in dummy. You will win one trick with dummy's trump and still have five heart tricks left in your hand, for a total of six.

You want to go out of your way to trump one of your clubs in dummy since you eliminate a loser. If you can maneuver to trump another club with one of dummy's hearts, you eliminate another loser and end up taking seven tricks in all, rather than the five you originally had.

In general, you eliminate a loser by *trumping in dummy;* you do not eliminate a loser by trumping in your own hand.

Sometimes, trumping your losers in dummy takes careful planning. Look for the following conditions to trump your losers in dummy successfully:

- More cards in the suit in your hand than in dummy;

- Enough trumps in dummy so you can trump your losers;

- High cards to get to your hand so you can lead the suit you want to trump in dummy.

Let's look at each of these conditions in turn.

The Opportunity for Trumping Losers

Side suits equally divided between your hand and dummy provide no opportunity to trump losers:

DUMMY:	9 4 3	8 2	7
DECLARER:	A 8 2	10 9	3

Even though dummy may have only a doubleton or singleton, declarer cannot trump a loser because declarer also has shortness. For there to be an opportunity to trump losers, the cards in a side suit must be unevenly divided, with declarer having more cards.

DUMMY: A 4	Here, declarer's hand has more cards than dummy. This provides a good opportunity to trump a
DECLARER: K 3 2	loser. Plan to start by playing the high card from the short side, the ace, and then lead the 4 to your king. Now lead your remaining low card and trump it in dummy.

DUMMY: —	Since dummy is void in the suit, you have the opportunity to trump your losers. You need at least
DECLARER: 8 4 2	three trumps in dummy and you also will need some way of getting back to your hand each time to lead the suit again.

DUMMY: 4	Since dummy has a singleton, the conditions are right to trump both your losers.
DECLARER: A 9 3	

DUMMY:	A 9 3
DECLARER:	4

When dummy has more cards in the suit than declarer, you have no opportunity to trump losers.

Let's see how trumping a loser in dummy works with a complete hand.

Contract: 4♡
Lead: ◇A

NORTH (DUMMY)
♠ A K 7
♡ K 9 7 6 3
◇ 10 7 4 2
♣ 6

WEST
♠ 9 6 3 2
♡ J
◇ **A** K Q J
♣ Q 8 5 3

EAST
♠ J 8 5
♡ 8 5
◇ 9 5
♣ K J 9 7 4 2

SOUTH (DECLARER)
♠ Q 10 4
♡ A Q 10 4 2
◇ 8 6 3
♣ A 10

In a contract of 4♡, you can afford three losers. You have three diamond losers and a club loser. You need to eliminate one of your losers. When you **Analyze your alternatives,** you can't do much about the diamond losers — West is poised to take the first three tricks; but the club suit provides an opportunity to trump your loser in dummy. After drawing trumps, play the ♣A and then trump a club in dummy to make your contract.

Creating the Opportunity to Trump Losers

In the previous example declarer could trump his club loser without losing a club trick. Sometimes, declarer has some work to do before the conditions are right for trumping losers in dummy.

DUMMY:	6
DECLARER:	9 7 5

You would like to trump your losers in dummy but cannot do so immediately since dummy is not void in the suit. Concede a trick to the opponents. When you regain the lead, dummy will be void, and the opportunity will be there to trump both your losers.

DUMMY:	7 4
DECLARER:	10 8 2

This time, you still can trump a loser in dummy because the suit is unevenly divided — declarer has more cards than dummy. You will have to give up the lead twice before the conditions are right to trump your remaining loser.

It can be nerve-wracking to give up the lead, since you may wonder what the opponents will do when they get the lead. The reward for your efforts, however, is that you eliminate one or more of your extra losers and frequently make your contract.

Consider this hand:

Contract: 4♠
Lead: ♡J

NORTH (DUMMY)
♠ A Q J 7 3
♡ A 6 4
◇ 9 5
♣ 10 8 2

WEST
♠ 9 5
♡ J 10 9 7
◇ A J 6 2
♣ Q 9 3

EAST
♠ 8
♡ Q 5 3 2
◇ K Q 8 4
♣ J 7 6 4

SOUTH (DECLARER)
♠ K 10 6 4 2
♡ K 8
◇ 10 7 3
♣ A K 5

In a contract of 4♠, you can afford three losers and you have three diamond losers and a club loser, one too many. When you **A**nalyze *your alternatives*, you can see the opportunity to trump one of your diamond losers in dummy since dummy has fewer diamonds than you.

However, some work must be done. When putting your plan together, decide to give up two diamond tricks, creating the right conditions to trump your loser in dummy. As you have seen, you generally want to take your losses early. Give up the diamond tricks (after drawing trumps) while you still have some trumps left in dummy (and some winners left in the other side suits so that you can regain the lead).

Managing Dummy's Trumps

Managing the trump suit is a very important part of your PLAN when you get to the fourth step, **N**ow *put it together*, and we will discuss it in more detail in Lesson 7. Since trump management is also important when trumping losers in dummy, we will look at that aspect now.

It is generally a good idea to draw the opponents' trumps — however small. They can be used to turn some of your winners into unexpected losers if you are not careful. However, declarer sometimes needs dummy's trumps to take care of losers and cannot afford to draw all the trumps right away.

Let's look at declarer's considerations when deciding whether to draw the opponents' trumps right away. The first consideration is how many trump cards are needed in dummy to take care of the losers in declarer's hand.

DUMMY: —

DECLARER: A 3

Declarer has one loser to get rid of, so dummy will need one trump to take care of it.

DUMMY:	4 2	Declarer only has two losers but will be able to trump only one of them in dummy since one trick
DECLARER:	A 6 3	must be lost before the remaining loser can be trumped. Therefore, one trump must remain in dummy when declarer is ready to trump the loser.

DUMMY:	5	Here declarer has a chance to trump two losers and will therefore need two trumps in dummy.
DECLARER:	A 9 7	

DUMMY:	—	In this case, declarer needs three trumps in dummy to trump all three losers.
DECLARER:	8 6 5	

Declarer must consider if enough trumps will be left in dummy if trumps are drawn first. If enough trumps will be left, declarer can start by drawing trumps.

Look at this example:

Contract: 4♠
Lead: ♡ K

NORTH (DUMMY)
♠ Q J 9 3
♡ 7 5 3
◇ K 3
♣ A K 6 2

WEST
♠ 8 4
♡ **K** Q 8 4
◇ 7
♣ Q 10 9 7 5 3

EAST
♠ 6 2
♡ A 10 9
◇ Q J 10 8 6 5 4
♣ J

SOUTH (DECLARER)
♠ A K 10 7 5
♡ J 6 2
◇ A 9 2
♣ 8 4

You can afford three losers and you have three heart losers and a diamond loser, one too many. To eliminate your extra loser, plan to trump your diamond loser in dummy. To do this, you need only one of dummy's trumps.

Suppose the opponents win the first three heart tricks and then lead a diamond. Win dummy's ◇ K (high card from the short side). Should you draw trumps first or trump your losing diamond? Since you need only one trump in dummy, start drawing the trumps. Since the opponents' trumps divide 2–2, this takes only two rounds and you have two trumps left in dummy, more than enough. You can now play the ◇ A safely and trump your diamond loser in dummy, making your contract.

Notice what happens if you do not draw trumps first. When you play your ◇ A, West trumps it and you are defeated. A little unlucky perhaps, but this is what you are trying to guard against by drawing trumps first.

Suppose we change the opponents' hands slightly:

Contract: 4♠
Lead: ♡K

```
                        NORTH (DUMMY)
                        ♠ Q J 9 3
                        ♡ 7 5 3
                        ◊ K 3
                        ♣ A K 6 2
        WEST                              EAST
        ♠ 8 6 4 2                         ♠ —
        ♡ K Q 8 4                         ♡ A 10 9
        ◊ 7 5 4                           ◊ Q J 10 8 6
        ♣ Q 10                            ♣ J 9 7 5 3
                        SOUTH (DECLARER)
                        ♠ A K 10 7 5
                        ♡ J 6 2
                        ◊ A 9 2
                        ♣ 8 4
```

From your perspective, it looks the same. The opponents take the first three heart tricks and lead a diamond. Win the ◊ K. Needing only one trump in dummy, you start to draw trumps so that the opponents cannot trump one of your winners.

This time, however, the missing trumps are divided 4–0 — it will take four rounds to draw them all. If you draw all the trumps first, dummy will have none left to trump your loser. Once you realize this (East discards when you lead a spade), stop drawing the missing trumps, play your ◊ A and trump your diamond loser. Now you can finish drawing West's trumps and make your contract.

Of course, the possibility exists that West started with only one diamond and will trump your ◊ A. However, you have no alternative but to take that risk. Your PLAN tells you that you need to trump a loser in dummy and you need at least one trump to do so. You cannot afford to draw all the trumps first.

Here is another example where declarer cannot afford to draw trumps first:

Contract: 4♡
Lead: ♠Q

```
                        NORTH (DUMMY)
                        ♠ A 7 6 5
                        ♡ A Q 7
                        ◊ J 7 6 5 3
                        ♣ 3
        WEST                              EAST
        ♠ Q J 10 9                        ♠ 8 2
        ♡ 5 3                             ♡ 6 4 2
        ◊ K 4                             ◊ A Q 10 8
        ♣ Q 10 7 5 2                      ♣ K 9 8 6
                        SOUTH (DECLARER)
                        ♠ K 4 3
                        ♡ K J 10 9 8
                        ◊ 9 2
                        ♣ A J 4
```

75

Your objective allows you to lose three tricks in your 4♡ contract. You have a spade loser, two diamond losers and two club losers — two too many. There appears to be a good opportunity to trump two club losers in dummy. Should you draw trumps immediately after winning the first trick?

You are missing five trumps, and hopefully they are divided 3–2. It will take three rounds of hearts to draw them all, leaving no hearts in dummy. Since you need two of dummy's trumps to trump your club losers, you must delay drawing trumps until your other work is done.

Win the ♠A, play the ♣A and trump a club in dummy. Come back to your hand (perhaps using one of your trumps for this purpose — we will discuss this shortly) and trump your remaining club loser in dummy. Now you are ready to draw trumps and make your contract.

Be careful about the number of trumps left in dummy if you must give up the lead to trump a loser. When the opponents get the lead, they have an opportunity to lead the trump suit themselves. If they see that you are planning to trump losers in dummy, they may try to prevent this. Consider this example:

```
Contract: 4♡            NORTH (DUMMY)
Lead: ♠J                ♠ K Q 6
                        ♡ A 8 7
                        ◇ J 7 6 5 3
                        ♣ J 3
        WEST                            EAST
        ♠ J 10 9 8                      ♠ 5 4 2
        ♡ 5 3 2                         ♡ 6 4
        ◇ K 4                           ◇ Q 10 9 8
        ♣ A 10 5 2                      ♣ K Q 8 6
                        SOUTH (DECLARER)
                        ♠ A 7 3
                        ♡ K Q J 10 9
                        ◇ A 2
                        ♣ 9 7 4
```

In your contract of 4♡, you have a diamond loser and three club losers, one more than you can afford. The club suit offers the opportunity to trump your third club loser in dummy. To do this, you must give up two club tricks.

You need only one heart in dummy to trump your loser. It would seem safe enough to draw two rounds of trumps before going to work on the club suit. However, you must let the opponents in twice before dummy is ready to trump the club loser. At either opportunity, the opponents, seeing your plan, can lead a heart themselves, getting rid of dummy's last trump.

Even one round of trumps is too many. Since the opponents will get the lead twice, they could lead trumps at both opportunities. By the time you are ready to trump your loser, dummy will have no trumps left. You need to start early and lead a club as soon as you win the first trick. Another example of taking your losses early!

Avoiding an Overruff

Don't send a boy to do a man's job (or a girl to do a woman's job). When you trump a loser in dummy, don't forget that the opponents also can play a trump if they have no cards in the same suit. Consider this hand:

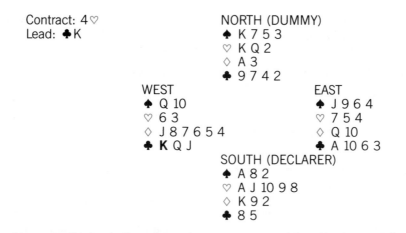

Contract: 4♡
Lead: ♣K

NORTH (DUMMY)
♠ K 7 5 3
♡ K Q 2
◇ A 3
♣ 9 7 4 2

WEST
♠ Q 10
♡ 6 3
◇ J 8 7 6 5 4
♣ K Q J

EAST
♠ J 9 6 4
♡ 7 5 4
◇ Q 10
♣ A 10 6 3

SOUTH (DECLARER)
♠ A 8 2
♡ A J 10 9 8
◇ K 9 2
♣ 8 5

You can afford only three losers in your contract of 4♡. You have a spade loser, a diamond loser and two club losers. You need to eliminate one of your losers. This looks simple enough, since the situation is ripe for trumping your diamond loser in dummy.

You need a trump left in dummy to trump your diamond loser, so you cannot afford to draw all the opponents' trumps right away. Suppose the opponents take the first two club tricks and play another club, which you trump in your hand. If you play the ◇A and ◇K and then trump your diamond loser with dummy's ♡2, look what happens. East can overruff (overtrump) your ♡2 with the ♡4 since he also has no diamond left.

You must be careful to trump your loser with as high a trump as you can afford. In this hand you can afford to trump with a man (the king) or a woman (the queen), since you have all the other high trumps. This avoids the possibility of an overruff and still leaves you with enough high trumps to draw the opponents' trumps.

Using Your High Cards Wisely

To trump a loser in dummy, you first must get to your (declarer's) hand to lead the loser. You often must be careful to take this into account when making your PLAN. Look at this example:

Contract: 2♠
Lead: ♣Q

NORTH (DUMMY)
♠ 10 8 6 5
♡ 3
◇ A 7 4 2
♣ K 6 5 3

WEST
♠ K 4
♡ K 10 7 6 2
◇ 10 8
♣ Q J 10 9

EAST
♠ A 3 2
♡ Q 9 8 4
◇ K Q 9 6
♣ 8 4

SOUTH (DECLARER)
♠ Q J 9 7
♡ A J 5
◇ J 5 3
♣ A 7 2

You can afford five losers in contract of 2♠. You must lose the ♠A and ♠K and you also have two heart losers, two diamond losers and a club loser — a total of seven losers. Trumping your two heart losers in dummy looks like the best way to eliminate the extra losers.

Does it matter whether you win the first trick with dummy's ♣K or your ♣A? Suppose you win it with the ♣A. You can play the ♡A and trump one of your heart losers in dummy, but how do you get back to your hand to lead your other heart loser? Whatever suit you lead, the opponents will win a trick. Now, seeing that you are trying to trump losers in dummy, they may play the ♠K, ♠A and another spade to eliminate dummy's remaining trumps.

It is important to look ahead — you will need to get back to your hand to trump your other heart loser. Win the first trick with dummy's ♣K. Then you can lead a heart to your ♡A and trump one of your heart losers. Next you can lead a club to your carefully preserved ♣A and be in the right hand to trump your remaining heart loser. Once this is done, you can start drawing the opponents' trumps by driving out their ace and king. You end up just making your contract.

We will discuss other examples of the careful utilization of your high cards in the next lesson.

The Crossruff

Sometimes, you have so many losers to trump that you never get around to drawing trumps at all. Consider the following hand:

Contract: 4♡
Lead: ◊K

NORTH (DUMMY)
♠ J 6 2
♡ K Q 10 7
◊ A 8 6 4 2
♣ 5

WEST
♠ K 7 4
♡ 6 5 2
◊ K Q 10 7 5
♣ 8 3

EAST
♠ A 10 9 3
♡ 4 3
◊ 9 3
♣ K Q J 9 6

SOUTH (DECLARER)
♠ Q 8 5
♡ A J 9 8
◊ J
♣ A 10 7 4 2

In a contract of 4♡, you can afford only three losers. You have three losers in spades, and four losers in clubs — far too many. However, dummy's singleton club offers some potential. You can plan to trump all four of your club losers with dummy's trumps.

You cannot afford to draw any trumps since you will need all of dummy's trumps for your losers. After winning the ◊A, you will start right away trumping your club losers by leading a club to your ♣A, leading another club and trumping it in dummy. But now you need to get back to your hand to lead another club. Since you have no high cards in your hand other than trumps, make use of the trump suit. You cannot lead one of dummy's trumps since you need all of them to trump your losers. However, you can lead a diamond from dummy and trump it in your hand.

Now you can lead another club and trump it in dummy. To get back to your hand, you again lead a diamond and trump it. You trump another club loser in dummy, lead another diamond and trump it. You lead your last club loser and trump it with dummy's last heart. The only trump you have left is the ace in your hand, but it is your tenth trick — your only remaining cards are the three spade losers. You have made your contract without ever drawing trumps.

Because you trumped (or ruffed) losers in both hands, crossing back and forth, this play is called crossruff. This is one occasion when you do benefit from trumping losers in your hand.

◆ DISCARDING LOSERS ◆

When you cannot trump your losers in dummy, another method of getting rid of losers is discarding them on extra winners available in dummy. Let's see how this works.

Discarding Losers on Extra Winners in the Dummy

When you are looking for alternative ways of disposing of losers in a trump contract, look to see if dummy has additional winners in a side suit (i.e., other than trumps) on which you can throw (discard) your losers. It often happens that weakness in one area is compensated for by extra strength somewhere else.

The advantage of discarding your losers in a side suit is that you then will be able to take advantage of your trump suit to prevent the opponents from taking tricks in that side suit. This technique is not useful in a notrump contract since, even if you were able to discard some of your *losers* on dummy's winners, you would have no trumps to prevent the opponents from taking tricks in the suit you discarded.

To discard a loser, you must have a side suit that is divided with more cards in dummy than in your hand. The suit also must contain more winners than you need to take care of your losers in that suit. Here are some examples:

DUMMY:	A K 4	In this suit you have one low card in your hand but dummy's ace will take care of it. So you have
DECLARER:	2	no losers in the suit. Dummy also has the king. This is an extra winner that you can use to take care of a loser in another side suit.
DUMMY:	A K Q	Dummy has two extra winners. You can discard two of your losers in another side suit.
DECLARER:	3	
DUMMY:	A Q 3	Dummy has a surplus winner in this suit. Start by playing the king (high card from the short side) and
DECLARER:	K 4	then lead the 4 to dummy's ace. The queen can now be played, allowing you to discard a loser.

Let's see how discarding a loser works in a complete hand.

Contract: 4♡
Lead: ◇ K

NORTH (DUMMY)
♠ Q 4 3
♡ 8 7 5 2
◇ A 6 4
♣ A K 7

WEST
♠ 8 7 2
♡ A 4
◇ **K** Q J 10
♣ 10 8 5 4

EAST
♠ 10 9 6 5
♡ K
◇ 8 7 2
♣ Q J 9 6 2

SOUTH (DECLARER)
♠ A K J
♡ Q J 10 9 6 3
◇ 9 5 3
♣ 3

You are in 4♡ and you can afford three losers. When you count your losers, you find two in hearts, since you are missing the ♡A and ♡K, and two in diamonds, since dummy's ◇A will take care of only one of your low diamonds. That's a total of four, one loser too many.

When analyzing your alternatives, you can see that dummy has an extra club winner — only the ♣A is needed to take care of the low club in your hand. Use this extra winner to discard one of your diamond losers. After winning the ◇A, play the ♣A and then the ♣K, throwing a diamond from your hand. Now you are left with only one diamond loser in your hand. If the opponents lead diamonds, you will trump after losing just one trick. Combined with your two heart losers, you are left with just three losers and can make your contract.

To Draw or not to Draw

Should you draw trumps before discarding your losers? In general, you want to draw the opponents' trumps as soon as possible. However, if you look at the previous hand, you can see that this won't always be correct.

In the above hand the opponents have led the ◇K, driving out your ◇A. You now have two *quick losers* in diamonds. That is, as soon as the opponents regain the lead, they will be in position to take two diamond tricks. To draw trumps, you must lose the lead since you are missing the ♡A and ♡K. If you start by leading trumps, the opponents will win, take their two diamond tricks and defeat your contract.

When you come to the fourth step of your PLAN, N*ow put it together,* consider whether to draw trumps before discarding your losers. If your losers are quick (as in the above example), and you must lose the lead to draw trumps, delay drawing trumps until you have disposed of your extra losers.

If you can draw trumps without giving up the lead, then it is safer to do this before discarding your losers. Look at this example:

Contract: 4♠
Lead: ♣K

NORTH (DUMMY)
♠ K 10 8
♡ J 5 2
◇ A K Q 4
♣ 7 5 2

WEST
♠ 7 6 5
♡ K 7 6 4
◇ 10 6
♣ **K** Q J 10

EAST
♠ 4
♡ A Q 10
◇ J 9 8 7 5 2
♣ 8 6 4

SOUTH (DECLARER)
♠ A Q J 9 3 2
♡ 9 8 3
◇ 3
♣ A 9 3

You can afford three losers in your contract of 4♠. You have three heart losers and two club losers — two too many — but dummy has two extra diamond winners on which you can discard two of your losers, allowing you to make your contract.

Should you draw trumps first or discard your losers? Once the ♣K has driven out your ace, all your losers are quick. However, you can draw trumps without giving up the lead, so you should do this before discarding your losers. Once the opponents' trumps are drawn, you can play the ◇A, ◇K and ◇Q and discard two of your losers.

Notice what happens if you don't draw trumps first. When you play your ◇A, ◇K and ◇Q, West trumps the ◇Q. Unlucky, but preventable if you draw trumps first.

If your losers are slow — that is, the opponents cannot take their winners in the suit right away when they get the lead — you generally can afford to draw trumps first, even if you must give up the lead. Take a look at this hand:

Contract: 4♡
Lead: ♠Q

NORTH (DUMMY)
♠ 8 7 4
♡ 10 7 5 2
◇ 10 5 2
♣ A K 4

WEST
♠ **Q** J 10 9
♡ A 6 3
◇ Q J 9 4
♣ J 5

EAST
♠ 6 3 2
♡ 4
◇ K 8 7
♣ 10 9 8 7 6 2

SOUTH (DECLARER)
♠ A K 5
♡ K Q J 9 8
◇ A 6 3
♣ Q 3

In your 4♡ contract you can afford three losers. You have one loser in spades, one in hearts and two in diamonds. Your club holding provides the opportunity to discard a loser on dummy's extra winner.

Should you draw trumps first? Then you must drive out the opponents' ♡A, giving up the lead. However, your losers are slow, not quick. When you win the ♠Q with your ♠K, you still will have the ♠A — when you give up the lead in the trump suit, the opponents will not be able to take their winners right away. Whatever they lead, you can win and draw the remaining trumps. Now it is safe to play the ♣Q (high card from the short side), and lead the ♣3 to dummy's ♣A and ♣K. On the last club you discard one of your losers.

If you don't draw trumps first, you will be defeated. When you play the third round of clubs, discarding your loser, West trumps it, turning one of your winners into a loser.

What if West leads the ◇Q instead of the ♠Q? After you win the ◇A, you have two quick losers left in diamonds. When the opponents get the lead with their ♡A, they will be able to take their two diamond winners. However, that is not enough to defeat your contract. You still have a slow loser in spades, and this is the loser you discard after drawing trumps. You must be careful not to give up the lead too soon only when you have too many quick losers.

Developing Extra Winners

Sometimes, dummy does not have an *immediate* extra winner on which to discard your loser; it may be possible to *establish* an extra winner by using one of the techniques you have seen earlier: promotion, length or the finesse. Consider these examples:

DUMMY:	K Q J	Dummy has no sure winners, but you can promote two tricks by driving out the opponents' ace. Since you have only two low cards in your hand, dummy's extra winner then can be used to discard one of your losers.
DECLARER	4 2	

DUMMY:	A K 8 6 2	If the missing cards are divided 3–2, you can develop two extra winners by giving up a trick. You then can use these winners to discard some of your losers.
DECLARER:	5 4 3	

DUMMY:	A Q J	With this combination you can take a finesse, hoping the opponent on your left has the king. If your finesse is successful, you can come back to your hand and repeat it. You then will have an extra winner in dummy on which you can discard one of your losers.
DECLARER:	7 3	

Here is a complete hand that illustrates promoting an extra winner on which to discard a loser.

Contract: 4 ♡
Lead: ◇K

NORTH (DUMMY)
♠ Q J 10
♡ Q 7 5 2
◇ A 8 6
♣ A 8 4

WEST
♠ A 7 6 2
♡ 6 3
◇ K Q J 10
♣ J 6 5

EAST
♠ K 9 8 5
♡ 9
◇ 7 5 4 2
♣ Q 9 3 2

SOUTH (DECLARER)
♠ 4 3
♡ A K J 10 8 4
◇ 9 3
♣ K 10 7

You can afford three losers and have two in spades, one in diamonds and one in clubs — one too many. Since you cannot trump any losers in dummy, you must consider whether you can discard one of them. Dummy has no immediate extra winners, but the spade suit offers an extra trick if you drive out the opponents' ♠A and ♠K.

After winning the first trick, you can afford to draw trumps since you don't have to give up the lead. You then can lead a spade and use dummy's ♠10 (or ♠J or ♠Q) to drive out the opponents' ♠K. They can take their diamond winner, but if they lead another diamond, you can trump it and lead another spade, using dummy's ♠J to force out their ♠A. Now you have established dummy's remaining spade as a winner and can use it to discard your club loser.

Here is an example of establishing an extra winner using length:

Contract 4♡
Lead: ◇4

NORTH (DUMMY)
♠ A K 5
♡ 6 5 2
◇ 8 7
♣ A 9 7 6 3

WEST
♠ 9 8 6 3
♡ 8 7
◇ K 10 5 **4** 2
♣ Q 5

EAST
♠ Q J 10
♡ 9 4 3
◇ A Q 9 6
♣ J 10 8

SOUTH (DECLARER)
♠ 7 4 2
♡ A K Q J 10
◇ J 3
♣ K 4 2

You can lose three tricks in 4♡ and you have a spade loser, two diamond losers and a club loser. You can't do much about the diamond losers since the opponents are poised to take the first two tricks. You cannot ruff your club loser and there is nowhere to discard it. So you must concentrate on getting rid of your spade loser.

The length in clubs offers an opportunity to develop extra winners. You have eight clubs and the opponents have five. If the missing clubs divide 3–2, your remaining clubs will be winners once you have given up a trick. You can use one of these extra winners to discard your spade loser.

Suppose the opponents win the first two diamond tricks and then lead a spade, driving out your ♠K. You can draw trumps and then play the ♣K, ♣A and another club to establish your remaining clubs as winners. If they lead another spade, driving out your ♠A, you then can play one of your club winners and discard your remaining low spade. You then have the rest of the tricks and make your contract.

Here is an example of establishing an extra winner using the finesse:

Contract 2♠
Lead: ♡Q

NORTH (DUMMY)
♠ J 10 8 2
♡ 7 4 2
◇ A J 4
♣ 7 6 5

WEST
♠ 9 4
♡ **Q** J 10 8
◇ Q 8 7 2
♣ K 10 8

EAST
♠ A 6
♡ K 6 3
◇ 10 9 6 5
♣ A Q 9 3

SOUTH (DECLARER)
♠ K Q 7 5 3
♡ A 9 5
◇ K 3
♣ J 4 2

In your partscore of 2♠, you can afford five losers. You have a spade loser, two heart losers and three club losers — one too many. Since the opponents will drive out your ♡A with their opening lead, all of your losers are quick. You cannot afford to start drawing trumps because the opponents will win the ♠A and take their two heart tricks and three club tricks.

How can you eliminate one of your losers? The only hope is to discard one of them on an extra winner in dummy. Dummy has no sure winners you can use, but a winning diamond finesse is possible. You can play the ◇K and then lead your ◇3 toward dummy's ◇A and ◇J. When West follows with a low diamond, you finesse dummy's ◇J, winning the trick, since East does not have the ◇Q. Now you can play dummy's ◇A and discard one of your losers. You are down to five losers and can safely start to play trumps and make your contract.

What if East held the ◇Q? Then your finesse would lose and you would be defeated two tricks — the opponents also would take their two heart tricks, three club tricks and the ♠A. That's the chance you have to take sometimes if you are going to try and make your contract — double or nothing!

 **GUIDELINES FOR DEFENSE**

If your partner leads a card, you will be contributing the third card to the trick. Here are some guidelines that will help you when you are the third hand to play.

Third Hand High

Consider the following layout of a suit:

DUMMY
7 6 5

PARTNER
K J 8 4 3

YOU
Q 9 2

DECLARER
A 10

Suppose your partner leads the 4, and dummy plays the 5. Which card should you play? You are the third hand to play and have the last opportunity for your side. A good guideline for this situation is *third hand high*. If it looks as though partner's card won't win the trick, play a high card, trying to win the trick for your side.

In this case play the highest card you can afford, the queen. Since declarer has the ace, your queen won't win the trick, but it will drive out declarer's ace and promote your partner's king and jack into winners. If you play the 2, or a halfhearted 9, declarer will win the trick with the 10 and still have the ace left. You will not have promoted any winners for your side.

The objective of the guideline *third hand high* is to win the trick for your side or promote other cards in the suit. You do not need to play third hand high if partner's card will win the trick, or if second hand has played a card higher than any you have. For example:

```
                    DUMMY
                    K 6 5
    PARTNER                     YOU
    Q J 10 9                    A 4 2
                    DECLARER
                    8 7 3
```

If partner leads the queen and dummy plays a low card, you do not need to play your ace since partner's queen is going to win the trick. Of course, if dummy plays the king, you would win the trick with your ace.

Only as High as Necessary

The principle of third hand high does not always require you to play your highest card. You need to play only as high a card as is necessary. Look at this layout:

```
                    DUMMY
                    Q 6 3
    PARTNER                     YOU
    10 7 4 2                    K J 9
                    DECLARER
                    A 8 5
```

Suppose your partner leads the 2, and the 3 is played from dummy. You do not need to play your king, since you can see the queen in dummy. Instead, play the jack. If your partner has the ace, your jack will win the trick. If declarer has the ace, the jack will force out the ace and you will have promoted your king into a winner.

The concept of *only as high as necessary* also applies in this situation:

```
                    DUMMY
                    9 6
    PARTNER                     YOU
    K 10 8 5 2                  Q J 3
                    DECLARER
                    A 7 4
```

If your partner leads the 5, and the 6 is played from dummy, your queen and your jack are *equals*. Either one can be used to force out declarer's ace. In such a case, play the

85

jack rather than the queen, following the principle of playing only as high a card as is necessary. When your jack forces out declarer's ace, your partner will know that you have the queen, since declarer would have won the trick with the queen if he held it (keeping the ace for a second trick). If you play the queen in such situations, your partner won't know who holds the missing jack (and probably should assume that declarer has it).

◆ **BIDDING REVIEW** ◆

The Takeout Double

One way to compete in the auction is by making a takeout double. You can tell when a double is for takeout by using the following guideline:

- If you and your partner have done nothing except pass, and the doubled contract is a partscore, the double is for takeout.

- If either you or your partner has bid, or the doubled contract is a game, the double is for penalty.

To make a takeout double, you need a hand that satisfies the following criteria:

REQUIREMENTS FOR A TAKEOUT DOUBLE

- 13 or more points (counting dummy points)

- Support for the unbid suits.

Responding to a Takeout Double

The takeout double is forcing, and responder must reply unless the opponent on his right bids. You choose your response using the following guidelines:

RESPONDING TO A TAKEOUT DOUBLE

- With a minimum hand (0–10 points):

    - Bid a four–card or longer major suit at the cheapest level.
    - Bid a four–card or longer minor suit at the cheapest level.
    - Bid 1 NT.

- With a medium hand (11–12 points):

    - Jump in a four–card or longer major suit.
    - Jump in a four–card or longer minor suit.
    - Jump to 2 NT.

- With a maximum hand (13 or more points):

    - Jump to game in a four–card or longer major suit.
    - Jump to 3 NT.

Rebids by the Takeout Doubler

Once you have made a takeout double, do not bid again unless partner shows better than a minimum hand or you have better than a minimum hand. Use the following guidelines:

REBIDS BY THE TAKEOUT DOUBLER

- With a minimum hand (13–16 points):

  - Pass if partner bids at the cheapest level.
  - Pass with 13–14 points if partner jumps a level. Bid a Golden Game with 15–16 points if partner jumps a level.

- With a medium hand (17–18 points):

  - Raise one level if partner bids at the cheapest level.
  - Bid a Golden Game if partner jumps a level.

- With a maximum hand (19–21 points):

  - Jump raise if partner bids at the cheapest level.
  - Bid a Golden Game if partner jumps a level.

◆ SUMMARY ◆

When you are playing in a trump contract and come to the third step in your PLAN, *Analyze your alternatives,* you may consider two techniques to eliminate losers:

- Trumping losers in dummy
- Discarding losers on extra winners in dummy

When planning to trump losers in dummy, ensure that sufficient trumps are left in dummy to accomplish your purpose. Sometimes, you must delay drawing trumps until you have trumped your losers. Use your high cards wisely — ensure that you are in the right hand at the right time.

When discarding losers, you also must be careful about drawing trumps. If you must give up the lead while drawing trumps and have too many quick losers, delay drawing trumps until you have discarded your extra losers. Sometimes, you must establish the extra winners you need in dummy using the techniques of promotion, development of long suits and the finesse.

A useful guideline when defending is *third hand high*. However, play only as high a card as necessary either to win the trick or promote winners for your side.

◆ *GROUP ACTIVITIES* ◆

Exercise One — Trumping Losers in Dummy

These are your holdings in various side suits in a trump contract. Which of them provide an opportunity to trump losers in dummy?

DUMMY:	1) 8	2) 10 9 8 7	3) 4 2	4) —	5) A K 6
DECLARER:	A 4 2	A K	Q J	9 6 5	5

_____   _____   _____   _____   _____

Exercise Two — Managing Trumps

How many trumps does declarer need to keep in dummy to take care of the losers in his hand in each of the following examples?

DUMMY:	1) K 4	2) —	3) A	4) Q 2	5) Q J
DECLARER:	A 8 5	10 5 3	7 5 4	A K 4	5 4 2

_____   _____   _____   _____   _____

Exercise Three — Preparing to Trump Losers

How many times must declarer give up the lead before he can trump losers in dummy in each of the following examples?

DUMMY:	1) A 4	2) J	3) 7 4	4) —	5) 5
DECLARER:	9 8 3	10 9 8	9 8 3	6 4 3	A 4 2

_____   _____   _____   _____   _____

Exercise Four — Discarding Losers

Each of the following side suits provides an opportunity for declarer to discard losers by throwing them on extra winners in dummy. How many losers can be discarded? What must declarer do to get the side suit ready for discarding losers?

DUMMY:	1) A K Q	2) K Q J	3) A K 7 6 4	4) A Q J	5) Q J 10 9
DECLARER:	9 8	7 4	9 8 3	8 3	6 5

_____   _____   _____   _____   _____

Exercise Five — Third Hand High

Your partner leads the 5 against a 3 NT contract, and the 3 is played from dummy. Which card do you play in each of the following examples?

1) DUMMY		2) DUMMY		3) DUMMY	
8 4 3		Q 6 3		9 3	
PARTNER	YOU	PARTNER	YOU	PARTNER	YOU
5	K 10 6	5	K J 2	5	K Q 4

_____   _____   _____

Exercise Six — Review of Takeout Doubles

The opponent on your right opens the bidding 1◇. What do you say with each of the following hands?

1) ♠ A J 6 3
   ♡ A J 7 5
   ◇ 4
   ♣ K 9 4 2

2) ♠ A K 7
   ♡ 9 3
   ◇ A J 7 3
   ♣ J 9 7 2

3) ♠ A Q J 8 3
   ♡ A 7
   ◇ 3 2
   ♣ K 8 5 2

4) ♠ K 10 9 3
   ♡ Q J 8 2
   ◇ —
   ♣ A 10 7 6 2

5) ♠ K J 10
   ♡ A Q 3
   ◇ A Q J
   ♣ 10 9 7 2

6) ♠ J 8 3
   ♡ 5 2
   ◇ A K J 9 8
   ♣ A 7 3

Exercise Seven — Review of Responses to Takeout Doubles

The opponent on your left opens the bidding 1◇. Your partner doubles, and the opponent on your right passes. What do you respond with each of the following hands?

1) ♠ 7 6 4
   ♡ J 9 8 3
   ◇ J 8 7 2
   ♣ 10 8

2) ♠ A 9 8 4
   ♡ 10 2
   ◇ 9 4 3
   ♣ Q J 8 5

3) ♠ 7 4
   ♡ A Q 10 9 7
   ◇ 10 6 3
   ♣ K J 4

4) ♠ K 10 8
   ♡ 8 5
   ◇ K 8 2
   ♣ K Q 10 9 7

5) ♠ J 10 8
   ♡ J 9 4
   ◇ K Q 10 8
   ♣ A J 2

6) ♠ A 10
   ♡ Q J 8 6 3
   ◇ 9 4 2
   ♣ A Q 4

Exercise Eight — Review of Rebids by the Takeout Doubler

The opponent on your right opens the bidding 1♡, and you double. The opponent on your left passes, partner responds 1♠ and opener passes. What do you rebid with each of the following hands?

1) ♠ K J 9 3
   ♡ 4
   ◇ K Q 8 2
   ♣ K 9 6 2

2) ♠ A K 10 8
   ♡ 9 5
   ◇ K Q J
   ♣ A 10 8 2

3) ♠ K Q 9 5
   ♡ 2
   ◇ A K J 3
   ♣ K J 10 9

Exercise Nine — Discarding a Loser

Turn up all the cards on the first pre–dealt hand. Put each hand dummy style at the edge of the table in front of each player.

Dealer: North

```
                        ♠ Q 10 9 7 6 3
                        ♡ A K
                        ◇ Q 3
                        ♣ A 8 2
        ♠ K 5                               ♠ A
        ♡ 8 7 5 2                           ♡ Q 9 6 3
        ◇ 10 9 8 4                          ◇ J 7 5 2
        ♣ 10 4 3                            ♣ K Q J 6
                        ♠ J 8 4 2
                        ♡ J 10 4
                        ◇ A K 6
                        ♣ 9 7 5
```

The Bidding

What is North's opening bid?

With an opening bid and support for all the unbid suits, what call does East make?

Can South support partner's major suit? What does South respond?

Does West have to respond to partner's takeout double when South bids? What does West call?

With a medium–strength hand, what rebid does North make to invite partner to carry on to game?

East passes. Does South accept North's invitation? What will be the contract? Who will be declarer?

The Play

Which player makes the opening lead? What will the opening lead be?

Declarer starts by making a PLAN:

1.   **P**ause to consider your objective
2.   **L**ook at your winners and losers
3.   **A**nalyze your alternatives
4.   **N**ow put it together

How many losers can declarer afford? How many losers does declarer have? How can declarer eliminate one of the losers? Should declarer draw trumps first? Why not?

Exercise Ten — More Discards

Turn up all the cars on the second pre–dealt hand. Put each hand dummy style at the edge of the table in front of each player.

Dealer: East

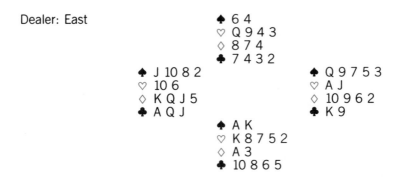

```
              ♠ 6 4
              ♡ Q 9 4 3
              ◇ 8 7 4
              ♣ 7 4 3 2
♠ J 10 8 2                    ♠ Q 9 7 5 3
♡ 10 6                        ♡ A J
◇ K Q J 5                     ◇ 10 9 6 2
♣ A Q J                       ♣ K 9
              ♠ A K
              ♡ K 8 7 5 2
              ◇ A 3
              ♣ 10 8 6 5
```

The Bidding

East does not have enough to open the bidding. What will South's opening bid be?

West has an opening bid and support for the unbid suits. How does West describe his hand?

North passes. With a medium hand of 11 points how does East show the strength of his hand?

South passes. Counting dummy points, does West have enough to accept East's invitation to bid on to game? What does West bid? What will be the contract? Who will be declarer?

The Play

Which player makes the opening lead? Assuming South chooses to lead a heart, which heart will he lead? When dummy plays a low card, which card will North play? Why?

Declarer starts by making a PLAN. How can declarer get rid of an extra loser? Should declarer draw trumps first?

Exercise Eleven — Trumping a Loser

Turn up all the cards on the third pre-dealt hand. Put each hand dummy style at the edge of the table in front of each player.

Dealer: South

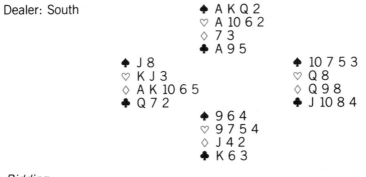

```
              ♠ A K Q 2
              ♡ A 10 6 2
              ◇ 7 3
              ♣ A 9 5
♠ J 8                         ♠ 10 7 5 3
♡ K J 3                       ♡ Q 8
◇ A K 10 6 5                  ◇ Q 9 8
♣ Q 7 2                       ♣ J 10 8 4
              ♠ 9 6 4
              ♡ 9 7 5 4
              ◇ J 4 2
              ♣ K 6 3
```

The Bidding

South passes. What is West's opening bid?

How does North describe his hand?

East does not have enough to respond. Can South pass his partner's takeout double? What does South bid?

West passes. What rebid does North make to show his medium–strength hand?

East passes. Knowing North has a medium–strength hand (17–18 points), does South bid again? What will be the contract? Who will be declarer?

The Play

Which player makes the opening lead? What will the opening lead be?

Declarer starts by making a PLAN. Assuming the missing trumps are divided 3–2, how many losers does declarer have? How can declarer eliminate one of the diamond losers? How does declarer plan to play the trump suit?

Exercise Twelve — More Losers to Trump

Turn up all the cards on the fourth pre–dealt hand. Put each hand dummy style at the edge of the table in front of each player.

Dealer: West

```
                          ♠ Q J 5 4
                          ♡ Q J 3
                          ◊ A 10 6
                          ♣ K 6 3
          ♠ 9 7 2                        ♠ A 8 6 3
          ♡ 9 8 6 2                      ♡ A K 7 5
          ◊ K J 8                        ◊ Q 9 2
          ♣ A 9 2                        ♣ 10 7
                          ♠ K 10
                          ♡ 10 4
                          ◊ 7 5 4 3
                          ♣ Q J 8 5 4
```

The Bidding

West does not have enough to open the bidding. Does North have enough to open? Which suit will North bid?

How can East compete in the auction?

What does South respond to North's opening bid?

Once South bids, West is no longer obliged to respond to partner's takeout double. However, with 8 points West should bid if possible since partner has invited him to compete. What does West bid?

With a minimum opening bid North passes. Does East have a minimum, medium or maximum hand? What does East rebid? What will be the contract? Who will be declarer?

The Play

Which player makes the opening lead? What will the opening lead be? Assuming North leads a low club, which card will South play to the first trick? Why?

Declarer starts by making a PLAN. Assuming the missing trumps divide 3–2, how many losers does declarer have? How can he eliminate one of the losers?

LESSON 5
Watching Out for Entries

Entries
Guidelines for Defense
Bidding — The Stayman Convention
Summary

Workshop Material
Group Activities

If declarer does not have enough tricks to make the contract in notrump or too many losers in a trump contract, he goes through the third step of the PLAN, *Analyze your alternatives*. In doing this, declarer looks at the opportunities in each suit for developing extra winners or eliminating losers.

Having looked at the possibilities, declarer moves on to the fourth step, *Now put it together*, to develop his overall strategy for playing the hand. In going through this step, declarer considers the overall picture, not just the individual suits — the best play in a particular suit may not be the best play for the entire hand. Declarer may have to choose between the available alternatives or consider in which order to play the suits.

Many of the techniques for developing extra winners or eliminating losers require declarer to be in his own hand or dummy. For example, declarer may need to lead toward a high card to take a finesse. When declarer plans his strategy, he must be able to get from one side of the table to the other as necessary. In this lesson we will look at how declarer builds this into his strategy.

◆ *ENTRIES* ◆

A way of getting from one hand to the other is called an entry. In some hands declarer has all the entries he needs. At other times he must create the entries needed.

Sure Entries

A sure entry is a winner on one side of the table accompanied by a low card on the other side — this allows declarer to cross over to the winner. Look at these examples:

DUMMY:	A 8 3	Dummy's ace is an entry. Declarer can play one of his low cards to dummy's winner.
DECLARER:	7 4 2	

DUMMY:	A K Q	In this case dummy has plenty of winners, but declarer has no low cards in the suit. This suit does not provide any sure entry to the dummy. In fact, declarer will need an entry in another suit to get to dummy to take the winners in this suit.
DECLARER:	—	

DUMMY:	—	Declarer has low cards in this suit, but dummy has no winners. The suit itself does not provide an entry to dummy. If this is a side suit in a trump contract, however, declarer may be able to lead one of the low cards and trump it in dummy, getting rid of a loser while providing an entry to dummy.
DECLARER:	6 5	

DUMMY:	Q 5 3	An entry does not need to be the highest card in a suit. In this example the queen is an entry since declarer has both the ace and king. Declarer can play the 4 to dummy's queen. The ace and king serve as entries to declarer's hand.
DECLARER:	A K 4	

DUMMY: 9 2	Even a low card can provide a useful entry. Declarer can play the 4 to dummy's 9 if he needs
DECLARER: A K Q J 10 4	an entry to dummy.

DUMMY: K Q J 10	Having a low card in the opposite hand is important. Declarer has lots of winners in dummy but
DECLARER: A	no entry — he has no low cards in his hand.

DUMMY: A 4 2	This is a useful suit — it provides an entry to either hand. If declarer is in dummy, he can lead a low
DECLARER: K 5	card to the king to get to his hand. If declarer is in his hand, he can lead the 5 to the ace to get to dummy.

If the opponents lead this suit, declarer must decide where to win the trick. If he wants to be in his hand now or needs to keep the ace as a later entry to dummy, he wins the king in his hand. If he wants to be in dummy or needs to keep the king as a later entry to his hand, he wins dummy's ace.

Creating an Entry

When dummy has no sure entry, it may be possible to create one through promotion, length or use of the finesse. Declarer may have to depend on the favorable location of a missing high card or a favorable division of a suit. Look at these examples:

DUMMY: K Q	Declarer has no quick entry to dummy in this suit, but he can create one by force. If the 4 is led to
DECLARER: 8 4	dummy's queen, and the opponents take their ace, the king becomes a sure entry. If the opponents do not take their ace, declarer is in dummy right away.

DUMMY: K 5 3	The king is a possible entry to dummy, depending on which opponent has the ace. Declarer can lead
DECLARER: 7 6 2	a low card toward dummy. If the opponent on his left has the ace and plays it, the king will be a dum-

my entry. If the ace is not played, declarer can win dummy's king immediately. If the ace is on declarer's right, the king will be taken by the ace — declarer will have no entry in the suit.

DUMMY: Q 4	Here is a similar example. Declarer can lead a low card toward dummy's queen. If the king is on
DECLARER: A 6 2	declarer's left, he will have an entry with dummy's queen. If the king is on his right, the queen will not be an entry.

DUMMY: 8 6 4 2	Dummy has no ready entry in this suit. If the missing cards are divided 3-2, however, declarer can
DECLARER: A K 5 3	establish an entry. He plays the ace and king and then leads the suit again. If the opponents' cards divide 3-2, dummy's 8 is a winner and provides an entry since declarer has the 5 (or 3) left.

Preserving Entries When Playing a Suit

To help preserve entries for when they are needed, declarer must remember to use some of the guidelines we looked at earlier: play the high card from the short side first; take your losses early. Here are some examples:

DUMMY:	A Q 9 8	When a suit is divided evenly between declarer and dummy, declarer can take his tricks in any
DECLARER:	K J 6 3	order. He can start by taking dummy's ace and queen or declarer's king and jack.

DUMMY:	Q 3	When the suit is unevenly divided between the two hands, declarer must be more careful. When tak-
DECLARER:	A K J 2	ing his winners in this suit, he starts by leading the 2 to dummy's queen — high card from the short

side first. Then the 3 can be led to the ace, king and jack. If declarer wins the first trick with a high card in his hand and then leads the 2 to dummy's queen, he will need an entry in another suit to get back to his hand and take the rest of his winners.

DUMMY:	K Q 10 3	When promoting tricks in this suit, declarer starts with the jack, the high card from the short side.
DECLARER:	J 2	If the opponents do not take the ace, declarer can continue by leading the 2 to dummy's high cards.

He will need only one entry in another suit to get over to the winners in dummy. If declarer starts by leading the 2 to dummy, he may need two outside entries to take all three of the tricks in dummy.

DUMMY:	A K 8 6 3	If declarer plays the ace and king and then leads the suit a third time, giving up a trick, dummy's
DECLARER:	5 4 2	remaining two low cards will be winners if the op- ponents' cards divide 3-2. However, declarer will

need an entry to dummy to get to them. Instead, declarer should take his losses early and give up (duck) the first or second trick, preserving his high cards as entries to dummy once the winners are established.

Now let's put it together and use all these carefully preserved entries in a complete hand.

◆ USING ENTRIES ◆

Entries are important when using any of the techniques discussed in earlier lessons: promoting high cards, developing long suits, finessing, trumping losers and discarding losers.

Promoting High Cards

Take a look at the following hand. You are in a 3 NT contract, and West leads the ♣Q.

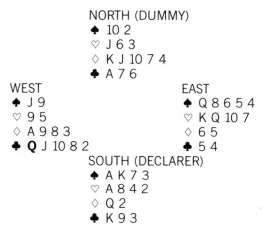

NORTH (DUMMY)
♠ 10 2
♡ J 6 3
◇ K J 10 7 4
♣ A 7 6

WEST
♠ J 9
♡ 9 5
◇ A 9 8 3
♣ Q J 10 8 2

EAST
♠ Q 8 6 5 4
♡ K Q 10 7
◇ 6 5
♣ 5 4

SOUTH (DECLARER)
♠ A K 7 3
♡ A 8 4 2
◇ Q 2
♣ K 9 3

You need nine tricks and have two sure tricks in spades, one in hearts and two in clubs. Four more tricks need to be developed. When you analyze your alternatives, the diamond suit appears to offer an excellent opportunity for all four.

In the fourth step of the PLAN, **N**ow *put it together*, you must consider exactly how you will play the hand, watching your entries carefully. You want to promote diamond winners in dummy. Once they have been established, you will need an entry to them. The ♣A looks like dummy's only entry, so you want to preserve it by winning the first trick with the ♣K in your hand. Next, you must be careful to start the diamonds by playing the ◇Q from your hand — high card from the short side first. Whether or not West wins the first trick with the ◇A, you can establish the diamonds and have the ♣A to get to them.

Developing Long Suits

In this hand you need to develop a long suit to make your contract and must be careful to watch your entries.

Contract: 3 NT
Lead: ♣Q

NORTH (DUMMY)
♠ 9 4
♡ A 8 5
◇ 10 7 4
♣ A K 6 4 2

WEST
♠ Q J 10 8
♡ J 7 4 3
◇ J 9 6 3
♣ 5

EAST
♠ 6 5 3 2
♡ 10 9 6
◇ K Q
♣ Q J 10 9

SOUTH (DECLARER)
♠ A K 7
♡ K Q 2
◇ A 8 5 2
♣ 8 7 3

Again, you need nine tricks in a 3 NT contract. You start with eight — two spades, three hearts, one diamond and two clubs — and need one more. The diamond suit offers some chance. You have seven diamonds, the opponents have six. However, you would need the missing diamonds to divide exactly 3-3, and they are more likely to divide slightly unevenly, 4-2. A more promising alternative is the club suit, in which you have eight cards. If the missing clubs divide 3-2, you can give up one trick and establish two extra winners, more than enough to fulfill the contract.

With the ♡ A in dummy you seem to have no entry problems, but do not be lulled into carelessness. Suppose you play the ♣ A and ♣ K, intending to give up the next trick and establish your remaining two clubs as winners. That would be fine if the missing clubs divided 3-2, since you still would have the ♡ A as an entry to dummy. On this hand, however, the missing clubs break 4-1. You can get to dummy with the ♡ A to lead the suit again and establish your remaining club, but now you have no way to get to it.

Instead, take your losses early. Win the first trick and give up a club trick right away by playing a low club from both hands. You have to lose at least one club trick anyway. (You also could win the first club trick and give up the second club trick.) Whatever the opponents lead, you win (being careful to keep the ♡ A in dummy if the opponents lead hearts) and lead clubs again. When they break 4-1, you give up a second club trick and you still have the ♡ A left in dummy as an entry to your established winner.

Finessing

Taking a finesse involves leading from one hand toward a high card in the other hand. Entries therefore play a vital part in the PLAN.

Contract: 4♡
Lead: ◇ Q

NORTH (DUMMY)
- ♠ A 9 2
- ♡ 10 7 5 3
- ◇ K 7 4
- ♣ 7 4 2

WEST
- ♠ Q 8 5
- ♡ 9 8
- ◇ Q J 10 9 6
- ♣ 9 5 3

EAST
- ♠ J 10 6 3
- ♡ 6 4
- ◇ A 8 3
- ♣ K 10 8 6

SOUTH (DECLARER)
- ♠ K 7 4
- ♡ A K Q J 2
- ◇ 5 2
- ♣ A Q J

You can afford three losers in a contract of 4♡. You have one spade loser, two diamond losers and one club loser. You can do nothing about the spade loser but you have good chances to avoid a loser in both diamonds and clubs. You have the ◇ K in dummy and, if West has the ◇ A, you will have only one diamond loser. Admittedly, things do not look good, since West has led the ◇ Q — it is quite likely that East has the ◇ A. In clubs you have the opportunity to take a repeated finesse against the king. If East has the ♣ K, you can eliminate your club loser.

When you put your plan together, you must lead twice from dummy toward your hand. This means you need two dummy entries. Where will they be? The ♠A is one entry, but if East has the ◇A, the ◇K will not be an entry. You do, however, have the ♡10 in dummy that can serve as a second entry. Since you have all the other high hearts, you plan to play the ♡2 to dummy's ♡10. This will allow you to take two club finesses.

Once again, be careful. The opening lead is the ◇Q. Suppose you play the ◇K from dummy at the first trick, hoping West started with the ◇A. It turns out East has the ◇A and wins the first trick. East returns his partner's suit and West wins a second diamond trick and leads another diamond. You trump this trick to avoid a third loser in the suit — but which card do you trump with? Having made your PLAN beforehand, you know you will need the ♡2 to lead to dummy's ♡10. Therefore, you cannot afford to use it to trump West's diamond lead. Instead, trump with one of your higher hearts, the ♡J for example.

Now you can draw the opponents' trumps with your high hearts. They break 2-2, and you now can lead your carefully preserved ♡2 to dummy's ♡10 so you can lead a low club toward your hand. When East plays low, finesse your ♣J, which wins the trick since West does not have the ♣K. You can get back to dummy by playing a low spade to dummy's ♠A and then lead another club. When East plays low, repeat the finesse by playing your ♣Q. This wins the trick, and you have avoided losing a club trick. You end up making your contract, losing only two diamond tricks and one spade trick.

This hand shows the importance of pausing to make your PLAN at the beginning of play. If you did not think ahead, you might trump the third round of diamonds with your ♡2 and no longer would be able to make the contract. Dummy's winner would be stranded. The PLAN warned you that the ♡2 was a very important card.

Trumping Losers in Dummy

When you want to trump a loser in dummy, you must be able to get to your hand to lead the loser. The more losers you have, the more entries you need. Look at this example:

Contract: 4♠
Lead: ♣10

NORTH (DUMMY)
♠ 10 8 5 3
♡ 9
◇ K J 7 4 3
♣ A Q 5

WEST
♠ A 4 2
♡ K 8 7 4
◇ 9 6 5
♣ 10 9 8

EAST
♠ K
♡ Q 10 6 3
◇ A Q 10 8
♣ 7 6 3 2

SOUTH (DECLARER)
♠ Q J 9 7 6
♡ A J 5 2
◇ 2
♣ K J 4

You can afford three losers. You have two losers in spades, three in hearts and one in diamonds. When analyzing your alternatives, you see that nothing can be done about the spade and diamond losers. You therefore concentrate on getting rid of the three heart losers. With a singleton heart in dummy, this looks like the perfect opportunity to trump your losers.

Since you plan to trump three losers in dummy, you will need to get to your hand three times. One entry is the ♡A. Where are the other two? You cannot use the spade suit, since the opponents have the ace and king. You also do not want to lead spades early because you need to leave three trumps in dummy to ruff your losers.

You might consider giving up a diamond trick — you then could trump one of dummy's diamonds to get to your hand. If you give up a diamond trick, however, the opponents may lead spades and remove some of dummy's trumps, leaving you with too few to trump your losers. The best suit to provide the entries you need is clubs.

Again, be careful to preserve your entries until you need them. If you win the first trick in your hand with the ♣J or ♣K, you use up one of your entries too soon. Even winning the first trick with dummy's ♣Q will not be good enough — dummy's clubs are not low enough to lead to your hand twice. You must win the first trick with dummy's ♣A. Once more, the importance of making a PLAN comes into play.

After winning the ♣A, lead dummy's ♡9 to your ♡A and trump one of your heart losers in dummy. Now lead dummy's ♣5 to your ♣J so you can trump another heart loser in dummy. Cross your fingers and play dummy's ♣Q, *overtaking* with the ♣K in your hand so you can lead your last heart loser and trump it in dummy. Why cross your fingers? You have six clubs and the opponents have seven. You must hope the missing clubs divide 4-3, otherwise one of the opponents could trump one of your club winners and defeat the contract.

After the clubs divide nicely and you trump your last heart loser, you are home free. Lead trumps, driving out the missing ace and king and make your contract. You lose only the ♠A, ♠K and a diamond trick.

Discarding Losers

Another way to eliminate losers in a trump contract is by discarding them on extra winners in dummy. If this is your PLAN, remember to watch those entries.

Consider the following hand. You are in a partscore of 2♡, and the opening lead is the ◇Q.

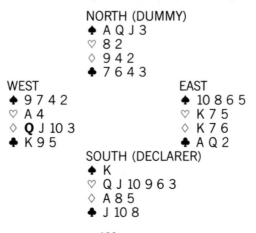

```
                    NORTH (DUMMY)
                    ♠ A Q J 3
                    ♡ 8 2
                    ◇ 9 4 2
                    ♣ 7 6 4 3
      WEST                              EAST
      ♠ 9 7 4 2                        ♠ 10 8 6 5
      ♡ A 4                            ♡ K 7 5
      ◇ Q J 10 3                       ◇ K 7 6
      ♣ K 9 5                          ♣ A Q 2
                    SOUTH (DECLARER)
                    ♠ K
                    ♡ Q J 10 9 6 3
                    ◇ A 8 5
                    ♣ J 10 8
```

You can afford five losers. You are missing the ♡A and ♡K and have two diamond losers and three club losers. Since all of the losers are quick, you cannot start by leading trumps. You must eliminate two of your losers before giving up the lead.

The extra spade winners in dummy will provide discards for some of your losers, but an entry to dummy is the problem. After winning the ◇A and taking a trick with your ♣K, how do you get to dummy's ♠A, ♠Q and ♠J to discard your losers?

The key again comes from your PLAN. You can afford five losers so you need to discard only two of your losers on dummy's spades. The spade suit itself can provide an entry if you *overtake* your ♠K with dummy's ♠A. This seems wasteful, but it gets you to dummy and allows you to play the ♠Q and ♠J and discard two of your losers. Now you can draw trumps by driving out the opponents' ♡A and ♡K and make your contract.

♦ GUIDELINES FOR DEFENSE ♦

If declarer leads a card from his hand or dummy, and you are next to play, you will be contributing the second card to the trick. Here are some guidelines that will help you when you are the second hand to play.

Second Hand Low

Consider the following situation. You are defending with dummy on your left — you cannot see declarer's or your partner's cards. Here is one of the suits, and declarer leads the 4 from his hand toward dummy's king:

```
                        DUMMY
                        K 8 3
        YOU                            PARTNER
        A 10 6 2                       ? ? ?
                        DECLARER
                        ? ? 4
```

Which card should you play? Since you are second to play, your partner will have the opportunity to play last for your side. A good guideline for this situation is *second hand low*. It does not seem as if it will make much difference. You will get only one trick with your ace, and declarer will get a trick with dummy's king, having followed the principle of leading toward a high card.

Let's see why it can make a difference. Suppose the complete layout of the suit is:

```
                        DUMMY
                        K 8 3
        YOU                            PARTNER
        A 10 6 2                       J 9 5
                        DECLARER
                        Q 7 4
```

If you play the ace, declarer will play a low card from dummy. Later, declarer will get a trick with the queen as well as the king.

Instead, suppose you follow the advice and play low. Declarer will play dummy's king and win the first trick. However, if declarer tries to get a second trick by leading toward his queen, you will win the trick. Since your side has the remaining high cards in the suit, declarer will get only one trick.

The objective of the guideline *second hand low* is to avoid expending your high cards while declarer is playing low cards. In the above example, if you play the ace when declarer leads the 4, you capture two low cards. It is better to wait to capture one of declarer's high cards with your ace.

Your partner, rather than declarer, may hold the queen, but you still lose nothing by playing second hand low. Declarer is entitled to one trick with the king once he leads toward it.

When Not to Play Low

The guideline *second hand low* should not be followed blindly. It is good advice only if you clearly have nothing better to do. In many situations you should not play low. Let's look again at our earlier example:

```
                    DUMMY
                    K 8 3
        YOU                     PARTNER
        A 10 6 2                ? ? ?
                    DECLARER
                    ? ? 4
```

If you are defending against a trump contract and this is a side suit, the possibility exists that declarer may have a singleton. The complete layout could be:

```
                    DUMMY
                    K 8 3
        YOU                     PARTNER
        A 10 6 2                Q J 9 7 5
                    DECLARER
                    4
```

If you play low, declarer can win the king — he will trump if you later try to take a trick with your ace. Declarer started with one loser in the suit but ended up with no losers! In such situations you must use the bidding and your holdings in other suits to guide you. If it looks as if declarer has a singleton or you can see enough tricks to defeat the contract if you win your ace, do not blindly play second hand low.

If you are not sure, playing low is usually correct. Even if declarer is leading a singleton and you do not take your ace, it may cost nothing — declarer may use the king to discard one of his other losers if you do play the ace.

Returning again to an earlier layout:

```
                    DUMMY
                    K 8 3
        YOU                     PARTNER
        A 10 6 2                J 9 5
                    DECLARER
                    Q 7 4
```

If declarer played the queen from his hand instead of a low card, this would not be a time to play low. You have an opportunity to win one of declarer's high cards with your ace and should do so. Declarer will get only one trick with his king. If you play low, declarer wins the queen and then can lead toward the king in dummy to get a second trick.

The above situation falls under another, seemingly conflicting, guideline: *cover an honor with an honor*. The idea is to promote the lower cards your side holds in the suit by playing your high cards on top of declarer's high cards. In this example, by covering the queen with your ace you promote partner's jack into a trick after declarer takes a trick with dummy's king.

Even if you exchange your ace with dummy's king, you still should cover if declarer leads the queen rather than playing low:

DUMMY
A 8 3

YOU   PARTNER
K 10 6 2   J 9 5

DECLARER
Q 7 4

By covering declarer's queen with your king, you make declarer use dummy's ace to win the trick. In effect, you eliminate two of declarer's high cards for one of yours. Now you have promoted your side's jack and 10 into winners. (As we saw in Lesson 3, declarer should lead *toward* the queen to try for a trick, hoping your partner has the king. In this layout, that would not work either.)

Here is another situation where second hand low clearly would not be the best play:

DUMMY
A J

YOU   PARTNER
K Q 10 9 2   ? ? ?

DECLARER
? ? 4

If declarer leads the 4 toward dummy, and you play low, declarer may play dummy's jack, winning the trick. Instead, you should play your queen to make declarer play dummy's ace. Now your king has been promoted into a winner, and declarer will not get a trick with dummy's jack.

This situation is called *splitting your honors*. You split your honors, rather than playing second hand low, to avoid letting declarer win an undeserved trick with a lower-ranking card.

The advice *second hand low* is very useful. Remember, however, to use it only when you clearly have no better alternative.

BIDDING

Having reviewed the bidding concepts covered in the *Club Series,* we can move on to some new ideas that will improve your ability to reach the best contract and add a new dimension to your game. In this lesson we will look at an artificial, or *conventional*, bid that is very useful when responding to an opening bid of 1 NT.

The Stayman Convention

When partner opens the bidding with 1 NT, responder, as captain, is responsible for deciding the level and denomination of the contract. When deciding on the denomination, responder wants to determine if the partnership has a *Golden Fit* — eight or more cards in the combined hands — in a major suit. The Stayman convention helps responder to uncover a Golden Fit in a major suit.

The *Stayman convention* is an artificial response of 2♣ to an opening bid of 1 NT. It is used to ask if opener has a four-card major suit. With a four-card (or longer) major suit, opener bids it. Without a four-card major suit, opener makes the artificial rebid of 2◇.

Here are some examples of the 1 NT opener's rebid when responder bids 2♣:

♠ A 8 7 3 ♡ Q J 10 ◇ A Q 8 ♣ K 8 5	Rebid **2♠** to show the four-card spade suit.
♠ A K ♡ 10 9 7 3 ◇ K Q 9 2 ♣ A Q 10	Rebid **2♡** to show the four-card heart suit. Responder is not interested in how good a suit you have, merely whether you have four of them.
♠ K 10 2 ♡ A K 5 ◇ 8 2 ♣ A Q 10 6 3	With no four-card major, rebid **2◇**. This says nothing about your diamond holding. It is an *artificial* response saying that you do not have a four-card major suit. Responder will bid again.

Let's see how the Stayman convention is used when responder has enough for a game contract.

When Responder Has 10 or More Points

If responder has 10 or more points, he knows that the partnership belongs in a game contract since opener has at least 16 points. The only question is the denomination. If there is a Golden Fit in a major suit, the partnership belongs in 4♡ or 4♠; otherwise, the partnership belongs in 3 NT.

With a six-card major suit responder knows that a Golden Fit exists since opener has a balanced hand. Responder therefore can bid game in the major suit. With a five-card major suit, responder can make a forcing response of 3♡ or 3♠ to tell opener to bid 4♡ or 4♠ with three-card or longer support; otherwise, to bid 3 NT. But what if responder has only four cards in a major suit? Look at this hand:

♠ K 7 6 4
♡ A J 7 3
◇ 6 2
♣ K 8 3

With 11 HCP responder wants to be in game when opener bids 1 NT — but which game? If opener has four spades, the partnership has a Golden Fit in that suit and belongs in

4♠. Similarly, if opener has a four-card heart suit, the partnership belongs in 4♡. Finally, if opener does not have four cards in either major, the contract should be 3 NT.

Responder can determine the best contract by using the Stayman convention. He starts by responding 2♣, asking opener to show a four-card major. If opener bids 2♠, showing a four-card spade suit, responder can place the contract in 4♠. Similarly, if opener bids 2♡, responder can raise to 4♡. Finally, if opener bids 2♦, denying four cards in either major, responder can jump to 3 NT, knowing there is no Golden Fit in a major suit.

Responder does not need four cards in both majors to use the Stayman convention. Suppose responder's hand is:

♠ Q J 7 4
♡ 9 3
♦ 7 2
♣ A K 8 4 3

Opener bids 1 NT and responder bids 2♣ to ask if opener has a four-card major. If opener rebids 2♠, responder can put the partnership in 4♠. If opener bids 2♦, showing no four-card major, or 2♡, showing four hearts, responder can place the contract in 3 NT.

This raises an interesting point. Suppose opener started with four hearts *and* four spades. When responder bids 2♣, asking for a major suit, opener has to pick one of them to bid. It does not matter which he bids first (some authorities recommend bidding hearts first, some recommend spades and others say to bid the better suit). Suppose he chooses to bid 2♡. Responder, with the above hand, would jump to 3 NT, since he is not interested in hearts.

Now opener must ask himself: "Why did responder bid 2♣ if he was not interested in hearing about my heart suit?" The answer must be that responder was interested only in spades. Thus, opener should bid 4♠ with a four-card spade suit when responder jumps to 3 NT over his 2♡ rebid. This puts the partnership in its Golden Fit.

Clearly, responder must be careful about bidding 2♣ unless he is interested in finding a Golden Fit in a major suit. Once the partnership agrees to use 2♣ as the Stayman convention, responder cannot suddenly change his mind and use it to show clubs — opener will be confused. A *conventional bid* is one that has a special (artificial) meaning to the partnership. Conventions, such as Stayman, can be very useful, but both partners must be on the same wavelength.

Here are some examples of responding to 1 NT when you and your partner have agreed to use the Stayman convention:

♠ 6 4 ♡ 9 7 5 3 ♦ A K 8 3 ♣ A J 5	Respond **2♣**. You are interested in finding a Golden Fit in hearts. If opener rebids 2♡, raise to 4♡. If opener rebids 2♦ or 2♠, jump to 3 NT.
♠ 9 6 2 ♡ 7 4 ♦ Q 7 2 ♣ A K J 8 6	Respond **3 NT**. Do not bid 2♣, since you are not interested in a major suit.

♠ A Q J 9 3
♡ K 5
◇ J 7 4
♣ 10 9 4

Respond **3♠**. With a five-card suit, you do not need to ask if opener has a four-card spade suit; three-card support will be sufficient. 3♠ asks opener to choose between 4♠ and 3 NT.

♠ A 9 6 4
♡ A 8 6 3
◇ 4
♣ Q 10 9 4

Use the Stayman convention, **2♣**, to find out if opener has a four-card major. If opener rebids 2♡ or 2♠, raise to game. If opener rebids 2◇, put the partnership in 3 NT.

When Responder Has 8 or 9 Points

The Stayman convention also can be used when responder has a hand of invitational strength and is interested in finding a Golden Fit in a major suit. Consider this hand as responder when opener bids 1 NT:

♠ 10 4
♡ K J 8 3
◇ 9 6 2
♣ A 10 8 3

With 8 HCP responder is not sure whether the partnership belongs in partscore or game. If opener has a minimum, 16 points, there isn't enough combined strength for game. If opener has a maximum, 18 points, there is enough for game. Responder could invite opener to bid on to game by responding 2 NT, but this would lose the opportunity to find a Golden Fit in hearts.

Instead, responder can start by using the Stayman convention, 2♣. If opener rebids 2♡, showing a four-card heart suit, responder can invite game by raising to 3♡. If opener has a maximum, he bids 4♡; otherwise, he passes. If opener rebids 2◇ or 2♠, responder can bid 2 NT, again inviting opener to bid game with a maximum or pass with a minimum. The Stayman convention gives responder the best of both worlds — he can invite game and look for a Golden Fit in a major suit along the way.

The Stayman convention is useful on another type of invitational hand. Consider the following hand when opener bids 1 NT:

♠ A J 9 7 4
♡ 8 3
◇ 9 6 2
♣ K 10 7

With 9 points — 8 HCP plus 1 point for the five-card suit — responder again wants to invite opener to carry on to game. At the same time, responder is interested in finding out whether there is a Golden Fit in spades. Responder cannot bid 2♠, since that is a signoff, showing 0-7 points — opener will pass. Responder also cannot bid 3♠, since that is a forcing bid, showing 10 or more points — opener will bid either 4♠ or 3 NT.

The solution is to start with 2♣, the Stayman convention. If opener rebids 2♠, showing four spades, responder raises to 3♠, showing the Golden Fit and inviting game. If opener rebids 2◇ or 2♡, responder bids **2♠**. This tells opener that responder has an invitational hand (8-9 points) with a five-card or longer spade suit.

How does opener know this? If responder had a weak hand (0-7 points), he would have signed off in 2♠ (and not have bid 2♣ first). If responder had a strong hand (10 or more points), he would have bid 3♠ with a five-card spade suit or 4♠ with a six-card or longer suit. So responder has an invitational hand (8-9 points). If responder had only a four-card spade suit, he would have rebid 2 NT rather than 2♠. So responder has five or more spades.

Opener can pass with a minimum hand, bid 3 NT with a maximum hand and only two spades or bid 4♠ with a maximum hand and three spades. Once again, the partnership has the best of all possible worlds.

Here are some examples of responding to an opening bid of 1 NT when you hold 8-9 points:

♠ Q 9 7 4 ♡ 5 3 ◇ K Q 8 3 ♣ J 10 3	Respond **2♣**. You are interested in finding a Golden Fit in spades. If opener rebids 2♠, raise to 3♠, inviting game with a maximum. If opener rebids 2◇ or 2♡, bid 2 NT, again inviting game.
♠ 10 8 3 ♡ 10 5 ◇ Q J 4 ♣ A J 8 6 3	Respond **2 NT** to invite opener to bid game with a maximum. Do not bid 2♣, since you are not interested in a major suit.
♠ 9 5 ♡ K J 8 7 6 3 ◇ 7 4 ♣ K 8 2	Respond **2♣**. With 7 HCP plus 2 points for the six-card suit, you are too strong to sign off in 2♡ but not strong enough to bid 4♡. If opener rebids 2♡, raise to 3♡. If opener rebids 2◇ or 2♠, you can bid your heart suit, showing an invitational hand with at least five hearts.
♠ 10 8 5 4 ♡ K 8 6 5 ◇ A J 5 ♣ 3 2	Use the Stayman convention, **2♣**, to find out if opener has a four-card major. If opener rebids 2♡, raise to 3♡. If opener rebids 2♠, raise to 3♠. If opener rebids 2◇, bid 2 NT.

When Responder Has Fewer Than 8 Points

Suppose opener bids 1 NT and responder holds this hand:

♠ Q 10 8 3
♡ Q 6 4 2
◇ 8 4
♣ 7 5 3

With 4 HCP responder wants to play in a partscore. Since responder is interested in playing in a Golden Fit, should he bid 2♣ to ask opener if he has a four-card major? At first glance this looks reasonable. If opener rebids 2♡ or 2♠, responder can pass and play a partscore in the Golden Fit. But what if opener rebids 2◇? Responder cannot pass since opener is not showing a diamond suit, just denying holding a four-card major suit. Responder also cannot bid 2 NT, since this would show an invitational hand (8-9 points) — opener might even bid on to 3 NT.

With 0–7 points responder is not strong enough to use the Stayman convention. The Bidding Scale leaves no room to go exploring. With a five-card suit, responder can sign off in 2 ◇, 2 ♡ or 2 ♠, but with a hand such as the one above, responder must pass and play in 1 NT.

Note, also, that responder cannot sign off in 2 ♣ with a weak hand and a long club suit. Opener will interpret this as the Stayman convention and bid something. Responder will have to rebid 3 ♣ to say that he really wants to play in a partscore in clubs.

◆ SUMMARY ◆

An entry is a way of getting from one hand to the other. When you come to the fourth step of the PLAN, *Now put it together*, you must be careful to watch out for the entries between your hand and dummy. Entries are important when using the techniques for establishing winners and eliminating losers: promoting high cards, developing long suits, finessing, trumping or discarding losers. Sometimes you will need to create an entry to a particular hand. At other times you will be concerned with preserving the entry to one of the hands.

When you are defending, a useful guideline is *second hand low*. You should not follow this blindly, however. For example, if declarer leads a high card and you have a higher card, you should *cover an honor with an honor* if doing so will promote tricks for your side.

When you respond to an opening bid of 1 NT, you can use the artificial response of 2 ♣, the Stayman convention, to find out if opener has a four-card major. If opener has a four-card (or longer) major, he bids it; otherwise, opener rebids 2 ◇, an artificial rebid showing no four-card major. Responder can use this information to help determine the partnership's best contract.

◆ *GROUP ACTIVITIES* ◆

Exercise One — Recognizing Entries

How many entries to dummy do each of the following examples contain?

DUMMY:	1) A Q 7	2) A K 3	3) 10 4	4) K 10 9	5) K Q J
DECLARER:	K 9 2	5	A K Q J 3	A Q J 3 2	A

_____ _____ _____ _____ _____

Exercise Two — Creating Entries

How could you try to create an entry to dummy in each of the following suits?

DUMMY:	1) K Q 6	2) K 8	3) Q 7 4	4) Q J 10	5) 9 7 5 4
DECLARER:	7 4 2	9 3	A 8 2	8 5 4	A K 3 2

_____ _____ _____ _____ _____

Exercise Three — Preserving Entries

How would you play each of the following suits so you do not need entries in other suits to take all your tricks?

DUMMY:	1) K 5	2) K 8 7 5 4	3) A K 7 4	4) A 7 6 3 2	5) A K J 10
DECLARER:	A Q J 6	A 9 3	Q J 2	8 5 4	Q

_____ _____ _____ _____ _____

Exercise Four — Estimating the Number of Entries Needed

How many entries would you need to dummy in other suits to try the finesse(s) in each of the following side suits?

DUMMY:	1) 8 5	2) 8 6 3	3) 6 5 2	4) 9 6 3	5) A 6 3
DECLARER:	A Q 4	A Q J	K Q 3	A Q 10	Q 5 4

_____ _____ _____ _____ _____

Exercise Five — Second Hand Low

Which card do you play in each of the following examples when declarer leads the indicated card from his hand toward the dummy?

1) DUMMY	2) DUMMY	3) DUMMY	4) DUMMY
Q 4 3	A Q 10	K Q 5	A 6 3
YOU	YOU	YOU	YOU
A 6 5	K J 3	A J 9	K 10 9
DECLARER	DECLARER	DECLARER	DECLARER
2	5	6	Q

_____ _____ _____ _____

Exercise Six — Using the Stayman Convention

Your partner opens the bidding 1 NT. What do you respond with each of the following hands?

1) ♠ A J 7 3
   ♡ K 10 8 6
   ◇ 10 5 2
   ♣ Q 8

2) ♠ A 5
   ♡ J 10 7 3
   ◇ A Q J 6
   ♣ 9 6 3

3) ♠ 10 5
   ♡ J 3
   ◇ A 8 4
   ♣ K Q 10 8 6 3

4) ♠ Q 9 8 5
   ♡ K 2
   ◇ K 10 8 4
   ♣ 9 8 4

5) ♠ 4 2
   ♡ Q J 9 7 3
   ◇ A 8 4
   ♣ J 10 5

6) ♠ K 8 6 3
   ♡ 10 9 6 4
   ◇ 10 5
   ♣ 8 7 5

Exercise Seven — Responding to the Stayman Convention

You open the bidding 1 NT, and your partner responds 2♣, the Stayman convention. What do you rebid with each of the following hands?

1) ♠ K 9
   ♡ A Q 8 3
   ◇ J 9 4
   ♣ K Q J 2

2) ♠ 9 7 4 2
   ♡ A K 3
   ◇ A J 8
   ♣ K Q 5

3) ♠ A J 9
   ♡ A K 7
   ◇ J 7
   ♣ K J 10 8 2

Exercise Eight — Responder's Rebid After Using the Stayman Convention

Your partner opens 1 NT, and you respond 2♣, the Stayman convention. Opener rebids 2♡. What do you rebid with each of the following hands?

1) ♠ K 9 7 3
   ♡ A J 7 4
   ◇ 8 4
   ♣ A 5 4

2) ♠ A K 5 3
   ♡ 10 9 3
   ◇ J 10 8 6
   ♣ Q J

3) ♠ Q 10
   ♡ Q J 3 2
   ◇ K 10 6 4
   ♣ 9 6 2

4) ♠ A Q 7 4
   ♡ J 2
   ◇ 10 6 3
   ♣ Q 9 8 6

5) ♠ K J 10 7 3
   ♡ 3
   ◇ A 9 8 5
   ♣ 10 7 5

6) ♠ K Q 7 6 3
   ♡ J 10 9 4
   ◇ A 10 5
   ♣ 5

Exercise Nine — Using Entries for a Finesse

Turn up all the cards on the first pre-dealt hand. Put each hand dummy style at the edge of the table in front of each player.

Dealer: North

```
              ♠ K Q 7 3
              ♡ Q 5 2
              ◇ 9 4
              ♣ A K Q J
  ♠ A J 9                    ♠ 10 5
  ♡ 10 7 3                   ♡ J 9 4
  ◇ A 7 6                    ◇ Q J 10 8 3
  ♣ 8 5 4 2                  ♣ 9 7 3
              ♠ 8 6 4 2
              ♡ A K 8 6
              ◇ K 5 2
              ♣ 10 6
```

The Bidding

With a balanced hand and 17 points, what is North's opening bid?

East passes. South has 10 points. Does the partnership belong in game or a partscore? Does South know if there is a Golden Fit in a major suit? How can South find out?

West passes. With a four-card spade suit what rebid does North make?

East passes. Now that South has found a Golden Fit, at what level and denomination does the partnership belong? What bid does South make?

What will be the contract? Who will be declarer?

The Play

Which player makes the opening lead? What will the opening lead be?

Declarer starts by making a PLAN:

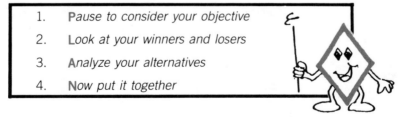

1. **P**ause to consider your objective
2. **L**ook at your winners and losers
3. **A**nalyze your alternatives
4. **N**ow put it together

How many losers can declarer afford? How many losers does declarer have? How can declarer avoid losing two trump tricks? Which suit provides entries to dummy? When declarer leads the first spade from dummy, which card should West play? Why?

Exercise Ten — Watching Entries While Promoting Winners

Turn up all the cards on the second pre-dealt hand. Put each hand dummy style at the edge of the table in front of each player.

Dealer: East

```
                          ♠ A 9 7 2
                          ♡ 7 5
                          ◇ J 10 8 6
                          ♣ A 9 8
         ♠ K J 6 5                        ♠ Q 10 3
         ♡ A 8 6 3                        ♡ K 2
         ◇ 9 5                            ◇ A K Q 4
         ♣ J 4 2                          ♣ Q 7 6 3
                          ♠ 8 4
                          ♡ Q J 10 9 4
                          ◇ 7 3 2
                          ♣ K 10 5
```

The Bidding

With a balanced hand of 16 points, what is East's opening bid?

South passes. West has 9 points. Does West know whether the partnership belongs in game or a partscore? Is West interested in finding a Golden Fit in a major suit? What does West respond?

North passes. How does East tell partner that he does not have a four–card major suit?

South passes. Since opener does not have a four–card major suit, what does West rebid to invite opener to bid game?

North passes. Does East have enough to accept West's invitation to bid on to game? What will be the contract? Who will be declarer?

The Play

Which player makes the opening lead? What will be the opening lead?

Declarer starts by making a PLAN. Which suit offers the best potential for developing extra tricks? How does declarer plan to play the suit? What can North do to make life difficult for declarer? In which hand should declarer win the first trick? Why?

If declarer were to play a club from either hand, which card should the first defender play? Why?

Exercise Eleven — Entries When Developing a Long Suit

Turn up all the cards on the third pre-dealt hand. Put each hand dummy style at the edge of the table in front of each player.

Dealer: South

```
                        ♠ J 9 6 2
                        ♡ 10 4
                        ◇ 7 3
                        ♣ A K 8 6 3
        ♠ 8 4 3                        ♠ Q 10 7 5
        ♡ K J 5                        ♡ Q 9 8 2
        ◇ Q 10 8 6 5                   ◇ J 9
        ♣ J 9                          ♣ Q 10 5
                        ♠ A K
                        ♡ A 7 6 3
                        ◇ A K 4 2
                        ♣ 7 4 2
```

The Bidding

With a balanced 18 points what is South's opening bid?

West passes. With 9 points, does North know if the partnership belongs in game or a partscore? Is North interested in finding a Golden Fit in a major suit? What does North respond?

East passes. Does South have a four-card major suit? What does South rebid?

West passes. Has North uncovered a Golden Fit? What does North rebid to invite South to bid game?

East passes. Does South accept North's invitation? What will be the contract? Who will be declarer?

The Play

Which player makes the opening lead? What will the opening lead be?

Declarer starts by making a PLAN. Which suit does declarer plan to establish to make the contract? What will declarer have to hope for? How does declarer ensure that dummy has an entry to the established winners?

Exercise Twelve — Creating an Entry

Turn up all the cards on the fourth pre-dealt hand. Put each hand dummy style at the edge of the table in front of each player.

Dealer: West

```
                      ♠ 10 8 4 2
                      ♡ K 3
                      ◇ 8 7 4
                      ♣ Q J 10 9
        ♠ A K                        ♠ Q 7 5
        ♡ J 9 6 5 4                  ♡ Q 10 8 7
        ◇ 10 9 5                     ◇ K Q J
        ♣ A K 3                      ♣ 8 6 2
                      ♠ J 9 6 3
                      ♡ A 2
                      ◇ A 6 3 2
                      ♣ 7 5 4
```

The Bidding

With a balanced hand and 15 HCP plus 1 point for the five–card suit, what is West's opening bid?

North passes. Does East have enough for game? Is East interested in finding a Golden Fit in a major suit? What does East respond?

South passes. Does West have a major suit? What does West respond?

North passes. Does East know the level and denomination in which the partnership belongs? What does East bid?

What will be the contract? Who will be declarer?

The Play

Which player makes the opening lead? What will the opening lead be?

Declarer starts by making a PLAN. How many losers can declarer afford? How many losers does declarer have? How does declarer plan to get rid of his extra loser?

Does declarer have an immediate entry to dummy? How does declarer plan to get to dummy? Can declarer start by drawing trumps? Why not?

LESSON 6
Watching Out for the Opponents

The Hold–Up Play
Avoiding the Dangerous Opponent
Guidelines for Defense
Bidding — Strong Opening Bids
Summary

Workshop Material
Group Activities

While you are working to develop the extra tricks you need to make the contract, the defenders are trying to prevent you from succeeding. When you consider the fourth step of the PLAN, **N**ow *put it together,* you must take into account what the defenders may do to interfere with your strategy.

The defenders can do things such as take tricks in their long suit once they have driven out your high cards, capture your high cards with a higher card and make you use up your entries before you are ready. Let's see what you can do about this.

◆ *THE HOLD-UP PLAY* ◆

Against a notrump contract, the defenders usually try to establish a long suit by driving out declarer's high cards. When the defenders regain the lead, they take their winners in that suit. The defenders have the advantage of making the opening lead. They can choose the suit they want to attack. Declarer may not be able to prevent the defenders from driving out his high cards in a suit, but sometimes he can make it more difficult for them to take their tricks when they regain the lead. Let's look at how declarer does this.

Holding Up the Ace

Timing is an important aspect of playing a hand. In the previous lesson we saw how by *ducking* a trick (letting the opponents win a trick he could win) declarer can help maintain an entry to a suit. He doesn't lose anything since he is still entitled to his winner(s) in the suit and has to lose one or more tricks sooner or later. However, declarer may gain by choosing exactly the right moment to win the trick.

When the opponents are trying to establish *their* suit, choosing the right time to take a winner can also make a difference. Consider this layout:

```
              NORTH (DUMMY)
              7 5
WEST                        EAST
K Q J 10 9                  8 3 2
              SOUTH (DECLARER)
              A 6 4
```

West leads the king against declarer's notrump contract. Declarer has only one sure trick, the ace, whether he plays it on the first, second or third round of the suit. However, *when* declarer takes the ace may make a big difference in the number of tricks the opponents get in the suit.

First, suppose declarer wins the first trick with the ace. The remaining cards in the suit are:

```
              NORTH (DUMMY)
              7
WEST                        EAST
Q J 10 9                    8 3
              SOUTH (DECLARER)
              6 4
```

Unless declarer has enough winners to make his contract, he must establish extra tricks. To do this, declarer may have to give up the lead. Whichever opponent gets the lead, the opponents can take all four of their winners in the above suit.

If declarer wins the second trick with the ace, the result will be the same. East will still have a low card left to lead back to West's remaining winners. The opponents take four tricks in the suit.

Suppose, however, that declarer waits until the third time the suit is led before taking the ace. Now the remaining cards are:

NORTH (DUMMY)

WEST   EAST
10 9

SOUTH (DECLARER)

If declarer has to lose a trick to West, West will take his remaining winners — the opponents once again get four tricks in the suit. However, if declarer loses a trick to East, East has no low cards left to lead. Unless West has some other way to win a trick, his winners are stranded. The opponents take only two tricks in the suit instead of four.

Declarer can make it difficult for the opponents to take all their winners by *holding up* his ace until one opponent has no cards left in the suit. Here is an example of the *hold-up play* in action:

Contract: 3 NT   NORTH (DUMMY)
Lead: ♡ 4   ♠ 10 4
                                  ♡ A 7 3
                                  ◇ Q J 9 6 3
                                  ♣ K 8 2
              WEST   EAST
              ♠ 9 6 2   ♠ Q J 8 5
              ♡ K J 9 4 2   ♡ Q 8 6
              ◇ 7 5   ◇ A 8 2
              ♣ 10 7 4   ♣ 9 6 5
                                  SOUTH (DECLARER)
                                  ♠ A K 7 3
                                  ♡ 10 5
                                  ◇ K 10 4
                                  ♣ A Q J 3

Declarer needs nine tricks in 3 NT and has two spades, one heart and four clubs, a total of seven. Two more tricks need to be developed, and four diamond tricks can be promoted by driving out the opponents' ace. That is more than enough, but when putting it together, declarer must watch out for the opponents.

The opponents have led hearts and will drive out declarer's only high card in the suit. If the hearts are divided as one might expect, 5-3, the opponents will have four winners in the suit. That, together with the ◇ A, will be enough to defeat the contract.

To give himself the best chance, declarer makes use of the hold-up play. He plays a low heart from dummy on the first trick, letting East win the ♡ Q. When East returns part-

117

ner's suit, declarer ducks again, holding up the ace. West leads hearts once more to establish two winners in the suit, and declarer wins dummy's ♡A.

Declarer now crosses his fingers and plays the ◇K, high card from the short side, to drive out the ◇A. When East wins, he has no hearts left to lead back to West's established winners. Whatever East leads, declarer wins the trick and takes his winners, ending up with an overtrick.

Why does declarer need to cross his fingers? If West had the ◇A instead of East, West would win the diamond trick and take his two heart winners to defeat the contract. Declarer needs luck, but it is combined with an element of skill. If declarer does not hold up the ♡A, he will be defeated no matter which defender has the ◇A. The hold-up play gives him a 50% chance.

Holding Up the King

The hold-up play involves letting the opponents win the trick instead of taking a sure winner. Sometimes, the hold-up play can be used when the sure winner is a king. Consider this situation:

```
                    NORTH (DUMMY)
                    10 4
        WEST                     EAST
        Q 9 7 6 3                A J 2
                    SOUTH (DECLARER)
                    K 8 5
```

West leads the 6 to East's ace, and East leads back the jack. Declarer's king is now a sure winner and he can hold up by playing his remaining low card. If East leads the suit again, declarer wins the king and now East has no cards left in the suit to lead to West's winners.

If the ace has not been played, the king is not a sure winner — declarer cannot afford to hold up. Look at this layout:

```
                    NORTH (DUMMY)
                    10 4
        WEST                     EAST
        A Q 9 6 3                J 7 2
                    SOUTH (DECLARER)
                    K 8 5
```

West leads the 6 and East plays the jack. If declarer lets East win the trick, he will lead the suit back — now the king is trapped by West's ace and queen. The opponents take the first five tricks in the suit and declarer gets no tricks. Declarer should take the king while he has the chance.

Here is an example of holding up with the king:

Contract: 3 NT
Lead: ♠ 4

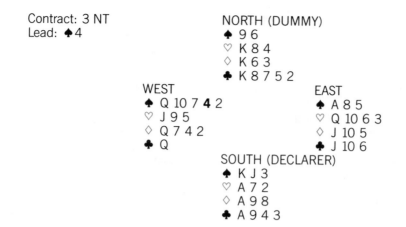

NORTH (DUMMY)
♠ 9 6
♡ K 8 4
◊ K 6 3
♣ K 8 7 5 2

WEST
♠ Q 10 7 **4** 2
♡ J 9 5
◊ Q 7 4 2
♣ Q

EAST
♠ A 8 5
♡ Q 10 6 3
◊ J 10 5
♣ J 10 6

SOUTH (DECLARER)
♠ K J 3
♡ A 7 2
◊ A 9 8
♣ A 9 4 3

West leads the ♠4 to East's ♠A and East returns the ♠8. Should declarer win the trick with the ♠K? He needs nine tricks. The ♠K is now a sure winner, and he has two tricks each in hearts, diamonds and clubs. Where will the two extra tricks come from?

The club suit looks promising. Declarer has nine clubs, the opponents have four. If the missing clubs divide 2-2, declarer's remaining three clubs will be winners after he takes the ♣A and ♣K. If, as is more likely, the clubs break 3-1, declarer must give up a trick to establish his remaining two low clubs as winners.

Since declarer may have to lose a trick, he does not want the opponents to take four spade tricks as well. Declarer should hold up the ♠K, and play the ♠J instead. This loses to West's ♠Q and West can lead the suit again to drive out the king. The hold-up play has the desired effect, however. When the clubs break 3-1, declarer must give up a trick to East to establish the suit. Since East has no spades left, declarer makes the contract.

How Long to Hold Up

Earlier, we examined this layout:

NORTH (DUMMY)
7 5

WEST
K Q J 10 9

EAST
8 3 2

SOUTH (DECLARER)
A 6 4

When the king was led, declarer held up twice, winning the ace on the third round. East was left with no cards in the suit and, provided West never got the lead, the opponents took two winners rather than four.

Suppose, instead, that the missing cards are divided in this fashion:

NORTH (DUMMY)
7 5

WEST
K Q J 10

EAST
9 8 3 2

SOUTH (DECLARER)
A 6 4

If the eight missing cards divide 4-4, then holding up the ace does no good but also does no harm. East still has a low card left, and whichever opponent gets the lead, the opponents get one more trick. Since the suit breaks 4-4, however, the opponents get only three tricks in all.

When deciding how long to hold up, consider how many tricks you can afford to lose. If you are in 3 NT, you can afford to lose four tricks. If you must give up a trick in another suit, you can afford to lose three tricks in the suit the opponents are trying to establish. In the above, example, holding up the ace until the third round ensures that you will still make the contract if East, rather than West, gets the lead. If the suit was originally divided 5-3, East will have none left. If it was 4-4, East will have one left but the opponents can take only three winners in the suit.

When deciding whether to hold up, declarer must take into consideration the possibility that the opponents may switch to another suit. That could be more dangerous. Look at this example:

Contract: 3 NT
Lead: ♠5

NORTH (DUMMY)
♠ 8 4 3
♡ K Q
◇ K J 5 3 2
♣ 9 4 2

WEST
♠ K J 7 **5**
♡ 10 6 4 2
◇ 9
♣ 7 6 5 3

EAST
♠ Q 10 2
♡ 9 7 5 3
◇ A 7
♣ K Q J 10

SOUTH (DECLARER)
♠ A 9 6
♡ A J 8
◇ Q 10 8 6 4
♣ A 8

In 3 NT, declarer has one sure spade trick, three sure heart tricks and one sure club trick. He can get the four extra tricks he requires to make his contract by driving out the opponents' ◇ A. The ♠5 has been led and East plays the ♠Q. Should declarer hold up?

Since declarer must let the opponents in the lead with the ◇ A, it may seem like a good time to employ the hold-up play. However, declarer's holding in the club suit is not very strong. If declarer lets East win the first trick, East may decide to try another suit and switch to clubs. Once declarer's ♣A is driven out, the defenders will have more than enough tricks to defeat the contract.

Declarer cannot afford to use the hold-up play. Instead, he wins the first trick with the ♠A and drives out the ◇ A to establish the extra winners he needs. When the opponents win the ◇ A, declarer must hope the missing spades are divided so that the opponents cannot take more than three tricks in the suit.

Holding Up With Two High Cards

If there is no danger of the opponents switching to another suit, declarer sometimes holds up even though he has two winners. Consider this example:

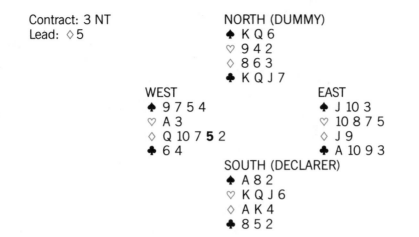

Contract: 3 NT
Lead: ◇ 5

NORTH (DUMMY)
♠ K Q 6
♡ 9 4 2
◇ 8 6 3
♣ K Q J 7

WEST
♠ 9 7 5 4
♡ A 3
◇ Q 10 7 **5** 2
♣ 6 4

EAST
♠ J 10 3
♡ 10 8 7 5
◇ J 9
♣ A 10 9 3

SOUTH (DECLARER)
♠ A 8 2
♡ K Q J 6
◇ A K 4
♣ 8 5 2

Declarer starts with three spade tricks and two diamond tricks. Four more tricks are needed to make 3 NT. Neither the club suit nor the heart suit alone will provide all the necessary tricks, so declarer must promote tricks in both suits by driving out the missing aces. This means declarer will have to let the opponents in twice.

The ◇ 5 is led to East's ◇ J. Since declarer has both the ◇ A and ◇ K, it may not seem necessary to hold up — but look what happens! Suppose declarer wins the first trick with the ◇ K and leads a club to dummy's ♣ J to drive out the ace. East wins the ♣ A and leads back the ◇ 9. Declarer may try holding up the ◇ A, but it is too late.

West wins the trick and leads another diamond to drive out declarer's ace. Since declarer still does not have enough winners, he must lead a high heart to drive out the ace. West wins the ♡ A and takes his established diamonds to defeat the contract. Declarer loses three diamond tricks and two aces.

Let's see what happens if declarer does not win the first diamond trick, holding up with both the ace and king. East wins and leads another diamond which declarer wins with the ◇ K. Next declarer leads a club and drives out East's ♣ A. Now the effect of the hold-up play becomes apparent. East has no more diamonds left and cannot drive out declarer's remaining ◇ A.

Suppose East leads a spade. Declarer wins and now drives out West's ♡ A. When West wins, he can lead another diamond to drive out declarer's ◇ A, but it too late for the defense. Declarer has established the tricks he needs — he can take all his winners, making the contract.

When the Defenders Try to Take Away Declarer's Entries

It is not only declarer who can make use of the hold-up play. The defenders do not have to win the first round of a suit declarer is trying to establish, and this can give declarer entry problems. We saw some examples of this in the previous lesson, where declarer had to be careful to watch his entries. Here is another hand:

Contract: 3 NT
Lead: ♡Q

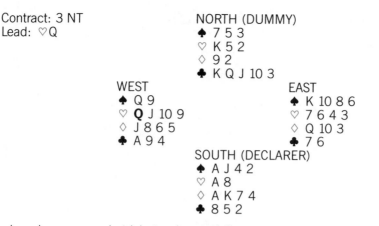

NORTH (DUMMY)
♠ 7 5 3
♡ K 5 2
◇ 9 2
♣ K Q J 10 3

WEST
♠ Q 9
♡ Q J 10 9
◇ J 8 6 5
♣ A 9 4

EAST
♠ K 10 8 6
♡ 7 6 4 3
◇ Q 10 3
♣ 7 6

SOUTH (DECLARER)
♠ A J 4 2
♡ A 8
◇ A K 7 4
♣ 8 5 2

Declarer has one spade trick, two heart tricks and two diamond tricks. To make 3 NT, declarer needs four more tricks. These can come from the club suit by driving out the opponents' ♣A. Declarer must be careful, however.

The opponents have led hearts, so declarer first needs to consider whether to use the hold-up play. Since the opponents will get the lead only once, with the ♣A, and declarer has two heart tricks, he doesn't need to hold up.

Declarer next must decide in which hand to win the first trick. Because the defenders may hold up their ♣A, declarer must win the first trick with the ♡A, keeping the ♡K as an entry to dummy. Now it is a simple task to drive out the ♣A and end up with nine tricks.

If declarer doesn't watch out for the opponents, the result may be different. Suppose declarer wins the first trick with dummy's ♡K and leads the ♣K to drive out the ace. West, seeing that declarer is trying to promote club tricks, holds up the ♣A, refusing to take the first trick. When declarer continues with the ♣Q, West can hold up again. If declarer persists by leading another club, West must win the ace — but now declarer has no clubs left in his hand and no entry to dummy. Dummy's club winners are stranded.

Declarer cannot always prevent the opponents from successfully holding up in a suit. Sometimes, declarer must use other countermeasures. Consider this hand:

Contract: 3 NT
Lead: ♠6

NORTH (DUMMY)
♠ A
♡ 9 5 2
◇ K Q 10 9 5 4
♣ 7 6 2

WEST
♠ Q 10 8 6 2
♡ Q 10 7
◇ 6
♣ A 9 4 3

EAST
♠ J 7 4 3
♡ J 6 4 3
◇ A 7 2
♣ 8 5

SOUTH (DECLARER)
♠ K 9 5
♡ A K 8
◇ J 8 3
♣ K Q J 10

Against your 3 NT contract, West leads the ♠6. You have no choice but to win the first trick with dummy's ♠A. Your only sure entry to dummy has been driven out at trick one. You have only two sure spade tricks and two sure heart tricks. You must develop five more tricks. The diamond suit looks like it can provide the tricks you need once the ◇A is driven out.

After winning dummy's ♠A, suppose you lead a diamond to your jack (high card from the short side) and a diamond back to dummy's queen, trying to drive out the ace. Realizing what you are doing, West refuses to take the ◇A. Should you lead another diamond to drive out the ace?

Leading another diamond would do no good. You could establish dummy's remaining three diamonds, but you have no entry to them. After winning the ◇A, East would lead another spade, driving out your ♠K. If you now tried to set up club tricks, West would win and take enough spade tricks to defeat the contract.

Instead, you must abandon the diamond suit and switch your attention to clubs. You already have two diamond tricks, so you need only three club tricks. After winning the second diamond trick, lead a club and drive out the opponents' ace. You will end up with two spade tricks, two heart tricks, two diamond tricks and three club tricks — nine in all.

East's hold-up play made you change your tactics. You no longer could use the diamond suit to provide all the extra tricks you needed. Fortunately, you had another option.

Sometimes, of course, you will have no suitable countermeasure to the opponents' defense. In that case congratulate the opponents on their fine defense and get on to the next hand. If you make every contract you bid, you are not bidding enough!

◆ *AVOIDING THE DANGEROUS OPPONENT* ◆

Sometimes, it is more dangerous to let one opponent have the lead than the other. In such cases you want to avoid giving the lead to the *dangerous opponent*. If you must lose a trick, try to lose it to the non-dangerous opponent.

The Dangerous Opponent

How do you know which opponent is the dangerous one? Let's return to the layout of a suit we examined earlier:

```
                    NORTH (DUMMY)
                    7 5
      WEST                          EAST
      K Q J 10 9                    8 3 2
                    SOUTH (DECLARER)
                    A 6 4
```

West leads the king against your notrump contract, and you use the hold-up play, winning your ace on the third round. The remaining cards are:

```
                    NORTH (DUMMY)

      WEST                          EAST
      10 9

                    SOUTH (DECLARER)
```

123

West is clearly the dangerous opponent. If West gets the lead, he can take his two remaining winners. If East gets the lead, he has no cards left in the suit and can do you no harm.

Dangerous opponents do not crop up only in notrump contracts. Suppose an opponent leads a singleton against your suit contract, hoping the suit will be led again so he can trump. Until the trumps are drawn, *the opening leader's partner* is the dangerous opponent. If he wins a trick, he can lead back the suit so the opening leader can trump it.

Here is another suit combination that provides a dangerous opponent in either a notrump contract or a suit contract:

```
                        NORTH (DUMMY)
                        7 5 2
          WEST                         EAST
          A 9 8 3                      Q J 10
                        SOUTH (DECLARER)
                        K 6 4
```

If declarer cannot afford to lose several tricks in this suit, which opponent is dangerous? There would be no danger if East held the ace, since declarer would get a trick with the king whichever opponent led the suit. (Declarer could even lead the suit himself, taking a finesse by leading toward the king.) But in the actual layout West holds the ace.

East is the dangerous opponent. If West gets the lead, he can take the ace, but now declarer gets a trick with the king. If East gets the lead, however, he can lead the queen. Whether declarer plays the king on the first trick or a subsequent trick, he never gets a trick with it — the opponents take all the tricks in the suit.

Here is a similar case. West leads the 5 against your notrump contract. You play dummy's 2, and East plays the jack:

```
                        NORTH (DUMMY)
                        7 2
          WEST                         EAST
          A 10 8 5 3                   J 9 6
                        SOUTH (DECLARER)
                        K Q 4
```

If you win the queen (or king), who is the dangerous opponent? Again, it is East. If East gets the lead, he can lead the suit and your remaining king is trapped. If West gets the lead, he can take the ace, but you will get a trick with the king.

Avoiding the Dangerous Opponent

Once you have identified the dangerous opponent, how do you avoid giving him the lead? Sometimes it will not be possible, but at other times you can control your own destiny. Consider the following hand:

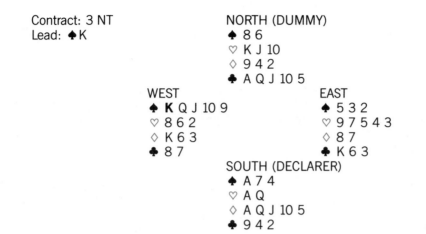

Contract: 3 NT
Lead: ♠K

NORTH (DUMMY)
♠ 8 6
♡ K J 10
◇ 9 4 2
♣ A Q J 10 5

WEST
♠ **K** Q J 10 9
♡ 8 6 2
◇ K 6 3
♣ 8 7

EAST
♠ 5 3 2
♡ 9 7 5 4 3
◇ 8 7
♣ K 6 3

SOUTH (DECLARER)
♠ A 7 4
♡ A Q
◇ A Q J 10 5
♣ 9 4 2

West leads the ♠K against your 3 NT contract. You have one spade, three hearts, one diamond and one club, for a total of six tricks. Either the club suit or the diamond suit will provide the tricks you need. In either suit you can finesse for the missing king. If the finesse works, you will take five tricks in the suit. If it loses, you still will end up with four tricks, enough for your contract.

Which finesse should you take? West has led a spade. If the missing spades divide 5-3 or worse, the danger is that you will lose four or more tricks in the suit. You therefore use the hold-up play, trying to leave East with no spades. Duck the first two rounds and win the third round. West is now the dangerous opponent. You therefore try the club finesse. You do not mind if it loses to East's ♣K since East can do you no harm.

If East wins the ♣K and leads back a diamond, do not take the finesse. Win the ◇A and scurry home with your nine tricks. You do not want to lose a trick to West, the dangerous opponent, if you can avoid it.

Sometimes you have a choice of which way to finesse within only one suit. This is called a *two-way finesse*. You want to arrange things so that, if a finesse loses, the dangerous opponent does not get the lead. Here is an example:

Contract: 3 NT
Lead: ♡6

NORTH (DUMMY)
♠ A 9 3
♡ 7 4 2
◇ K J 6 3
♣ A 10 4

WEST
♠ J 7 5
♡ A J 9 **6** 3
◇ 8 7
♣ 8 7 2

EAST
♠ Q 10 8 4
♡ 10 8
◇ Q 9 2
♣ J 9 6 3

SOUTH (DECLARER)
♠ K 6 2
♡ K Q 5
◇ A 10 5 4
♣ K Q 5

You start with two spade tricks, two diamond tricks and three club tricks. You will get at least one trick from the heart suit since you hold both the king and queen. Where is your ninth trick to come from if you are to make your 3 NT contract?

In the diamond suit you have all the high cards except the queen. You can develop another trick in this suit simply by playing the ace and king and then driving out the queen or by taking a finesse for the missing queen. If you think West has the ◇ Q, win a trick with the ◇ A and lead a low diamond toward dummy, finessing the ◇ J if West plays a low card. If you think East has the ◇ Q, win a trick with dummy's ◇ K and lead a low diamond toward your hand, finessing the ◇ 10 if East plays low. Since you have a choice, this is a *two-way finesse*.

Before deciding how to play the diamond suit, you need to think about the whole hand. West has led the ♡ 6, and when you play low from dummy, East plays the ♡ 10. When you win this trick with the ♡ Q, who is the dangerous opponent? In this case, it is East — if East gets the lead, he can lead a heart, and your remaining ♡ K will be trapped. However, if West gets the lead, he cannot trap your ♡ K.

This tells you how to play the diamond suit. After winning the ♡ Q, lead to dummy's ◇ K, lead a low diamond from dummy and finesse the ◇ 10 when East plays low. If the finesse works, you make the contract with an overtrick. If the finesse loses, you are still safe — West cannot take more than one heart trick without giving you a trick with the ♡ K. If he leads anything else, you have established the extra diamond winner you need.

On the actual layout of the cards, you are rewarded with an overtrick by playing the diamond suit in this fashion. If you had finessed in the other direction, East would have won the ◇ Q and led back a heart, trapping your king. West would have taken four heart tricks to defeat the contract. It pays to know about avoiding the dangerous opponent!

Here is an example of watching out for the opponents in a suit contract:

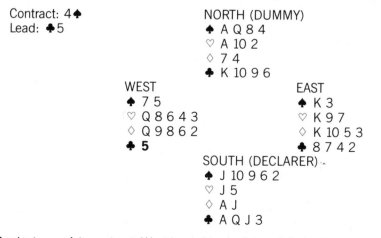

Contract: 4♠
Lead: ♣5

NORTH (DUMMY)
♠ A Q 8 4
♡ A 10 2
◇ 7 4
♣ K 10 9 6

WEST
♠ 7 5
♡ Q 8 6 4 3
◇ Q 9 8 6 2
♣ 5

EAST
♠ K 3
♡ K 9 7
◇ K 10 5 3
♣ 8 7 4 2

SOUTH (DECLARER)
♠ J 10 9 6 2
♡ J 5
◇ A J
♣ A Q J 3

Against your 4♠ contract, West leads his singleton club, hoping to trump some of your winners. When you look at your losers, you see one in spades, since you are missing the ♠ K, one in hearts and one in diamonds. There appears to be no problem, but you must not get careless.

The spade suit offers the opportunity for a finesse. You could win the first trick with a high club in your hand and lead the ♠J. If West plays a low spade, you could play low from dummy. If West has the ♠K, your finesse will work and you will end up with an over-trick. If the finesse loses — well, you could afford to lose one spade trick anyway.

On this hand, however, when the spade finesse loses, East leads back a club. West trumps your winner and down you go, losing two trumps instead of one — unfortunate but avoidable.

Since you can afford one trump loser but not two, you should avoid letting the dangerous opponent, East in this case, get the lead until trumps are drawn. Instead of taking a finesse, play the ♠A and another spade to drive out the ♠K, drawing trumps as quickly as possible. When East wins the king, all the trumps are gone and the danger is past. If West started with the king, he would win a trick with it but there no longer would be any danger. Safety first!

As we will see in the next lesson, you cannot always draw all the missing trumps right away because of other considerations. But when you can afford to draw trumps, draw them as quickly possible, to avoid letting a dangerous opponent do you some damage.

When Both Opponents Are Dangerous

On some hands, you cannot afford to let either opponent win a trick since they are both dangerous. In such cases, you will have to look for a way of making the contract without giving up the lead. Here is an example:

```
Contract: 3 NT              NORTH (DUMMY)
Lead: ♡4                    ♠ K 7 4
                            ♡ 9 5
                            ◇ K Q J 8
                            ♣ Q J 6 3
        WEST                                EAST
        ♠ J 9 6                             ♠ 10 8 3
        ♡ K 10 7 4 2                        ♡ Q J 6 3
        ◇ A 5 2                             ◇ 7 4 3
        ♣ 9 5                               ♣ 8 7 2
                            SOUTH (DECLARER)
                            ♠ A Q 5 2
                            ♡ A 8
                            ◇ 10 9 6
                            ♣ A K 10 4
```

In 3 NT you have three spades, one heart and four clubs — eight tricks in all. It looks easy enough to develop extra tricks by driving out the ◇A, but you must watch out for those opponents! West has led a heart, and even if you hold up the ♡A, you can do so for only one round. Even if the missing hearts divide 5-4, the opponents will get four heart tricks to go along with the ◇A if you give up the lead.

Is there any alternative to conceding the ◇A? The spade suit does provide some poten-tial. You have seven spades and the opponents have six. If the missing spades divide 3-3, your remaining low spade will be a winner after you take the ♠A, ♠K and ♠Q. This goes against the odds, since you expect an even number of missing cards to divide slightly unevenly, 4-2 and they could even be divided 5-1 or 6-0. However, when it is your only legitimate chance, go for it!

In such a situation it does no harm to take your four club winners first. This gives you the added chance that an unsuspecting opponent who started with four spades may discard a spade when he runs out of clubs. Even though the spade suit started out breaking 4-2, it might suddenly become 3-2. It is not always easy for the defenders to know which cards to keep when declarer is taking tricks in a long suit.

◆ GUIDELINES FOR DEFENSE ◆

During the play, the defenders will have many decisions to make. Should they win this trick or hold up? If they win the trick, what should they do next. Many of declarer's techniques are just as useful to the defenders: the hold-up play, ducking to keep an entry, leading toward high cards. The difficulty comes from recognizing when they apply, since the defenders cannot see each other's hands. Here are a couple of the techniques we have discussed presented from the defenders' point of view.

Defensive Hold-up Play

The hold-up play is not solely the prerogative of declarer. The defenders can put it to good use also. Consider the following layout of a suit in a notrump contract:

```
                    NORTH (DUMMY)
                    Q J 10 8 7 5
        WEST                        EAST (YOU)
        2                           A 9 3
                    SOUTH (DECLARER)
                    K 6 4
```

If you hold the ace of this suit, and dummy has no entries outside the suit, choosing when to win your ace is very important. Suppose declarer starts by leading the king (high card from the short side), trying to drive out the ace and establish the remaining cards in dummy. If you take the ace, declarer still will have two low cards left in his hand for entries to dummy's winners.

Instead, use the hold-up play and refuse to win the first trick. If declarer leads the suit again, hold up again. How do you know declarer still has a low card left without peeking into his hand? Partner will have to discard. Since you can see all the cards in dummy and your own hand, and each suit has 13 cards, declarer still has one left. If declarer leads the suit again, you must win the ace. But now your hold-up play has done its job. Declarer has no low cards left in his hand, and dummy's winners are stranded. Declarer gets only two tricks rather than five.

The principle is the same as when declarer holds up, hoping a defender will have no cards left in the suit when he gets the lead. Just as declarer cannot see the exact division of the cards in the defenders' hands, you cannot see how many cards declarer has in the suit. However, you often will be able to tell, as in the above example. Suppose we change the layout of the suit slightly:

NORTH (DUMMY)
Q J 10 8 7 5

WEST
6 2

EAST (YOU)
A 9 3

SOUTH (DECLARER)
K 4

Again, declarer leads the king, and you hold up. This time, when declarer leads the suit again, your partner follows suit. Since you now can see all 13 cards in the suit, it is safe to win the ace on the second round. Declarer gets only one trick, and four winners are stranded in the dummy.

Let's take a look at the defensive hold-up play in action:

Contract: 3 NT
Lead: ♠7

NORTH (DUMMY)
♠ A 6
♡ 8 6 5
◇ 7 6 4
♣ K Q 10 8 3

WEST
♠ J 9 8 **7**
♡ J 9 3 2
◇ A 9 2
♣ 7 4

EAST (YOU)
♠ K 10 3 2
♡ Q 10
◇ 8 5 3
♣ A 9 6 5

SOUTH (DECLARER)
♠ Q 5 4
♡ A K 7 4
◇ K Q J 10
♣ J 2

Your partner leads the ♠7 against declarer's 3 NT contract. The ♠6 is played from dummy, and you win the ♠K. Being a good partner, you return partner's lead — declarer wins dummy's ♠A. Declarer now leads a low club to his ♣J. You play low, holding up your ace. Declarer leads another club to dummy's ♣K. What do you do?

With five clubs in dummy originally and four in your hand, only four clubs were missing. You now have seen two in declarer's hand and two from your partner. Win the ♣A since declarer has no clubs left. Three club winners are left in dummy but they are stranded. You now lead another spade, driving out declarer's queen — eventually, declarer goes down to defeat. Declarer gets two spade tricks, two heart tricks and three diamond tricks (by driving out partner's ace), but only one club trick.

Had you won the first club trick, declarer would have ended up with four club tricks. Had you held up with your ♣A until the third round, declarer would have gotten two club tricks. In either case declarer would have made the contract. Well defended!

Ducking to Keep an Entry

In an earlier lesson we saw how declarer can preserve an entry within a suit by taking his losses early and giving up a trick. The defenders also can use this technique. Look at the following layout:

NORTH (DUMMY)
Q J 8

WEST (YOU)   EAST
A 9 7 3 2   K 6 4

SOUTH (DECLARER)
10 5

You lead the 3 against a notrump contract, and your partner wins the first trick with the king. Partner then leads the suit back. Do you win the second trick with the ace?

If you have an entry in another suit, it is all right to win the ace and lead the suit again, establishing your remaining cards as winners. If partner subsequently gets the lead, he can lead the suit in which you have an entry, and you can take your winners.

But what if you do not have an entry in another suit? If you win the ace and lead the suit again, you set up two winners, but now they are stranded. If partner gets the lead, he will have no low cards in this suit to lead. Instead, duck the second trick, keeping the ace as an entry. Declarer is entitled to one trick anyway. Now if your partner subsequently gets the lead, he can lead his remaining low card back to your ace, and you can take your other two winners.

Again, this is identical to the way declarer would handle this suit if he had to watch his entries.

Let's see how the defenders make use of this technique in an actual hand:

Contract: 3 NT   NORTH (DUMMY)
Lead: ♡ 5   ♠ A 8 5
                            ♡ Q 7 2
                            ◇ K J 8 3
                            ♣ Q 9 6

WEST (YOU)   EAST
♠ 9 4 3   ♠ J 10 7 2
♡ K 9 8 5 4   ♡ A 6 3
◇ 7 4   ◇ A 6 5
♣ 10 4 2   ♣ 8 5 3

                    SOUTH (DECLARER)
                    ♠ K Q 6
                    ♡ J 10
                    ◇ Q 10 9 2
                    ♣ A K J 7

You lead the ♡ 5 against declarer's 3 NT contract. Your partner wins the first trick with the ♡ A and leads back a heart. Do you win the trick with the ♡ K?

Since you have no other entry to your heart winners and can see declarer always will win one heart trick, duck this trick. Declarer has three spade tricks and four club tricks to go along with the heart trick, but sooner or later, he will have to lead a diamond to try to establish a ninth trick. Your partner can win the ◇ A and lead back his remaining heart. You win the ♡ K and take your remaining two heart winners to defeat the contract.

◆ *BIDDING* ◆

Opening bids at the one level are used with hands in the range of 13-21 points. Responder passes with fewer than 6 points since enough combined strength for a game contract is very unlikely. With a very strong hand of 22 or more points, opener wants responder to bid, even with fewer than 6 points. In this lesson we will look at how opener and responder handle such hands.

Balanced Hands

With a balanced hand of 22-24 points, opener bids 2 NT. With a balanced hand of 25-27 points, opener bids 3 NT. (Balanced hands of 28 or more points are extremely rare.) Here are some examples:

♠ K Q 8 3 ♡ A Q 3 ◇ K Q 8 4 ♣ A Q	With a balanced hand and 22 HCPs, open the bidding **2 NT**.
♠ A Q J ♡ K Q ◇ A K J 8 2 ♣ K Q J	Here you have 26 HCPs plus one for the five-card suit. Open **3 NT** to show a balanced hand in the 25-27 point range.
♠ K J 8 ♡ A Q J ◇ K 10 9 7 ♣ K Q 10	Although this is a balanced hand, you have only 19 HCPs. While this hand is too strong to open 1 NT, it is too weak to open 2 NT. Instead, open **1◇**, intending to jump in notrump at your next opportunity. You show a balanced hand in the 19-21 point range.

Responding to a 2 NT Opening Bid

If your partner opens 2 NT, you are the captain and are responsible for determining the level and denomination in which the partnership belongs. Use the following guidelines.

- Bid 4♡ or 4♠ with a six–card or longer major suit.

- Bid 3♡ or 3♠ with a five–card major suit. This is a forcing bid, asking opener to bid 4♡ or 4♠ with three-card or longer support; otherwise, to bid 3 NT.

- Bid 3♣ with one or two four-card major suits. This is the *Stayman convention*, asking opener to bid a four-card major suit if he has one; otherwise, to bid 3◇.

- Bid 3 NT with 3 or more points and no interest in a major suit.

- Pass with 0-2 points. Game is unlikely.

Here are some examples when your partner opens the bidding 2 NT:

♠ 10 9 6 4 3 2 ♡ 3 ◇ K 8 3 ♣ 7 5 3	With 3 HCPs plus 2 points for the six-card suit, you have enough combined strength for game since opener has at least 22 points. Since opener has a balanced hand, you must have a Golden Fit in spades. Knowing the level and denomination in which the partnership belongs, respond **4♠**.

♠ 10 7
♡ K 10 8 6 3
◇ J 5
♣ J 10 8 3

You have enough combined strength for game but you are not sure if there is a Golden Fit in hearts. Respond **3♡**. With three or more hearts, opener will bid 4♡ ; otherwise, 3 NT.

♠ K 9 6 2
♡ Q 5
◇ Q 10 9 7
♣ 7 4 2

You are interested in finding out whether partner has four spades. Respond **3♣**, the Stayman convention. If opener bids 3♠, raise to 4♠. If opener bids 3◇, denying a four-card major or 3♡, bid 3 NT.

♠ J 10 6
♡ 7 5
◇ Q 9 6 5 2
♣ 7 4 2

With no interest in a major suit, raise to **3 NT**. Even though you have only 3 HCPs and 1 point for the five-card suit, opener has at least 22 and could have as many as 24.

♠ 9 6
♡ 7 4 3
◇ J 6 4 2
♣ 10 8 6 3

Since you have only 1 point, things do not look hopeful for game even if opener has 24 points. **Pass** and wish partner luck when you put down the dummy.

If partner opens the bidding 3 NT, you don't have much room to explore. Bid 4♡ or 4♠ with a six-card or longer major suit. Otherwise, pass. (We will discuss slam bidding in the next lesson.)

Unbalanced Hands

With an unbalanced hand of 22 or more points, open the bidding at the two level in your longest suit. This is called a *strong two-bid* and tells partner you want to keep the bidding going until a game contract is reached. Here are some examples:

♠ A K 3
♡ A K Q J 6 5
◇ 5
♣ A Q J

With 24 HCPs plus two for the six-card suit, open **2♡**. This is a forcing bid — partner cannot pass until game is reached.

♠ A K 10 8 7
♡ A Q
◇ 5
♣ A K Q 7 3

With 22 HCPs plus 1 point for each of the five-card suits, you are strong enough to open the bidding at the two level. With a choice of suits, use the same guideline as with opening bids at the one level. Bid the higher-ranking of two five-card suits, **2♠**.

Responding to Strong Two-Bids

If partner opens with a strong two-bid, the partnership is forced to game. Responder must bid, even with no points. With a weak hand of 0-5 points, responder makes the *artificial* (conventional) response of 2 NT. With 6 or more points, responder raises opener's suit with three-card or longer support, bids a new suit of his own or jumps to 3 NT with a balanced hand. Here are some examples of responding when opener bids 2♡ :

♠ J 8 5 2
♡ 7 4 3
◇ 10 9 6
♣ 8 7 2

Even though you have only 1 point, you cannot pass when opener bids 2♡. Respond **2 NT**. This is an artificial response showing 0-5 points. Remember, you must keep bidding until game is reached. For example, if opener rebids 3♡, raise to 4♡.

♠ A 8 4
♡ Q 7 5
◇ 10 9 6 3
♣ J 8 2

With 7 points and three-card support for opener's suit, raise to **3♡**.

♠ A Q 9 7 3
♡ 7 6
◇ Q 7 3
♣ 8 4 2

With 8 HCPs plus 1 point for the five-card suit, but without three-card support for opener, bid a new suit. Respond **2♠**.

◆ **SUMMARY** ◆

When going through the fourth step of the PLAN, *Now put it together*, you often must watch out for the opponents. If you have to give up the lead, you do not want the opponents in a position to take enough tricks to defeat your contract.

One technique to make it difficult for the opponents to take their tricks is the *hold-up play*. If the opponents lead a suit in which you have only one winner, you may not have to play it at the first opportunity. By *holding up* (delaying taking your winner), you may exhaust one of the opponents of the suit. If he subsequently gets the lead, he will have no low cards left to lead back to his partner's winners.

Sometimes it is advantageous to hold up even with two winners in the suit. However, do not hold up your winners any longer than necessary, and be careful that you can afford to hold up at all. The opponents may be able to do even more damage in another suit.

If you have to give up the lead, it is often more dangerous to give up the lead to one opponent than the other. One opponent may have winners to take or be able to lead a suit, trapping one of your high cards. In such cases you want to avoid the dangerous opponent. If you must lose a trick, try to arrange your play so you lose the trick to the non-dangerous opponent.

When defending, you can make use of the same techniques declarer employs. A defender can use a hold-up play to make it difficult or impossible for declarer to get all his winners in a suit. The defenders also can duck a trick, letting declarer win it, if that will maintain entries between their two hands.

Strong hands of 22 or more points are opened at the two level or higher:

2♣, 2◇, 2♡, 2♠	22 or more points, unbalanced hand
2 NT	22–24 points, balanced hand
3 NT	25–27 points, balanced hand

An opening bid of 2♣, 2◇, 2♡ or 2♠ (*strong two-bid*) is a forcing bid. Responder cannot pass until game is reached. With 0–5 points responder bids 2 NT, an artificial response showing a weak hand.

◆ *GROUP ACTIVITIES* ◆

Exercise One — Holding Up

Your left-hand opponent leads the following suit against your notrump contract. If you do not take your ace until you have to, how many cards will your right-hand opponent have left in the suit if it divides as you expect?

DUMMY:	1) 8 6	2) 7 4 3	3) 7 6 4 2	4) 9 7 4	5) 10 7
DECLARER:	A 9 2	A 6 5	A 3	A 8	A 6

_____   _____   _____   _____   _____

Exercise Two — How Long to Hold Up

The hold-up play is such an exciting concept that it is tempting to use it whenever you get the chance. West leads the ♡ K against your 3 NT contract. Should you hold up? State the reason for your answer.

Contract: 3 NT
Lead: ♡ K

NORTH (DUMMY)
♠ 8 6 2
♡ 7 4
♢ K 9 7 3
♣ A Q J 5

WEST

♡ K

SOUTH (DECLARER)
♠ Q 3
♡ A 6 5
♢ A Q J 10
♣ K 9 4 2

Exercise Three — The Dangerous Opponent

Who is the dangerous opponent in each of the examples in Exercise One? If you cannot afford to lose three tricks in the following suits, which opponent is the dangerous one?

DUMMY:	1) K 8 4	2) 5 4 2
DECLARER:	7 5 2	K 7 3

_____   _____

Exercise Four — Avoiding the Dangerous Opponent

The opponent on your right is the dangerous opponent. How would you play each of the following suits to avoid giving up the lead to the dangerous opponent whenever possible?

DUMMY: 1) A J 10 5 2) 10 7 5 3 3) J 10 3   4) A 9 7 5 2 5) A Q J 8 3

DECLARER: K 9 8 3   A Q J 8   A K 8 7 2   K J 3   10 7 6 4

_____   _____   _____   _____   _____

Exercise Five — Defensive Hold-up

If dummy has no outside entries, when should you win your ace in each of the following examples if your partner has one card in the suit? What if your partner has two cards in the suit?

1)   DUMMY   2)   DUMMY
    K Q J 10 9   K Q J 10 9 8
            YOU   YOU
        A 7 5 2   A 6 2

_____   _____

Exercise Six — Strong Opening Bids

What would be your opening bid with each of the following hands?

1) ♠ K J 10   2) ♠ A K   3) ♠ A K J 10 9 7
   ♡ A K J   ♡ A Q J 8   ♡ A
   ◇ K Q J 9 4   ◇ K Q J   ◇ K Q J 7
   ♣ A J   ♣ A Q 10 5   ♣ K J

Bid:_____   Bid:_____   Bid:_____

Exercise Seven — Responding to 2 NT

Your partner opens the bidding 2 NT. What do you respond with each of the following hands?

1) ♠ J 7 3   2) ♠ A J 8 6 2   3) ♠ 10 5
   ♡ Q 9 8 6 4 3   ♡ 7 3   ♡ K J 8 3
   ◇ 5   ◇ J 6 5   ◇ Q 8 4 2
   ♣ Q 9 3   ♣ 9 7 6   ♣ 10 7 3

Response: _____   Response: _____   Response: _____

4) ♠ J 9 5   5) ♠ 10 4 2   6) ♠ J 5
   ♡ 8 4 2   ♡ 10 7 3   ♡ 6 4
   ◇ 10 7 6   ◇ 9 8 5   ◇ 10 5 3
   ♣ K J 8 5   ♣ 10 6 5 2   ♣ Q J 8 6 4 2

Response: _____   Response: _____   Response: _____

Exercise Eight — Responding to a Strong Two-bid

Your partner opens 2♠, a strong two-bid. What do you respond with each of the following hands?

1) ♠ 7 3
   ♡ J 9 7 6 3
   ◊ 10 8 4
   ♣ 7 5 2

   Response: _____

2) ♠ K 8 6
   ♡ 10 9 7
   ◊ Q 10 8 5
   ♣ K 9 3

   Response: _____

3) ♠ 6 4
   ♡ 3 2
   ◊ K Q 10 6 4
   ♣ K 9 8 4

   Response: _____

Exercise Nine — The Hold-up Play

Turn up all the cards on the first pre-dealt hand. Put each hand dummy style at the edge of the table in front of each player.

Dealer: North

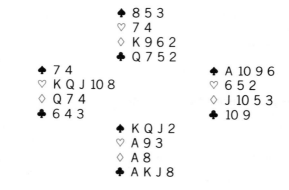

```
                    ♠ 8 5 3
                    ♡ 7 4
                    ◊ K 9 6 2
                    ♣ Q 7 5 2
    ♠ 7 4                          ♠ A 10 9 6
    ♡ K Q J 10 8                   ♡ 6 5 2
    ◊ Q 7 4                        ◊ J 10 5 3
    ♣ 6 4 3                        ♣ 10 9
                    ♠ K Q J 2
                    ♡ A 9 3
                    ◊ A 8
                    ♣ A K J 8
```

The Bidding.

North and East pass. With a balanced hand and 22 points, what is South's opening bid?

West passes. North has 5 points. Does the partnership belong in game or a partscore? Is North interested in a Golden Fit in a major suit? What does North respond?

How would the auction proceed? What will be the contract? Who will be declarer?

The Play

Which player makes the opening lead? What will the opening lead be?

Declarer starts by making a PLAN:

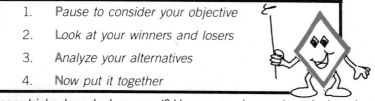

1. **P**ause to consider your objective
2. **L**ook at your winners and losers
3. **A**nalyze your alternatives
4. **N**ow put it together

How many tricks does declarer need? How many winners does declarer have? How can declarer develop the extra winners he needs? Is there any danger? What can declarer do to minimize the danger?

Exercise Ten — Holding Up With a King

Turn up all the cards on the second pre-dealt hand. Put each hand dummy style at the edge of the table in front of each player.

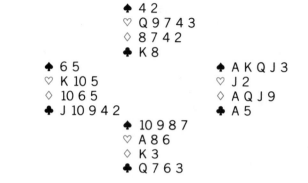

Dealer: East

♠ 4 2
♡ Q 9 7 4 3
◇ 8 7 4 2
♣ K 8

♠ 6 5
♡ K 10 5
◇ 10 6 5
♣ J 10 9 4 2

♠ A K Q J 3
♡ J 2
◇ A Q J 9
♣ A 5

♠ 10 9 8 7
♡ A 8 6
◇ K 3
♣ Q 7 6 3

The Bidding

With an unbalanced hand of 23 points, what is East's opening bid?

South passes. West has 5 points. Can West pass? How does West show a weak hand?

North passes. How does East further describe his hand? Why is East not concerned about being left in a partscore?

South passes. Can West pass? With no known Golden Fit, what looks like the best contract? What does West bid?

North passes. Does East have any reason to disagree with West's decision? What will be the contract? Who will be declarer?

The Play

Which player makes the opening lead? What will be the opening lead? Which card will leader's partner play to the first trick? To the second trick?

Declarer starts by making a PLAN. Which suit offers the best potential for developing extra tricks? How does declarer plan to play the suit? Is there any danger? How can declarer minimize the danger?

Exercise Eleven — Defensive Hold-up

Turn up all the cards on the third pre-dealt hand. Put each hand dummy style at the edge of the table in front of each player.

Dealer: South

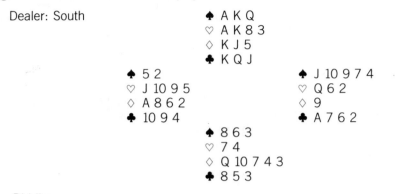

```
                        ♠ A K Q
                        ♡ A K 8 3
                        ◇ K J 5
                        ♣ K Q J
        ♠ 5 2                           ♠ J 10 9 7 4
        ♡ J 10 9 5                      ♡ Q 6 2
        ◇ A 8 6 2                       ◇ 9
        ♣ 10 9 4                        ♣ A 7 6 2
                        ♠ 8 6 3
                        ♡ 7 4
                        ◇ Q 10 7 4 3
                        ♣ 8 5 3
```

The Bidding

South and West pass. With a balanced 26 points, what is North's opening bid?

East passes. What does South do? What will be the contract? Who will be declarer?

The Play

Which player makes the opening lead? What will the opening lead be?

Declarer starts by making a PLAN. Which suit can provide the extra tricks declarer needs to make the contract? How does declarer plan to play the suit? What can West do to make things difficult for declarer? What can declarer do to counter West's efforts?

Exercise Twelve — Creating an Entry

Turn up all the cards on the fourth pre-dealt hand. Put each hand dummy style at the edge of the table in front of each player.

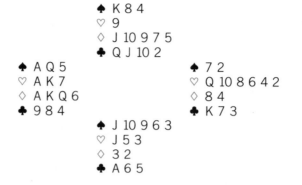

Dealer: West

```
                        ♠ K 8 4
                        ♡ 9
                        ◇ J 10 9 7 5
                        ♣ Q J 10 2
        ♠ A Q 5                         ♠ 7 2
        ♡ A K 7                         ♡ Q 10 8 6 4 2
        ◇ A K Q 6                       ◇ 8 4
        ♣ 9 8 4                         ♣ K 7 3
                        ♠ J 10 9 6 3
                        ♡ J 5 3
                        ◇ 3 2
                        ♣ A 6 5
```

The Bidding

With a balanced hand and 22 HCP, what is West's opening bid?

North passes. Does East have enough for game? Is there a Golden Fit? What does East respond?

How does the auction proceed? What will be the contract? Who will be declarer?

The Play

Which player makes the opening lead? What will the opening lead be?

Declarer starts by making a PLAN. How many losers can declarer afford? How many losers does declarer have? What are declarer's alternatives for eliminating a loser?

Is there a dangerous opponent? Should declarer take the spade finesse? If not, why not? How should declarer play?

LESSON 7
Managing the Trump Suit

Drawing Trumps
Delaying Drawing Trumps
Maintaining Control
Developing Long Suits
Guidelines for Defense
Bidding — Slam Bidding
Summary

Workshop Material
Group Activities

If you are playing in a suit contract, managing the trump suit is a most important task. After all, the lowest trump card can have more value than an ace in another suit. You also can use the trump suit to help control the opponents' long suits and help establish your suits. Although the general guideline is to *draw the opponents' trumps* at the first opportunity, it is often best to delay drawing trumps altogether — or to draw some trumps, play another suit and then go back to drawing trumps.

Before deciding whether to draw trumps you must consult your PLAN to determine how many losers you can afford and how many you have. You need to know whether your losers are *quick* or *slow*. The trump suit is so important that managing it skillfully is a key to improving your game.

 ## ◆ DRAWING TRUMPS ◆

Generally, it is a good idea for declarer to draw trumps as soon as possible since *any* outstanding trumps in the opponents' hands have the potential to defeat a contract if they can be used to ruff your winners. Let's start by looking at how to handle the trump suit itself.

Playing the Trump Suit

In many respects the trump suit is like any other suit. Winners can be developed through promotion, length or finessing. Since your side has named the trump suit, you probably have more than the opponents. You have a comfortable advantage when you hold eight or more trumps — the opponents have five or fewer. Depending on how the trump suit is distributed between your hand and dummy and which high cards are missing, drawing trumps can be handled in a variety of ways.

DUMMY:	A J 8 3	When you have nine trumps, the opponents have only four. With the four highest cards in the suit, you can draw trumps without losing a trick, even if the missing trumps divide 4-0.
DECLARER:	K Q 7 4 2	

Most of the time, you will not need to play four rounds of the suit to draw all the missing trumps. If the missing trumps divide 3-1, you will need only three rounds. If they are 2-2, you need to play the suit only twice.

DUMMY:	Q 10 7 4	You are missing the ace but can use one of your high cards to drive it out, promoting the rest of your trumps into winners. When you regain the lead, draw the remainder of the opponents' trumps.
DECLARER:	K J 8 5 3	

When drawing trumps, you often must give up the lead. Generally, you should not be afraid to let the opponents have the lead when it is necessary to draw trumps. We will see, however, that at times you cannot afford to give up the lead too early. Your PLAN will tell you whether you must do other work first.

DUMMY:	7 6 4	Develop the trump suit through length. The op-ponents have five trumps. If they divide 3-2, you must give up two tricks to draw all the trumps. If they divide 4-1, you will end up losing three tricks. If they are 5-0, you will have four losers. Fortunate-ly, suits are rarely distributed 5-0.
DECLARER:	A 8 5 3 2	

DUMMY:	10 9 7 3	You are missing the king. If you can afford a loser in the trump suit, you could play the ace and then drive out the king, losing only one trick (unless the king is singleton).
DECLARER:	A Q J 8 5	

If you cannot afford a loser, you must hope the king is on your right and can be trapped using a finesse. Cross to dummy with an entry in another suit and lead the 10. If a low card appears on your right, take a finesse by playing low from your hand. If the 10 wins the trick, you are still in dummy and can repeat the finesse.

When drawing trumps, you do not want to play more rounds of the suit than necessary. There are 13 trumps. If you have eight, the opponents have five. The easiest way to keep track of the missing trumps is to deduct the number of opponents' trumps that appear each time you play the suit so you will know how many are still outstanding. After a little practice this will become second nature to you.

When to Draw Trumps

To decide whether to draw trumps, consult your PLAN. One of the times to draw trumps right away is when *you have no more losers than you can afford*. You do not have to trump or discard any losers. Usually, the only thing that can go wrong is that the opponents may trump one of your winners. This is why you want to draw trumps as soon as possible, even if you must give up the lead. Look at this example:

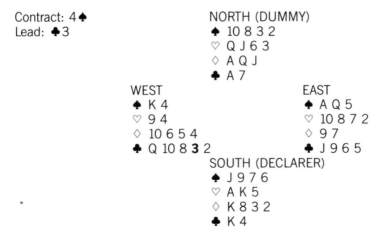

Contract: 4♠
Lead: ♣3

NORTH (DUMMY)
♠ 10 8 3 2
♡ Q J 6 3
◇ A Q J
♣ A 7

WEST
♠ K 4
♡ 9 4
◇ 10 6 5 4
♣ Q 10 8 3 2

EAST
♠ A Q 5
♡ 10 8 7 2
◇ 9 7
♣ J 9 6 5

SOUTH (DECLARER)
♠ J 9 7 6
♡ A K 5
◇ K 8 3 2
♣ K 4

You can afford three losers, and the only losers are in the trump suit, where you are missing the ace, king and queen. In such situations, start playing the trump suit right away. After winning the first trick, lead a trump to drive out one of the opponents' winners. As soon as you regain the lead, lead trumps again to drive out another high trump. In this fashion you lose only three trump tricks, and it will be safe to take your winners in the other suits.

If you were afraid to draw trumps, either because of your anemic-looking trump suit or because you did not want to give up the lead, you would be defeated. When you tried to take your heart winners, West would trump the third round with the ♠4. The opponents still would have three winners left in the trump suit. If you continued the policy of not drawing trumps, East would trump the third round of diamonds with the ♠5 and you might be defeated two tricks.

It is not the opponents' high trumps, but their low trumps that could lead to defeat. In driving out the high trumps, you also are drawing out the low trumps, making it safe for you to take your winners.

Most of the time, when you compare the number of losers you can afford with the losers you have, you find that you need to eliminate a loser or two. For example, you may need to throw away a loser on an extra winner in dummy. It is still a good idea to get rid of the opponents' trumps first, but you may not always be able to do this.

If you can draw trumps without giving up the lead, do so. However, you cannot afford to give up the lead if you have too many *quick losers* — tricks the opponents can take right away. It is safe to give up the lead only if some of your losers are *slow* — the opponents cannot immediately take enough tricks to defeat you.

Contract: 4♡
Lead: ♠K

NORTH (DUMMY)
♠ A 7 3
♡ Q 10 6
◇ A K 8 6
♣ 9 4 2

WEST
♠ **K Q J 9**
♡ 8
◇ 10 7 5 3 2
♣ K 10 8

EAST
♠ 8 5 4
♡ J 7 4
◇ J 9
♣ A J 7 5 3

SOUTH (DECLARER)
♠ 10 6 2
♡ A K 9 5 3 2
◇ Q 4
♣ Q 6

You can afford three losers. You have two in spades and two in clubs — one too many. Fortunately, dummy has an extra diamond winner on which you can discard one of your losers. After you win the ♠A, all your losers are quick. If the opponents get the lead, they will take all four of their tricks. Should you draw trumps or discard your loser first?

You can draw trumps without giving up the lead, so you should play them first. It takes three rounds to draw all the trumps, but then you can safely play the ◇Q and lead the ◇4 to dummy's ◇A and ◇K to discard one of your losers.

What if you do not draw trumps first? When you try to take your diamond winners, East plays a trump on the third round. You can overtrump to win the trick, but now you have no extra winner left in dummy on which to discard a loser. Down you go.

On the next hand you must give up the lead to draw trumps. Should you do that before discarding your loser?

Contract: 3♠
Lead: ♡K

NORTH (DUMMY)
♠ J 10 8 6
♡ 10 5 4
◇ A K 3
♣ K Q 8

WEST
♠ K 5 2
♡ **K Q J 9**
◇ J 7 5 2
♣ 10 7

EAST
♠ A
♡ 7 6 2
◇ Q 10 6
♣ J 9 5 4 3 2

SOUTH (DECLARER)
♠ Q 9 7 4 3
♡ A 8 3
◇ 9 8 4
♣ A 6

In a partscore of 3♠ you can afford four losers. You have two spade losers, two heart losers and one diamond loser. One of the losers can be discarded on the extra club winner in dummy. Drawing trumps is a good idea, but you will have to give up the lead twice. Should you play clubs first?

When considering giving up the lead, you need to look at your quick losers. The opponents have driven out your ♡A, so you have two quick heart losers to go with the two sure trump losers. However, the opponents cannot take a diamond trick right away if you give up the lead since you still have the ◇A and ◇K. (Your diamond loser is slow.) Therefore, it is safe to start drawing trumps.

When East wins the ♠A, the opponents can take their two heart tricks. Whatever they lead next, you can win. You then can lead spades again to drive out the ♠K. Whatever they lead back, you can win and lead spades once more, drawing West's last trump. Now it is safe to play the club suit and discard your diamond loser.

If you do not draw trumps first, West trumps the third round of clubs — you end up with five losers instead of four.

Now let's look at situations where you cannot afford to draw trumps right away.

◆ *DELAYING DRAWING TRUMPS* ◆

On many hands you cannot afford to draw trumps right away. You cannot give up the lead because you have too many quick losers or you may need your trump suit for other purposes.

When You Have Too Many Quick Losers

If you have more quick losers than you can afford, you cannot give up the lead without being defeated. You must eliminate some of your losers first. Look at this hand:

Contract: 2 ◇
Lead ♡ 2

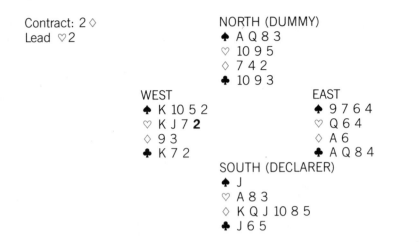

NORTH (DUMMY)
♠ A Q 8 3
♡ 10 9 5
◇ 7 4 2
♣ 10 9 3

WEST
♠ K 10 5 2
♡ K J 7 **2**
◇ 9 3
♣ K 7 2

EAST
♠ 9 7 6 4
♡ Q 6 4
◇ A 6
♣ A Q 8 4

SOUTH (DECLARER)
♠ J
♡ A 8 3
◇ K Q J 10 8 5
♣ J 6 5

In 2 ◇ you can afford five losers, but you have six — two hearts, one diamond and three clubs. After you win the ♡ A, all your losers are quick. If you start to draw trumps right away by driving out the ◇ A, the opponents will take their winners. You must get rid of a loser first.

The only hope is dummy's ♠ A and ♠ Q. You can try a spade finesse. If West has the ♠ K, you can create an extra winner in dummy on which to discard one of your losers. Then you can afford to draw trumps. After winning the ♡ A, lead the ♠ J. If West covers with the ♠ K, win the ♠ A and play the ♠ Q, discarding a loser. If West does not cover, be careful to overtake the jack with dummy's queen; otherwise, you will have no entry to dummy to play the ♠ A and discard your loser.

If East had the ♠ K, you would have ended up with an extra spade loser and gone down an extra trick. Nothing ventured . . . .

Here is a hand where you must be careful to analyze whether your losers are quick or slow:

Contract: 4 ♡
Lead: ♣ Q

NORTH (DUMMY)
♠ K Q J
♡ Q 9 6 4
◇ J 7 2
♣ A 7 5

WEST
♠ 9 7 5 3
♡ A 7
◇ 9 4 3
♣ Q J 10 4

EAST
♠ A 10 6 4
♡ 10 2
◇ A 10 6 5
♣ 9 6 2

SOUTH (DECLARER)
♠ 8 2
♡ K J 8 5 3
◇ K Q 8
♣ K 8 3

You are missing the ♠A, ♡A and ◇A and also have a club loser. When analyzing your alternatives, you see the possibility of discarding your club loser on an extra spade winner in dummy once the ♠A has been driven out. Can you afford to draw trumps first?

On the surface it looks as though you can. You must give up the lead to draw trumps but you have only three quick losers — the three aces. Your club loser is slow. Even after winning the first club trick, you will have another club winner left to stop the opponents from taking a trick in that suit.

Looking ahead, however, you can see that you will lose the race if you play the trump suit first. Upon winning the ♡A, the opponents will lead another club to drive out your remaining high card. Now you will have a quick loser in the clubs. When you establish your extra spade winner, you must let the opponents in with their ♠A, and they can take a club trick to defeat your contract.

Instead, win the first trick with the ♣K, keeping the ♣A in dummy as a potential entry to your extra spade winner (if the opponents do not take their ♠A on the first round). Immediately lead a spade to drive out the opponents' ace. When the opponents lead back a club, you can win and play your extra spade winner to discard your club loser. Now it is safe to draw trumps and, when that is done, drive out the opponents' ◇A to make your contract. You, not the opponents, win the race.

When You Need to Trump Losers

As we saw in Lesson 4, if you plan to trump losers in dummy, be careful to keep a sufficient number of trumps in dummy for that purpose. This often affects your decision whether to draw trumps. Here is an example:

Contract 2♠
Lead: ♡10

```
                        NORTH (DUMMY)
                        ♠ 9 6 2
                        ♡ A K 7
                        ◇ 10 7
                        ♣ 9 7 5 4 2
        WEST                            EAST
        ♠ Q 5                           ♠ J 4 3
        ♡ 10 9 8 5 3                    ♡ Q J
        ◇ A 9 6 5                       ◇ K Q 4 2
        ♣ K 10                          ♣ Q J 8 3
                        SOUTH (DECLARER)
                        ♠ A K 10 8 7
                        ♡ 6 4 2
                        ◇ J 8 3
                        ♣ A 6
```

The opponents lead the ♡10 against your 2♠ contract and the race is on. You can afford five losers. You have one trump loser if the missing trumps are 3-2, one heart loser, three diamond losers and one club loser. One of the losers will have to disappear. There is the possibility of trumping one of your diamond losers in dummy. Should you start by drawing trumps?

You must preserve a trump in dummy to take care of your diamond loser and you must give up the lead twice in diamonds before you are ready to trump your loser. Each time you give up the lead, the opponents can lead trumps, trying to stop you from ruffing your loser in dummy. Therefore, you cannot afford to play even one round of trumps.

Win the first trick and immediately lead a diamond. Suppose East wins and, seeing your plan, leads a spade. Win the trick and lead diamonds again. If East wins and leads another trump, win and lead your last diamond, trumping it in dummy. You win the race and end up losing only a spade, two diamonds, a heart and a club, making the contract.

When You Need the Trump Suit for Entries

Because the trump suit is usually the longest and most powerful suit in the combined hands, it often is needed as a source of entries to declarer's hand and dummy. Here is an example:

Contract: 2 ♡
Lead: ♣4

NORTH (DUMMY)
♠ Q 10 8 3
♡ K 10
◇ 9 7 2
♣ J 8 5 2

WEST
♠ A J 5 2
♡ 5 4
◇ K 8 4
♣ K 10 7 4

EAST
♠ K 7 6
♡ 9 7 3
◇ Q 6 5 3
♣ A Q 9

SOUTH (DECLARER)
♠ 9 4
♡ A Q J 8 6 2
◇ A J 10
♣ 6 3

Once again, you can afford five losers if you are to make your contract of 2 ♡. You have two spade losers, two diamond losers and two club losers — one too many. You cannot do much about the spade and club losers, but you have a chance to eliminate one of the diamond losers. Recalling the lesson on finesses, you want to lead a diamond from dummy and, when East plays low, insert the ◇10 (or ◇J). If the first finesse loses, you plan to lead another diamond from dummy and repeat the finesse. If East has either the ◇K or the ◇Q, you will lose only one diamond.

The problem with this plan is that it requires two entries to dummy so you can lead twice toward your hand. Where are the entries to come from? Your strong heart suit provides the answer. Both the ♡K and ♡10 can be used as entries. This means you must delay drawing all the trumps.

Suppose East wins the ♣A and ♣Q and leads a third club, which you trump. Lead a low heart to dummy's ♡10 and then temporarily stop drawing trumps. Lead a diamond from dummy and finesse the ◇10 when East plays small. West wins the ◇K. Suppose he leads back the ♣K, which you trump. Lead a low heart to dummy's ♡K and lead another diamond from dummy, finessing the jack when East plays low. This time, the finesse works since East has the ◇Q. Now finish drawing trumps and take the ◇A to make the contract.

Here is another example of using the trump suit to provide an entry.

Contract: 4 ♡
Lead: ♣Q

NORTH (DUMMY)
♠ A K 5 4
♡ K 6 2
◇ 7 6 2
♣ K 6 3

WEST
♠ 9 8 7 2
♡ J 8
◇ K 10 9 4
♣ Q J 10

EAST
♠ 10 6 3
♡ 10 7 4
◇ Q J 5
♣ A 8 7 2

SOUTH (DECLARER)
♠ Q J
♡ A Q 9 5 3
◇ A 8 3
♣ 9 5 4

With the ♣A placed unfavorably your ♣K is trapped and you lose the first three club tricks. Now the opponents lead a diamond and drive out your ◇A. You cannot afford any more losers in your contract of 4♡. Missing five trumps, you must hope they divide 3-2 so you have no losers in that suit. You still have two diamond losers, but it may be possible to discard them on the extra spade winners in dummy. Since you need to take all four of your spade winners, you must be careful about entries. The only entry to dummy outside the spade suit is the ♡K.

You plan to play the ♠Q and ♠J and then use the ♡K to get to dummy. Then you can play the ♠A and ♠K, discarding your diamond losers. But what about drawing trumps? If you do not draw all of them, the opponents may trump one of your spade winners, and down you go. If you do draw all the trumps, you will have no entry left in dummy.

The key is to delay drawing the last trump until you are ready to use it as an entry to dummy. After winning the ◇A, play the ♡A and the ♡Q. (This is not the time to start with the high card from the short side since you will need the ♡K later.) You watch with satisfaction as both opponents follow suit when you play the first two rounds of trumps. The missing trumps divide 3-2. However, you cannot yet draw the opponents' final trump. First, play the ♠Q and the ♠J, hoping the opponents cannot trump. Now you are ready to play a low heart to dummy's ♡K, drawing the last trump and putting you in dummy at the same time. Play the ♠A and the ♠K, discarding your diamond losers, and you are home. A well-played hand!

When You Need a Finesse in the Trump Suit

Sometimes you cannot draw trumps right away because you need to take a finesse in the trump suit itself and you are not in the appropriate hand. Here is an example:

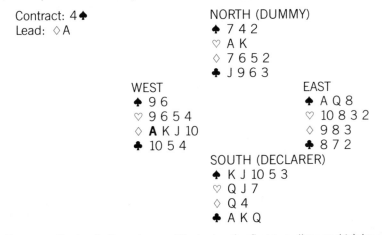

Contract: 4♠
Lead: ◇A

NORTH (DUMMY)
♠ 7 4 2
♡ A K
◇ 7 6 5 2
♣ J 9 6 3

WEST
♠ 9 6
♡ 9 6 5 4
◇ **A** K J 10
♣ 10 5 4

EAST
♠ A Q 8
♡ 10 8 3 2
◇ 9 8 3
♣ 8 7 2

SOUTH (DECLARER)
♠ K J 10 5 3
♡ Q J 7
◇ Q 4
♣ A K Q

You can afford only three losers. West wins the first two diamond tricks and leads another high diamond, which you trump. You have no losers in hearts or clubs but you must avoid two trump losers to make your contract of 4♠. You must hope East has the ♠Q so you can take a successful finesse.

You need to lead from dummy toward your hand so you must delay playing the trump suit — first, play a low heart to dummy's ♡K. Now lead a spade from dummy and, if East plays a low spade, finesse the ♠10 (or ♠J). When this is successful, you again abandon playing trumps until you can get back to dummy with the ♡A to lead another spade. With East having the ♠Q, the opponents cannot prevent you from making the contract.

◆ *MAINTAINING CONTROL* ◆

One advantage of the trump suit is that it can be used to stop the opponents from taking their winners in a long side suit. But, if you run out of trumps, and the opponents get the lead and start taking their winners, you have *lost control* of the hand. Maintaining control involves keeping enough trumps to prevent this.

When the Opponents Have the Outstanding High Trumps

One consideration in maintaining control of the trump suit is whether you can afford to draw trumps when an opponent has the highest remaining trump. Since he will take a trick with his high trump anyway, it usually is not necessary to use your trumps to drive it out. The reason for drawing trumps is to get rid of the opponents' low trumps so they can do you no harm. If an opponent is entitled to a high trump, why not save your remaining trumps and let him use the high trump to trump one of your winners? You will get the trick back since your remaining trump will now be promoted into a winner.

Knowing when not to draw an outstanding high trump is one of the keys to maintaining control in a suit contract. Consider the following hand:

Contract: 4♠
Lead: ♡J

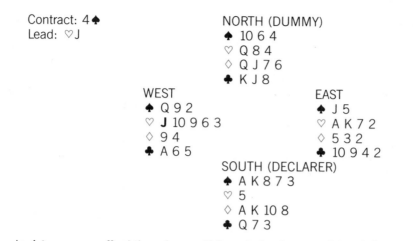

NORTH (DUMMY)
♠ 10 6 4
♡ Q 8 4
◇ Q J 7 6
♣ K J 8

WEST
♠ Q 9 2
♡ J 10 9 6 3
◇ 9 4
♣ A 6 5

EAST
♠ J 5
♡ A K 7 2
◇ 5 3 2
♣ 10 9 4 2

SOUTH (DECLARER)
♠ A K 8 7 3
♡ 5
◇ A K 10 8
♣ Q 7 3

In 4♠ you can afford three losers. If the missing trumps divide 3-2, you have only one spade loser. There are also one heart loser and one club loser. Since you have the number of losers you can afford, this appears to be a simple case of drawing trumps and then taking your winners.

Let's look a little more closely. You will have to give up the lead when you drive out the ♣A to promote your club tricks, so you must be careful to maintain control — keep enough trumps to stop the opponents from taking their heart winners. This will affect how you handle the trump suit.

The opponents win the first heart trick and lead another high heart which you trump. Start drawing trumps by playing the ♠A and ♠K. Both opponents follow suit, so the only outstanding trump is the ♠Q, a winner for the opponents. Should you play another round of spades to draw it out?

Let's see what happens if you do. You must play two of your trumps, one from each hand, to drive out the ♠Q. Since you trumped the opponents' heart winner earlier, that leaves you with only one trump in your hand. Suppose West wins the ♠Q and plays another high heart. You can trump this with your last spade and take your diamond winners, but now you must lead a club to drive out the opponents' ace. When West wins the ♣A, he still has some hearts — since you have no trumps left, West can take his remaining heart tricks to defeat the contract. You have lost control of the hand.

Suppose you do not draw the outstanding high trump. Instead, after playing the ♠A and ♠K, leave West with the ♠Q and go about your business of driving out the ♣A. When West wins the ♣A, you still have two low trumps left in your hand. Even if West plays the ♠Q to draw your trump, you still have one trump left. If West next leads a heart, you can trump and play your remaining winners. You make the contract, losing just one spade, one heart and the ♣A. You have successfully maintained control by not drawing the outstanding high trump.

Incidentally, the above hand illustrates that it is often advantageous for the defenders to force declarer to ruff their winners. If declarer runs out of trumps, the opponents may be able to defeat the contract with their winners, if they can regain the lead.

Ducking to Maintain Control

We have seen in earlier lessons that *ducking* (not taking a trick when you could win it) is a useful technique to maintain entries in your suits or remove entries in the opponents' hands (hold-up play). Playing the trump suit may offer another opportunity for taking your losses early through ducking. This time, the reason for ducking is to maintain control of the trump suit.

When your trump suit is weak, but you do have the ace, ducking a trick is a useful way of maintaining control while drawing trumps. You keep your ace to prevent the opponents from drawing too many of your trumps and then taking their winners. You still will lose the same number of trump tricks but you keep control. Let's see how this helps on the following hand:

Contract: 4♠
Lead: ♡J

NORTH (DUMMY)
♠ A 8 6 3
♡ Q 5 2
◇ K Q J 8
♣ J 7

WEST
♠ K Q 9
♡ J 10 9 7
◇ 9 5
♣ 8 6 4 2

EAST
♠ 10 4
♡ A K 8 4 3
◇ 7 6 3 2
♣ 9 5

SOUTH (DECLARER)
♠ J 7 5 2
♡ 6
◇ A 10 4
♣ A K Q 10 3

You can afford three losers in 4♠. Provided the missing trumps divide 3-2, you have only two losers in spades and one in hearts. With such a weak trump suit, however, you must be careful not to lose control.

The opponents win the first heart trick and lead another heart which you trump. Now you have only three spades left in your hand. You want to draw some of the opponents' trumps so they cannot use their low trumps on your winners. You are willing to let them have two trump tricks but not three. Suppose you start by playing the ♠A and then another spade. West will win the ♠Q and play the ♠K to draw the last trump left in your hand. Now West can lead a heart and you have no trump left in your hand to stop the opponents from winning the trick. You lose two trump tricks and two heart tricks to go down in your contract.

Instead, after trumping the second round of hearts, play a low spade from both hands, giving up a trick. If the opponents lead another spade, you can win the ♠A and start taking your winners, leaving the remaining high trump outstanding — the opponents can have it whenever they want.

If the opponents win the first spade trick and play a high heart, you can trump it and now lead another round of trumps, winning the ♠A. Again, leave the remaining high trump outstanding and go about the business of taking your winners. You end up losing only two spades and a heart.

By ducking the first round of trumps, you maintain control of the trump suit while drawing the opponents' low trumps.

When to Draw the Outstanding High Trump

Declarer does not always leave a high trump outstanding. If declarer still can maintain control, drawing it may be necessary. Consider this hand:

Contract: 4♡
Lead: ♠J

NORTH (DUMMY)
♠ A 4
♡ 6 4 3
◇ 8 6 2
♣ A K J 10 4

WEST
♠ J 10 9 6 3
♡ Q 9 2
◇ K 7 3
♣ 6 5

EAST
♠ K Q 5 2
♡ J 5
◇ Q J 10 5
♣ 9 7 2

SOUTH (DECLARER)
♠ 8 7
♡ A K 10 8 7
◇ A 9 4
♣ Q 8 3

You have one spade loser, one heart loser if the suit breaks 3-2, and two diamond losers. That is one more than you can afford in 4♡. You plan to discard two of your losers on dummy's extra club winners.

After winning the ♠A and playing the ♡A and ♡K, should you draw the remaining high trump or start playing your club winners? Suppose you leave the high trump outstanding and start leading clubs. On the third round of clubs West trumps with the ♡Q. The opponents take their spade trick and then lead diamonds, driving out your ◇A. You have two club winners in dummy but no entry to them. You end up losing two diamond tricks and going down in the contract.

Instead, since you are in no danger of losing control, you should drive out the opponents' ♡Q. The opponents can win this trick and take a spade trick, but now you are in control. Whatever they lead next, you win and peacefully take your club tricks, discarding your two diamond losers. You make an overtrick, losing just a spade and a heart, rather than being defeated in your game.

◆ *DEVELOPING LONG SUITS* ◆

The trump suit often can be helpful when trying to develop tricks in a side suit.

Establishing Declarer's Side Suit

Consider the following hand:

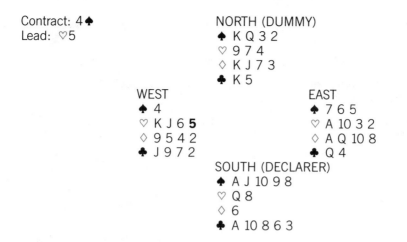

Contract: 4♠
Lead: ♡5

NORTH (DUMMY)
♠ K Q 3 2
♡ 9 7 4
◇ K J 7 3
♣ K 5

WEST
♠ 4
♡ K J 6 **5**
◇ 9 5 4 2
♣ J 9 7 2

EAST
♠ 7 6 5
♡ A 10 3 2
◇ A Q 10 8
♣ Q 4

SOUTH (DECLARER)
♠ A J 10 9 8
♡ Q 8
◇ 6
♣ A 10 8 6 3

In 4♠ you can afford three losers. You must lose two heart tricks and the ◇A, so you cannot afford to lose any club tricks. You have three possible club losers, but with only two clubs in dummy you can trump your losers.

How many losers do you need to trump? If the six missing clubs divide 3-3, after playing the ♣K and ♣A, you need to trump only one of your losers in dummy. Your remaining clubs will be established as winners. If, as is more likely, the missing clubs divide 4-2, you must trump two of your losers to establish your remaining club. If the missing clubs break 5-1 or 6-0, you must ruff all three of your club losers — you will be defeated since an opponent will trump the second or first round of clubs — you cannot draw trumps and still have three trumps left in dummy.

Suppose the opponents win the first two heart tricks and lead another heart, which you trump. Since you do not know how the missing clubs will divide and you will need trumps as entries back to your hand, delay drawing any trumps. Lead a low club to dummy's king (high card from the short side) and the ♣5 back to your ♣A. Now lead one of your club losers, planning to trump it in dummy.

When West follows with a club, recall the advice in Lesson 5: *never send a boy to do a man's job*. When trumping losers, use as high a trump as you can afford. Since you have enough high trumps in your hand to draw the opponents' trumps, you can afford to trump with dummy's ♠Q (or ♠K). This prevents East from overruffing if he also has no clubs left.

If the missing clubs are divided 3-3, you would not need to trump any more losers — you could draw the missing trumps and take your established club winners. On this hand, however, the clubs divide 4-2, so your remaining clubs are not yet established. Lead a spade to your hand and trump another club high, using dummy's ♠K. Your last club is now a winner, so you can lead dummy's remaining spade to your hand and draw the missing trumps. Then you take your established club trick and make the contract, losing only two hearts and a diamond.

Notice how carefully you managed the trump suit on this hand. You delayed drawing trumps because you had to trump some losers. You also used the trump suit for entries back to your hand, drawing some of the opponents' trumps in the process. Finally, once your side suit was established, you drew the remaining trumps so the opponents could not trump your winner.

Establishing Dummy's Side Suit

Sometimes, you do not have enough winners in dummy on which to discard your losers. You often can create extra winners with the help of the trump suit. Look at this hand:

Contract: 4♡
Lead: ♠K

```
                    NORTH (DUMMY)
                    ♠ J 8 7
                    ♡ Q 9 2
                    ◇ J 5
                    ♣ A K Q 3 2
        WEST                        EAST
        ♠ K Q 10 4                  ♠ A 5 2
        ♡ 6 5                       ♡ 8 7 4
        ◇ 10 9 4 2                  ◇ K Q 3
        ♣ 9 5 4                     ♣ J 10 8 6
                    SOUTH (DECLARER)
                    ♠ 9 6 3
                    ♡ A K J 10 3
                    ◇ A 8 7 6
                    ♣ 7
```

After losing the first three spade tricks, you must take the rest to make your 4♡ contract. You have three diamond losers to worry about. Two of them can be discarded on dummy's extra club winners, but what can be done with the third loser?

The club suit does offer a further possibility. You have six clubs and the opponents have seven. If the missing clubs divide 4-3, you can establish a low club as a winner. You cannot afford to give up a club trick, so you must establish the suit by trumping one of dummy's low clubs.

Suppose the opponents win the first three spade tricks and then lead a diamond to drive out your ◇ A. Once again, you must be careful in managing the trump suit. Can you afford to draw all the missing trumps? If the missing trumps divide 3-2, this will take three rounds, using up all of dummy's trumps. You do not need dummy's trumps to ruff your losers, but you do need an entry to dummy once you have established the club suit. The ♡ Q will serve that purpose.

After winning the ◇ A, play the ♡ A and ♡ K to draw some of the opponents' trumps. Now you must delay drawing the final trump and go to work on the club suit. Lead a club to dummy's ♣ Q. Take dummy's ♣ A and ♣ K and discard two of your diamond losers. Now lead a low club and trump it high in your hand, to avoid an overruff. Now lead a low trump to dummy's ♡ Q, drawing the last trump and putting you in dummy — you can take your established club winner and discard your remaining diamond loser.

(You also could have trumped a low club before playing the ♣ A and ♣ K and then crossed back to dummy with the ♡ Q to take your three club winners. This usually is a safer approach to keep the opponents from ruffing one of your club winners.)

◆ *GUIDELINES FOR DEFENSE* ◆

The defenders work together to try to defeat the contract. One of their disadvantages is that they cannot see each other's hands. They can only see their own hand and dummy. This makes it difficult for them to tell where their strengths and weaknesses lie.

One way to overcome this is through the use of defensive signals. The defenders can give each other information through the cards that they play when a suit is led. We already have seen one way they can exchange information — by leading the top of touching honors. If your partner leads the queen, you know he doesn't have the next-higher card, the king, but probably has the next-lower card, the jack. Here is another way the defenders can help each other.

Attitude Signals

The most common form of defensive signal is *the attitude signal*. This is the play of a card to tell partner whether or not you like (i.e., have high cards in the suit and/or wish to have the suit led or continued) a particular suit. Traditionally, *a high card is encouraging and a low card is discouraging*. The terms *high card* and *low card* have no absolute meaning. Depending on what cards are available, an 8 may be low, a 4 may be high. A *high card* is ideally a card higher than a six and a *low card* is something smaller. You may not always have a perfect card available, but when you do, you can help partner out. Here is an example:

```
Contract: 3 NT              NORTH (DUMMY)
Lead: ♡4                     ♠ 9 5 2
                             ♡ A 7
                             ◇ K Q J 6
                             ♣ 9 7 6 5
        WEST (PARTNER)                    EAST (YOU)
        ♠ Q 10 6 3                        ♠ K J 7 4
        ♡ Q 10 6 4 3                      ♡ K 9 2
        ◇ 5 2                             ◇ 10 8 4 3
        ♣ A 8                             ♣ 3 2
                             SOUTH (DECLARER)
                             ♠ A 8
                             ♡ J 8 5
                             ◇ A 9 7
                             ♣ K Q J 10 4
```

Your partner leads the ♡4 against a contract of 3 NT. Declarer plays the ♡A from dummy at the first trick. Which card do you (East) play? Holding the ♡K, you like the suit partner has led and want to *encourage* him to lead it again when he gets the opportunity. You therefore play the ♡9, an encouraging card.

This makes the defense easy for your partner. Declarer cannot make the contract without establishing some club winners and therefore leads a club from dummy to his ♣K to drive out the ♣A. When your partner wins the ♣A, he knows from your encouraging signal that you like hearts — he continues by leading another heart. You win the ♡K and lead the ♡2 back to partner, who takes his three heart winners to defeat the contract. Bridge is such an easy game!

Did it matter whether you played the ♡9 or the ♡2? After all, partner may have led another heart anyway and still have defeated the contract. Let's give your partner and dummy the same hands but exchange a couple of your cards and declarer's:

Contract: 3 NT
Lead: ♡4

NORTH (DUMMY)
♠ 9 5 2
♡ A 7
◇ K Q J 6
♣ 9 7 6 5

WEST (PARTNER)
♠ Q 10 6 3
♡ Q 10 6 **4** 3
◇ 5 2
♣ A 8

EAST (YOU)
♠ A K 7 4
♡ 9 5 2
◇ 10 8 4 3
♣ 3 2

SOUTH (DECLARER)
♠ J 8
♡ K J 8
◇ A 9 7
♣ K Q J 10 4

Your partner makes the same lead and the same dummy comes down. Again, declarer wins the first trick with dummy's ♡A and leads a club to his ♣K. What does your partner do when he wins the ♣A?

If partner leads another heart, declarer will end up with 11 tricks: three hearts, four diamonds and four clubs. On this hand your partner must abandon the heart suit and lead a spade instead. The defense then can take four spade tricks along with the ♣A, defeating the contract.

How will partner know to shift to a spade? When declarer wins the first trick with dummy's ♡A, you want to *discourage* partner from continuing hearts since you have no interest in the suit. You can do this by playing a discouraging card, the ♡2. When partner wins the ♣A, he knows you do not like hearts. So he can try something else. Since declarer is establishing club tricks, and dummy has diamond strength, it is quite likely that partner will lead a spade.

A Ruff for the Defense

The attitude signal also can be useful on a hand such as the following:

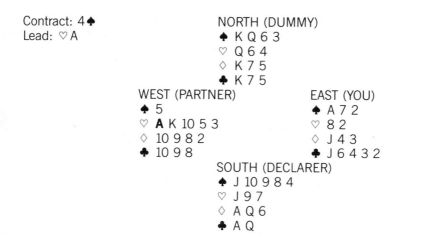

Contract: 4♠
Lead: ♡ A

NORTH (DUMMY)
♠ K Q 6 3
♡ Q 6 4
◇ K 7 5
♣ K 7 5

WEST (PARTNER)
♠ 5
♡ **A** K 10 5 3
◇ 10 9 8 2
♣ 10 9 8

EAST (YOU)
♠ A 7 2
♡ 8 2
◇ J 4 3
♣ J 6 4 3 2

SOUTH (DECLARER)
♠ J 10 9 8 4
♡ J 9 7
◇ A Q 6
♣ A Q

Your partner leads the ♡ A against the opponents' 4♠ contract. You want to encourage partner to continue playing the suit, even though the ♡ Q is in dummy. Why? If, as seems likely, partner also has the ♡ K, he can win it and then lead a third round of hearts which you can trump. You still will have the ♠ A for the fourth defensive trick.

To encourage partner to continue leading hearts, play the ♡ 8 on the first trick. Partner may wonder why you like hearts, but trusting your attitude signal, he should continue by leading the ♡ K and another heart. Signaling requires partnership cooperation. One partner must make the appropriate signal, and the other partner must be watching for it.

Suppose we exchange several of your cards with declarer's:

Contract: 4♠
Lead: ♡ A

NORTH (DUMMY)
♠ K Q 6 3
♡ Q 6 4
◇ K 7 5
♣ K 7 5

WEST (PARTNER)
♠ 5
♡ **A** K 10 5 3
◇ 10 9 8 2
♣ 10 9 8

EAST (YOU)
♠ 8 7 2
♡ 8 7 2
◇ J 4
♣ A Q 4 3 2

SOUTH (DECLARER)
♠ A J 10 9 4
♡ J 9
◇ A Q 6 3
♣ J 6

This time, you discourage partner from continuing hearts by playing the ♡ 2. This play tells partner you would prefer that he switch to another suit. If he chooses clubs, you will win the ♣ A and ♣ Q since you have dummy's king trapped. Partner's ♡ K then will be the fourth defensive trick. If partner chooses diamonds, you again can discourage by playing the ◇ 4. When partner later wins the ♡ K, he can try clubs — again, you will defeat the contract.

What if your partner continued leading hearts? Then declarer would discard one of his club losers on the ♡Q and make the contract. By playing the ♡2, and having partner interpret this as a discouraging signal, you give the defense the opportunity to defeat the contract.

It is not always possible to give a clear-cut signal. On this hand, for example, you might have held the ♡9, ♡8 and ♡7. You want to discourage partner from continuing but the lowest heart you have is the ♡7. You must play it and hope partner can see enough of the missing low cards to realize that this is your lowest heart.

Similarly, on the previous hand, when you wanted to encourage partner to lead hearts, you might have been dealt the ♡3 and ♡2. You would have had to play the ♡3 and hope partner figured it out. Of course, nothing will help if partner does not watch the cards you play — and you don't watch his.

◆ *BIDDING* ◆

There are large bonuses in the scoring for bidding and making a *small slam* (a contract to take 12 tricks) or a *grand slam* (a contract to take 13 tricks). Deciding whether to bid a slam adds a great deal of drama to the auction.

Slam Bidding

The decision whether to bid a slam is similar to the decision whether to play in a part-score or game. The partnership must determine if they have enough combined strength to play at the slam level and which denomination to play.

With 33-36 combined points the partnership generally has enough strength to play in a small slam. With 37 or more points the partnership should have enough strength for a grand slam.

At the game level the partnership usually plays in 3 NT, 4♡ or 4♠ since these contracts require fewer tricks than 5♣ or 5◇. At the slam level the same number of tricks is required for every denomination — 12 for a small slam and 13 for a grand slam. Since playing in a Golden Fit often will produce one more trick than playing in notrump, slams generally should be played in a Golden Fit if one can be found. Otherwise, the slam should be played in notrump.

Here are some examples of bidding a slam when your partner opens the bidding 1 NT.

♠ K Q J ♡ A Q 5 ◇ J 10 7 4 ♣ K J 5	With 17 HCPs you know there is enough combined strength for slam since partner has at least 16 points to open 1 NT. With no known Golden Fit, bid slam in notrump by jumping directly to **6 NT**.
♠ A 10 8 ♡ A J 5 ◇ 10 ♣ A Q J 8 5 2	With 16 HCPs plus 2 points for the six-card club suit, you have enough combined strength for a small slam. Since opener has a balanced hand, he must have at least two clubs — so there is a Golden Fit in clubs. Bid **6♣**.

♠ A K 6
♡ K J 10
◇ A 8 5
♣ A K 8 2

With 22 HCPs you should have enough for a grand slam. Jump directly to **7 NT** since there is no known Golden Fit.

If you have enough combined strength for slam but you are not sure of the best denomination, make a forcing bid and make your decision when you have more information. For example, suppose your partner opens the bidding 1♡, and you hold the following hand:

♠ K Q 7 2
♡ A J
◇ A 9 5
♣ A Q 10 5

You have 20 points, and since partner has at least 13 points, the partnership should have enough combined strength for slam. What denomination? At this point you do not know if a Golden Fit exists, so you must do some exploring. Respond 1♠, a forcing bid, and wait to hear what partner does next. Maybe partner will raise your suit and you can play in slam in spades. If partner rebids his own suit, showing a six-card suit, you could bid slam in hearts. Partner may show a second suit with a 2♣ rebid. Now you can bid a slam in clubs. Partner may rebid 1 NT to show a balanced hand — then the partnership belongs in 6 NT.

Inviting a Slam

Sometimes, you know the best denomination but are not certain whether there is enough combined strength for slam. In this case you can invite partner to bid a slam by bidding one level beyond game. If partner has extra strength, he can accept the invitation and bid slam. If partner has the minimum of the range he has promised, he can pass, turning down the invitation.

Here are some examples of inviting slam when your partner opens the bidding 1 NT:

♠ Q J 6
♡ K 10 8
◇ K Q 7
♣ A J 9 3

Partner has 16-18 points. With 16 points yourself you know the partnership has at least 32 combined points and could have as many as 33 or 34. Invite partner to slam by bidding one level beyond game, **4 NT**. With a minimum hand of 16 points partner will pass. With some extra strength (17-18 points), partner will accept the invitation and bid 6 NT.

♠ A Q J 10 8 3
♡ A 5
◇ 10 4
♣ K 6 5

With a total of 16 points — 14 HCPs plus 2 points for the six-card spade suit — you again have enough to invite a slam contract. Since there must be a Golden Fit in spades, invite slam by bidding one level beyond game, **5♠**.

Slam Conventions

Suppose partner opens the bidding 1♡, and you have the following hand:

♠ A 8 5 2
♡ Q J 9 4
◇ A K Q J
♣ 5

Since you have 17 HCPs plus 3 dummy points for the singleton club, the combined partnership strength is at least 33 points, enough for a small slam. Since there is a known Golden Fit in hearts, you could jump directly to 6♡. This would work out unfortunately if partner had this hand:

♠ K Q J
♡ K 10 8 7 4
◇ 10 6
♣ K Q 10

The partnership does have enough combined strength for slam, but there are two quick losers, the ♡A and ♣A. Given time, partner might discard his three clubs on your extra diamond and spade winners and make the slam. More likely, the opponents will be only too eager to take their two aces and defeat you.

It is obviously not a good idea to bid a slam missing two aces, since the opponents can take their two tricks before you get an opportunity to develop your extra winners or discard your extra losers. Similarly, in a grand slam you do not want to be missing an ace. How can you avoid such situations?

One way to avoid bidding a slam when too many aces are missing is to use the *Blackwood convention*. Once you have agreed on a trump suit, a bid of 4 NT is used as an artificial (conventional) bid to ask partner how many aces he has. Partner responds artificially as follows:

5♣	No aces or all four aces
5◇	One ace
5♡	Two aces
5♠	Three aces

Once you know how many aces your partner has, you will know if the combined hands are missing too many aces. If they are, you can stop below slam. If not, you can bid slam.

Let's return to our earlier hand when partner opens the bidding 1♡ and you hold the following hand:

♠ A 8 5 2
♡ Q J 9 4
◇ A K Q J
♣ 5

Instead of jumping directly to 6♡, use the Blackwood convention (assuming partner is familiar with it) to find out if two aces are missing. Respond 4 NT to ask partner how many aces he has. Since you have not bid another suit, partner will assume that hearts is the agreed trump suit.

If partner rebids 5♣, showing no aces, you can sign off in 5♡. If he bids 5◇, showing one, you know that the partnership is missing only one ace — you can bid 6♡. Note that the Blackwood convention does not tell you which aces partner has, only how many. If you needed to know the specific aces partner held, you would have to use more sophisticated methods that are beyond the scope of this text.

If partner bids 5♡, showing two aces, you know that you have them all. Sometimes, after finding out that the partnership has all the missing aces, you will be interested in a grand slam. In a grand slam you generally do not want to be missing any kings, and you can use an extension of the Blackwood convention, a bid of 5 NT, to ask partner how many kings he has. Partner responds in the same fashion as over 4 NT, this time at the six level (6♣ with no kings, etc.).

One other common slam convention is the *Gerber convention*. When your partner opens the bidding in notrump, you cannot use the Blackwood convention since no trump suit has been agreed. If you bid 4 NT, one level beyond game in notrump, partner would interpret it as an invitation to bid 6 NT, as we saw earlier. Instead, jump to an artificial 4♣, the Gerber convention, to ask for aces. Partner responds in a similar manner as when responding to the Blackwood convention:

4♢	No aces or all four aces
4♡	One ace
4♠	Two aces
4 NT	Three aces

If your side does not have enough aces, you can sign off in a contract below the slam level. If you have enough aces, you can bid a slam. If you have all the aces and are interested in a grand slam, you can use the artificial bid of 5♣ to ask for kings. Opener will respond in a similar fashion (5♢ with no kings, etc.).

◆ *SUMMARY* ◆

Managing the trump suit is one of the key considerations when you come to the fourth step of the PLAN, *Now put it together*. You must decide whether or not to draw trumps right away. You should draw trumps right away when you do not need the trump suit for other purposes and:

- You have no more losers than you can afford.
- You have more losers than you can afford but can draw trumps without giving up the lead.
- You have more losers than you can afford but do not have too many quick losers.

You may have to delay drawing trumps when:

- You would have to give up the lead and have too many quick losers.
- You need the trumps for other purposes (trumping losers, entries).
- You need to get to the other hand to take a finesse in the trump suit.

When drawing trumps, you must be careful to *maintain control* of the trump suit. If you run out of trumps, you can no longer stop the opponents from taking their winners and may lose control. One way to maintain control is to avoid spending a trump to draw an outstanding high trump unless you can afford to do so. If your trump suit is weak, you sometimes can *duck a trick to the opponents* to help maintain control.

The trump suit also can be used to help develop a long side suit, either in declarer's hand or in dummy.

When defending, you can use an *attitude signal* to tell partner whether or not you like a particular suit. A *high card is encouraging* and a *low card is discouraging*.

If the partnership holds 33-36 combined points, it generally should play in a small slam. With 37 or more points, the partnership should be in a grand slam. Slam can be played in any Golden Fit.

You can invite your partner to bid a slam by bidding one level beyond game. With extra strength partner will accept the invitation; otherwise, partner will pass.

If you have agreed on a trump suit and are interested in slam, you can find out the number of aces partner has by bidding 4 NT, the *Blackwood convention*. If partner opens the bidding in notrump, you can find out how many aces he has by bidding 4♣, the *Gerber convention*.

◆ *GROUP ACTIVITIES* ◆

Exercise One — Playing the Trump Suit

If you decide the best plan is to draw *all* the missing trumps, how would you draw the opponents' trumps with each of the following trump suits (high cards, promotion, length, finesse)? How many tricks would you have to lose if the missing high cards are favorably located and the suit is divided as you expect? How many times would you have to play the trump suit to draw all the missing trumps?

DUMMY:	1) K Q 6	2) J 9 8 5	3) A 9 5	4) Q J 10	5) K 9 6 3
DECLARER:	A J 9 5 4 2	Q 10 7 4	8 7 6 4 2	A 9 8 7 6	A 7 5 2
METHOD:	_____	_____	_____	_____	_____
# of Losers:	_____	_____	_____	_____	_____
# of Rounds:	_____	_____	_____	_____	_____

Exercise Two — Looking at Quick and Slow Losers

The opening lead is the ♡ Q against your 4♠ contract. How many losers do you have in each of the following examples after winning the first trick with the ♡ A? Are they quick or slow?

	DUMMY		DUMMY		DUMMY
1)	♠ A Q 8 6	2)	♠ Q 10 8 2	3)	♠ J 9 6 4
	♡ A 9 5		♡ A K 3		♡ A 8 4
	◇ 7 4 2		◇ J 8		◇ A Q 3
	♣ K 5 4		♣ K Q J 5		♣ Q 7 4

	DECLARER		DECLARER		DECLARER
	♠ K J 7 5 4		♠ K J 9 7 6		♠ Q 10 8 7 3
	♡ 10 8 3		♡ 9 8 4		♡ 7 6 2
	◇ Q		◇ Q 10		◇ K 5
	♣ A Q J 2		♣ A 8 2		♣ A K 8

Quick Losers: _____	Quick Losers: _____	Quick Losers: _____
Slow Losers: _____	Slow Losers: _____	Slow Losers: _____
Total Losers: _____	Total Losers: _____	Total Losers: _____

Exercise Three — Drawing Trumps

In each of the examples in Exercise Two, should declarer start by drawing trumps? Give a reason for your answer.

1) Draw Trumps?: _____   2) Draw Trumps?:____   3) Draw Trumps?:____

Reason: _____   Reason: _____   Reason: _____

Exercise Four — Side Suit Establishment

How do you expect the missing cards to be divided in each of the following side suits? Assuming you have lots of entries to dummy, how many trumps will you need to establish the side suit if the missing cards are divided as you expect?

DUMMY: 1) A K 8 6 4   2) A K 9 6 4   3) A 9 7 6 3 2   4) A K 9 8 4 2   5) A Q 7 4 2

DECLARER: 3 2   2   5   5 3   K 5

Expected
Division: _____   _____   _____   _____   _____

Trumps
Required: _____   _____   _____   _____   _____

Exercise Five — Attitude Signals

You are defending a 3 NT contract, and your partner leads the ♠5. Declarer plays the ♠A from dummy. Circle the spade you would play in each of the following examples?

1)   DUMMY   2)   DUMMY
                ♠ A 6   ♠ A 6
                ♡ K Q 10 5   ♡ K Q 10 5
                ◇ 8 6 4   ◇ 8 6 4
                ♣ Q 9 7 3   ♣ Q 9 7 3

                YOU   YOU
                ♠ K 8 2   ♠ 8 4 2
        ♠ 5   ♡ J 4 3   ♠ 5   ♡ J 4 3
                ◇ Q 9 7 3   ◇ A Q 9 7
                ♣ 10 4 2   ♣ 10 4 2

Exercise Six — Bidding Slams

Your partner opens the bidding 1 NT. What do you respond with each of the following hands?

1) ♠ K J 9   2) ♠ A   3) ♠ A K Q
   ♡ A Q 3   ♡ 10 8 2   ♡ A 7 2
   ◇ J 9 4   ◇ K Q J 8 6 3   ◇ Q J 10 7
   ♣ K Q J 2   ♣ A Q 5   ♣ K Q J

Opener's   Opener's   Opener's
Range: 16—18   Range: 16—18   Range: 16—18

Responder's   Responder's   Responder's
Points:_____   Points:_____   Points:_____

Combined   Combined   Combined
Range: _____ —   Range: _____ —   Range: _____ —

Response: _____   Response: _____   Response: _____

Exercise Seven — Inviting Slam

Your partner opens the bidding 1 NT. What do you respond with each of the following hands?

1) ♠ J 7 3
    ♡ K Q
    ◇ A K 10 2
    ♣ K 10 9 5
    Opener's
    Range: 16—18

    Responder's
    Points: _____

    Combined
    Range: _____

    Response:_____

2) ♠ K J 10 8 7 3
    ♡ Q 3
    ◇ A Q 8
    ♣ Q 5
    Opener's
    Range: 16—18

    Responder's
    Points: _____

    Combined
    Range: _____

    Response:_____

Exercise Eight — Responding to Blackwood

You open the bidding 1♠, and your partner responds 4 NT, the Blackwood convention. What do you rebid with each of the following hands?

1) ♠ A K 9 7 3
    ♡ J 7 4
    ◇ 8 4
    ♣ A 5 4

    # of Aces: _____

    Response: _____

2) ♠ K J 10 5 3
    ♡ K Q 10 9 3
    ◇ K J
    ♣ 5

    # of Aces: _____

    Response: _____

3) ♠ Q 10 8 6 2
    ♡ A 2
    ◇ K Q 6 4
    ♣ J 2

    # of Aces: _____

    Response: _____

4) ♠ A 10 8 7 4
    ♡ J 2
    ◇ A 6 3
    ♣ A 8 6

    # of Aces: _____

    Response: _____

5) ♠ A J 10 7 3
    ♡ A 3
    ◇ A 9
    ♣ A 10 7 5

    # of Aces: _____

    Response: _____

Exercise Nine — Delaying Drawing Trumps

Turn up all the cards on the first pre-dealt hand. Put each hand dummy style at the edge of the table in front of each player.

Dealer: North

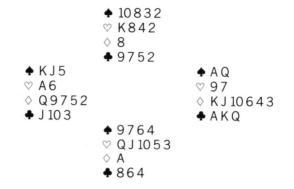

```
                    ♠ 10 8 3 2
                    ♡ K 8 4 2
                    ◇ 8
                    ♣ 9 7 5 2
 ♠ K J 5                              ♠ A Q
 ♡ A 6                                ♡ 9 7
 ◇ Q 9 7 5 2                          ◇ K J 10 6 4 3
 ♣ J 10 3                             ♣ A K Q
                    ♠ 9 7 6 4
                    ♡ Q J 10 5 3
                    ◇ A
                    ♣ 8 6 4
```

The Bidding

North passes. What is East's opening bid?

South passes. West has 12 total points and support for opener's suit. What does West respond?

North passes. How many points does East have? How many points is West showing? At what level does the partnership belong? Is there a Golden Fit? What does East rebid?

How does the auction proceed? What is the contract? Who is declarer?

The Play

Which player makes the opening lead? What will be the opening lead? Assuming dummy wins the first trick, which card will North play?
Declarer starts by making a PLAN:

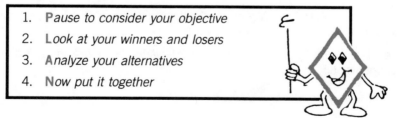

1. **P**ause to consider your objective
2. **L**ook at your winners and losers
3. **A**nalyze your alternatives
4. **N**ow put it together

How can declarer get rid of a loser? Should declarer draw trumps first? If not, why not?

Exercise Ten — Care in the Trump Suit

Turn up all the cards on the second pre-dealt hand. Put each hand dummy style at the edge of the table in front of each player.

Dealer: East

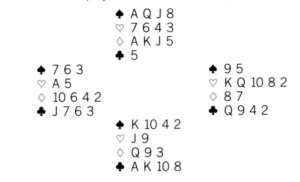

```
              ♠ A Q J 8
              ♡ 7 6 4 3
              ◇ A K J 5
              ♣ 5
  ♠ 7 6 3                    ♠ 9 5
  ♡ A 5                      ♡ K Q 10 8 2
  ◇ 10 6 4 2                 ◇ 8 7
  ♣ J 7 6 3                  ♣ Q 9 4 2
              ♠ K 10 4 2
              ♡ J 9
              ◇ Q 9 3
              ♣ A K 10 8
```

The Bidding

East passes. With a balanced hand too weak to open 1 NT, what is South's opening bid?

West passes. North has three suits he can bid at the one level. Which suit does he bid first? Why?

East passes. Without support for partner's suit, South still has room to bid a new suit at the one level. What does South rebid?

West passes. Counting dummy points, how many points does North have in support of opener's major? If opener has a minimum hand, is there enough combined strength for slam? What if opener has more than a minimum? What does North bid to invite partner to bid slam?

East passes. Does South accept partner's invitation? Why not? What will be the contract? Who will be declarer?

The Play

Which player makes the opening lead? With the opponents having bid three suits, what might be a good suit to lead? If West leads the ♡A, which card should East play?

Declarer starts by making a PLAN. How does declarer plan to get rid of his club losers? If the opponents start by playing three rounds of hearts, why must declarer be careful?

Exercise Eleven — Maintaining Control

Turn up all the cards on the third pre-dealt hand. Put each hand dummy style at the edge of the table in front of each player.

Dealer: South

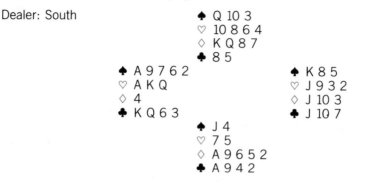

```
              ♠ Q 10 3
              ♡ 10 8 6 4
              ◇ K Q 8 7
              ♣ 8 5
♠ A 9 7 6 2              ♠ K 8 5
♡ A K Q                 ♡ J 9 3 2
◇ 4                     ◇ J 10 3
♣ K Q 6 3               ♣ J 10 7
              ♠ J 4
              ♡ 7 5
              ◇ A 9 6 5 2
              ♣ A 9 4 2
```

The Bidding

South passes. What is West's opening bid?

North passes. With 6 points and support for partner's five-card suit, what does East respond?

South passes. Does West have a minimum, medium or maximum hand? What does West rebid?

How does the auction proceed from there? What will be the contract? Who will be declarer?

The Play

Which player makes the opening lead? What will the opening lead be? What is South's attitude toward the opening lead? Which card does South play?

Declarer starts by making a PLAN. How many losers can declarer afford? How many losers does declarer have? How must the missing trumps divide so declarer has only one trump loser? Should declarer draw any trumps before playing his winners? Why? Should declarer draw the last outstanding trump? Why not?

Exercise Twelve — Establishing a Side Suit

Turn up all the cards on the fourth pre-dealt hand. Put each hand dummy style at the edge of the table in front of each player.

Dealer: West

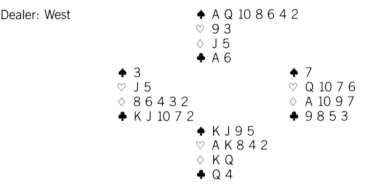

```
                          ♠ A Q 10 8 6 4 2
                          ♡ 9 3
                          ◇ J 5
                          ♣ A 6
          ♠ 3                              ♠ 7
          ♡ J 5                            ♡ Q 10 7 6
          ◇ 8 6 4 3 2                      ◇ A 10 9 7
          ♣ K J 10 7 2                     ♣ 9 8 5 3
                          ♠ K J 9 5
                          ♡ A K 8 4 2
                          ◇ K Q
                          ♣ Q 4
```

The Bidding

West passes. What is North's opening bid?

East passes. How many dummy points does South have in support of partner's major suit? Is there enough combined strength for slam? What does South respond?

How does the auction proceed from there? What will be the contract? Who will be declarer?

The Play

Which player makes the opening lead? Assuming that the opening lead is the ◇ A (you should not lead away from an ace against a suit contract), which card will partner play? Why?

Declarer starts by making a PLAN. How many losers can declarer afford? How many losers does declarer have? How does declarer plan to get rid of his extra loser? How many entries to dummy will declarer need to establish and take a heart trick if hearts break as expected? Can declarer afford to draw trumps first?

LESSON 8
Putting It Together

Combining Techniques
Choosing Among Techniques
Combining Alternatives
Choosing Among Alternatives
Guidelines for Defense
Bidding — Preempts
Summary

Workshop Material
Group Activities

When not enough tricks are available to make the contract, the third step of the PLAN is to **A**nalyze *your alternatives*. We have looked at several techniques for developing extra tricks or eliminating losers: promotion, length, finesses, discarding or trumping losers. Within each suit, it is sometimes possible to combine two or more techniques. At other times you must choose among the techniques available.

Coming to the final step of the PLAN, **N**ow *put it together*, you must look at the hand as a whole rather than the individual suits. There may be a number of alternatives from which to choose. In some cases you must combine the alternatives to give yourself the best chance. In other cases you must choose the best alternative because you won't have the luxury of trying more than one.

Let's see how to go about making these decisions.

◆ *COMBINING TECHNIQUES* ◆

When establishing tricks in a suit, it is often possible to combine the techniques of promoting high cards, developing long suits and finessing. In a suit contract the trump suit provides additional possibilities. Some of these combinations have been discussed in earlier lessons, but there is an almost endless variety of suit combinations — this is part of the fascination of the game.

Promotion, Length and Finesses

Here are some examples of combining various techniques to get the maximum number of tricks from each suit. Assume you have sufficient entries and no more important considerations for the hand as a whole.

DUMMY: K Q 6 3 2

DECLARER: J 5 4

This suit can be developed with a combination of promotion and length. The king can be used to drive out the ace, promoting the queen and jack into winners. Since there are eight cards, if the missing cards divide 3–2, dummy's low cards also will be tricks, giving you four tricks in all. If the missing cards divide 4–1, you still can develop one extra trick through length by giving up a second trick. You would end up with three tricks.

DUMMY: A Q J 2

DECLARER: 6 5 4 3

You can combine a finesse with length to try for all four tricks. Lead a low card toward dummy and, if the opponent on your left has the king, your finesse will win. You then need an entry back to your hand to repeat the finesse. Take the ace and, if the missing cards divide 3–2, your remaining low card will be a winner.

DUMMY: A Q 4 3 2

DECLARER: 6 5

Lead toward dummy, taking a finesse. If the finesse is successful, play the ace and give up a trick. If the missing cards divide 3–3, your remaining two low cards are winners, and you get four tricks. If the missing cards divide 4–2, you must give up a second trick and will end up with three tricks.

DUMMY: Q 3

DECLARER: A 7 6 5 2

Start by leading low toward dummy's queen. If your left-hand opponent has the king, you will win a trick with the queen sooner or later. You also have a trick with the ace and, if the missing cards divide 3–3, will end up with four tricks. If they are 4–2, you must give up a second trick to establish a third winner.

DUMMY: Q 10 4 3 2

DECLARER: K 5

Start by using the king to drive out the opponents' ace, promoting the queen into a winner. Next, lead the 5 and finesse dummy's 10, hoping your left-hand opponent has the jack. If the finesse wins, play the queen. If the suit divides 3-3, your two low cards will be winners, giving you four tricks in all.

This last suit is developed through a combination of promotion, length and finesse. In an actual hand a number of things may go differently. The opponents may hold up their ace when you play the king. That does not stop you from leading toward dummy to try the finesse. The finesse may not work, but you still may get tricks through length. The suit will more likely break 4–2 than 3–3, but you still can establish one additional trick through length. In the end you may get anywhere from one to four tricks from this suit. Combining good technique with a little luck will do wonders in making tricks appear from thin air!

Knowing the best way to handle a particular suit combination still must be put into the context of a complete hand. Other considerations, such as entries, then come into play. Let's look at a hand where you needs lots of luck together with a knowledge of how to play a particular suit to bring home your contract.

Contract: 3 NT
Lead: ♣6

NORTH (DUMMY)
♠ 9 5 3
♡ 10 6 4
◇ A Q 7 5 3 2
♣ 7

WEST
♠ Q 10 8 6 4
♡ J 3
◇ K 9 4
♣ Q 10 8

EAST
♠ J 7
♡ Q 9 8 7 2
◇ J 10
♣ K 9 6 5

SOUTH (DECLARER)
♠ A K 2
♡ A K 5
◇ 8 6
♣ A J 4 3 2

You need nine tricks in 3 NT and start with six sure tricks: two spades, two hearts, a diamond and a club. It looks as if the diamond suit has some potential for producing extra tricks, but how should you handle this combination?

One extra trick can come from taking a finesse, hoping West has the ◇ K. In addition, if the five missing cards divide 3–2, three extra tricks will come from length by giving up one trick. Is that good enough?

When putting it together, do not forget to consider entries. The only entry to dummy is in the diamond suit itself. You can't take the finesse and then give up a trick, since you will have no entry to dummy's winners. Instead, since you must give up a trick even if the finesse works and the suit divides 3–2, incorporate a ducking play as well.

Win the first trick and play a low diamond from both hands, ducking a trick. Now the stage is set. When you win the next trick, lead your other low diamond and finesse dummy's queen. You breathe a sigh of relief when this works since you would take *no* diamond tricks if it lost. Now you can play the ◇A. When the suit divides 3–2, your remaining diamonds are all winners and you are in dummy to take them.

You end up with five diamond tricks and make an overtrick. You were lucky — East could have held the ◇K, you would have taken no diamond tricks and the contract would have been defeated by four tricks — quite a swing! Nonetheless, you needed to know how to play the diamond suit to give yourself a chance.

Using the Trump Suit

When you have a trump suit, there are further opportunities to develop tricks in side suits. Here are some examples:

DUMMY: 5 2

DECLARER: A Q 8 3

You potentially have three losers. However, you can lead a low card from dummy and finesse the queen. If this wins, you can take the ace and trump both your remaining losers in dummy, ending up with no losers in the suit.

DUMMY: A Q 8 6 3

DECLARER: 5 4

You have only one loser in your hand and can avoid losing a trick by taking a successful finesse. In addition, you can establish an extra winner by leading the suit again and trumping it. If the suit breaks 3–3, dummy's remaining two cards will be winners and you can use them to discard losers in other side suits. Even if the suit breaks 4–2, you can establish one extra winner by crossing back to dummy, leading the suit again and trumping it.

DUMMY: J 8 6 5 4 2

DECLARER: 7

This is a similar situation. If you need to develop an extra trick on which to discard a loser, start by giving up a trick. When you regain the lead, lead the suit from dummy and trump it. Cross back to dummy, lead the suit again and trump it. If the missing cards divide 3–3, your remaining cards in dummy are winners. If not, you must go to dummy, lead the suit again and trump it.

DUMMY: —

DECLARER: K Q J 10

You can promote three tricks by leading the king to drive out the ace. In a trump contract you may be able to take three tricks without losing one. Lead the king and, if your left-hand opponent plays the ace, trump it in dummy. Now the remaining cards are winners. If the ace is not played, discard from dummy. If right-hand opponent follows low, you can continue by leading the queen to see whether your left-hand opponent wants to play the ace. Whenever he does, you trump it and end up with no losers in the suit. This technique is called a ruffing finesse, since you are *finessing* against the ace on your left and will use dummy's trumps to ruff the ace when it appears.

◆ *CHOOSING AMONG TECHNIQUES* ◆

Sometimes, you cannot employ more than one technique to handle the suit. How you play the suit may depend on such factors as how many tricks you need or can afford to lose and whether there is a dangerous opponent.

Eight Ever, Nine Never

Consider the following layout where the only missing high card is the queen:

                        NORTH (DUMMY)
                        K J 10 6
        WEST   EAST

                        SOUTH (DECLARER)
                        A 5 3 2

Declarer could take the ace and king. If the queen had not yet appeared, he could play the jack to drive it out, promoting the 10 into a winner. Alternatively, declarer could take the ace and lead low toward dummy. If West produced a low card, declarer could take a finesse against the queen by playing the 10 (or jack). Which way should declarer play the suit?

If declarer needs just three tricks from the suit and can afford to lose a trick, then either way is fine. However, if declarer needs all four tricks and cannot afford to give up the lead, a useful guideline for this situation is: *eight ever, nine never*.

Use this advice when you are missing a queen and must decide whether to take a finesse. With eight or fewer cards, take the finesse (ever). With nine or more cards, do not finesse (never) — play the ace and king and hope one of the opponents has to play the queen. The *ever* and *never* are a bit extreme. When you look at the entire hand, you may see valid reasons for not finessing with eight cards or taking a finesse with nine cards.

Here are some examples of suits where you would consider using the guideline *eight ever, nine never.*

DUMMY:	A K J 6 5 2	With nine cards in the combined hands, play the ace and king. This is the *nine never* case — meaning don't take the finesse for the queen.
DECLARER:	8 7 3	
DUMMY:	A K J 6 3	With only eight cards plan to take the finesse by leading low to dummy's jack. If you have enough entries, win the first trick with dummy's ace (or king) and then come to your hand to finesse. This gives you an extra chance in case your right-hand opponent started with a singleton queen.
DECLARER:	7 5 4	
DUMMY:	A J 3	Win the first trick with the king and lead low toward dummy, finessing the jack if a low card appears — *eight ever* applies when you have fewer than eight cards.
DECLARER:	K 6 2	

DUMMY: K J 7 6 3 2

DECLARER: A 5 4

With nine cards you normally play the ace and king. However, if you could afford to lose a trick in this suit, and dummy had no other entries, it would be safer to take the ace and then finesse the jack if the queen did not appear. If the finesse lost, you still would have a low card left to lead to dummy's winners. If you play the ace and king instead, the queen may not appear if the suit was originally divided 3–1. You can drive out the queen, but you have no way to get to dummy. This is the type of consideration that makes *never* too extreme.

Let's look at a complete hand and put the guideline to work:

Contract: 7 NT
Lead: ♡10

NORTH (DUMMY)
♠ K Q J
♡ K J 5
◇ A Q J
♣ K J 7 2

WEST
♠ 7 6 4
♡ **10** 9 8 7
◇ 10 7 3
♣ ? 9 5

EAST
♠ 10 9 5 3
♡ 6 3 2
◇ 9 6 5 2
♣ ? 4

SOUTH (DECLARER)
♠ A 8 2
♡ A Q 4
◇ K 8 4
♣ A 8 6 3

With nearly every high card in the deck, you have bid 7 NT, as high as you can go. Unfortunately, the one high card you lack is the ♣Q. You have three tricks each in spades, hearts and diamonds. You must take all four tricks in clubs to make the grand slam.

You can delay things by taking your spade, heart and diamond winners, but eventually, you must play the ♣A and lead a low club toward dummy. Naturally, West produces the ♣9 (if the ♣Q appeared, all the excitement would be over). Do you finesse dummy's ♣J or play the ♣K, hoping East has just the ♣Q left?

The guideline is there to help you out. *Eight ever* guides you to take the finesse. Does it work? If it does, you and your partner can score up your large bonus. If it doesn't, you can be content knowing you made the *right* play.

Counting Tricks

Here is a suit combination we have looked at before:

NORTH (DUMMY)
7 4 2

WEST

EAST

SOUTH (DECLARER)
K Q 3

The best way to play this suit is to lead from dummy toward declarer's hand. If East has the ace and plays low, declarer wins the first trick with the queen (or king). Declarer then goes back to dummy and leads toward his hand again. Whether or not East plays the ace, declarer ends up with two tricks. If West started with the ace, declarer gets only one trick.

Alternatively, declarer can lead the king from his hand, driving out the ace and promoting the queen. Declarer gets one trick no matter which opponent has the ace but gives up the chance to get two tricks.

Why would declarer ever settle for one trick? While the finesse may be the best play for a particular suit, declarer must take the whole hand into consideration. Declarer may need only one trick and not two. Dummy may not have two entries to allow declarer the luxury of leading twice toward his hand. Dummy may have two entries, but declarer cannot afford to use one of them because he needs it for another purpose.

Here are some other examples of suits where declarer must choose the technique for developing them based on how many tricks he needs and whether he can afford to give up the lead:

DUMMY: A Q J

DECLARER: 8 7 2

If declarer needs only two tricks and can afford to give up the lead, he can play the ace and lead the queen to drive out the king and promote the jack into a second winner. If declarer needs all three tricks or cannot afford to lose a trick, he must try the finesse. Declarer will need two entries to his hand so he can finesse twice.

DUMMY: A Q 3

DECLARER: 10 9 6 5 4 2

If declarer needs all six tricks in this suit, he must lead a low card to dummy's queen, hoping the opponent on his left has the king. Then declarer plays the ace and hopes the suit divides 2–2. If declarer can afford to lose one or two tricks or is short of entries to his hand, he can play the ace and then lead the queen to drive out the king. If the suit breaks 2–2, declarer will get five tricks. If it is 3-1, he will get at least four tricks (five if the singleton is the king or the jack) provided he has an entry to his hand to take his winners.

DUMMY: K 2

DECLARER: 5 4 3

Normally, declarer will lead toward dummy's king, hoping the ace is on his left. If this were a side suit in a suit contract, however, declarer might want to trump one of his losers in dummy. If declarer were short of entries to his hand, he could lead the suit from dummy, giving up two tricks. In the end he would get to trump his loser in dummy.

Here is a hand where declarer cannot afford to play a suit in the manner he would like:

Contract: 1 NT
Lead: ◇ Q

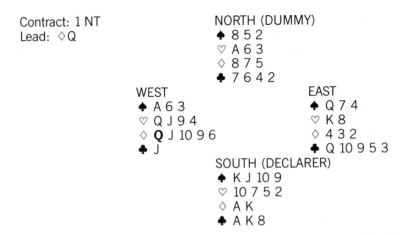

NORTH (DUMMY)
♠ 8 5 2
♡ A 6 3
◇ 8 7 5
♣ 7 6 4 2

WEST
♠ A 6 3
♡ Q J 9 4
◇ **Q** J 10 9 6
♣ J

EAST
♠ Q 7 4
♡ K 8
◇ 4 3 2
♣ Q 10 9 5 3

SOUTH (DECLARER)
♠ K J 10 9
♡ 10 7 5 2
◇ A K
♣ A K 8

Declarer has one heart trick, two diamond tricks and two club tricks. Two more tricks are needed to make 1 NT. Ideally, declarer would like to take a spade finesse, hoping East has the ♠ Q. By repeating the finesse, declarer could take three tricks.

However, dummy has only one entry — even if East has the ♠ Q, declarer cannot repeat the finesse. Using the ♡ A as an entry to dummy is also dangerous. Once the ♡ A is gone, the opponents can take all their heart winners along with any winners *they* establish.

Since declarer needs only two spade tricks, he can develop them simply by using promotion. After winning the first trick, declarer leads the ♠ K to drive out the ace. The opponents drive out one of declarer's remaining high cards, but declarer then leads the ♠ J to drive out the ♠ Q. The defenders can take the winners they have established, but not enough to defeat the contract. When declarer regains the lead, he can take his promoted ♠ 10 and ♠ 9 along with his other winners to make the contract.

Safety Plays

Another reason for playing a suit in a particular manner is *safety*. Sometimes, you can afford one loser in the suit but you want to avoid two losers. Look at this layout:

NORTH (DUMMY)
K J 4 2

WEST

EAST

SOUTH (DECLARER)
A 7 5

If you need four tricks in this suit, you play the ace, lead a low card toward dummy and finesse the jack when West plays low, hoping West has the queen. If the finesse works, you play the king and hope the suit divides 3–3.

If you need only three tricks in the suit and can afford to lose one, the safest play is take the king and ace and then lead low toward dummy's jack. You still will take three tricks if the suit breaks 3-3, although one of the opponents will win a trick with the queen. You also will take three tricks when West has the queen, even if the suit breaks 4–2 or 5–1 since you end up leading toward dummy's jack.

Why is this called a safety play? Suppose the actual layout of the missing cards is:

NORTH (DUMMY)
K J 4 2

WEST   EAST
10 9 6 3   Q 8

SOUTH (DECLARER)
A 7 5

If you try for all four tricks, playing the ace and finessing dummy's jack, you lose to East's queen. When you later play dummy's king, the suit divides 4-2 — you get only the two tricks you started with. By making the safety play of taking the king and ace first, you find out about East's doubleton queen and no longer need to risk the finesse. By sacrificing the potential for a fourth trick, you increase your chance of safely winding up with three tricks.

Safety plays are generally beyond the scope of this text. This example is included so you can see another reason why you may choose one method of playing a particular suit over another method. Now let's move on to look at how you choose which suit to play when you have a choice.

◆ *COMBINING ALTERNATIVES* ◆

When putting it together, you often have more than one suit from which you can get extra tricks or from which you must eliminate losers. In some cases you must develop two or more suits. At other times you must combine your chances so, if you cannot get the tricks you need in one suit, you can turn to an alternative suit.

Which Suit First?

On many hands you must be careful of the order in which you take your tricks, even if you do not have to develop them. Here is a simple example:

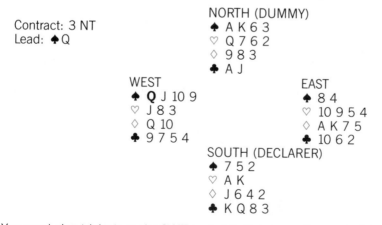

Contract: 3 NT
Lead: ♠Q

NORTH (DUMMY)
♠ A K 6 3
♡ Q 7 6 2
◇ 9 8 3
♣ A J

WEST
♠ Q J 10 9
♡ J 8 3
◇ Q 10
♣ 9 7 5 4

EAST
♠ 8 4
♡ 10 9 5 4
◇ A K 7 5
♣ 10 6 2

SOUTH (DECLARER)
♠ 7 5 2
♡ A K
◇ J 6 4 2
♣ K Q 8 3

You need nine tricks to make 3 NT and at first glance you seem to have everything you need. You have two sure tricks in spades, three in hearts and four in clubs. Suits in which you cannot take all your winners without using an entry in another suit are said to be *blocked*. In this hand, both the heart and club suits are blocked.

After winning the first trick with the ♠K, play the ♣A and ♣J to *unblock* that suit. Now lead a heart to your king so you can take the ♣K and ♣Q. Next, take the ♡A to unblock that suit. Now lead a spade to dummy's ♠A and take the ♡Q as the ninth trick.

If you play the suits in a different order, you may find that you have trouble getting all nine of your winners. For example, if you play the ♡A and ♡K, unblocking the heart suit, you will have no entry to your club winners.

Here is a hand where you must develop two suits and be careful to play them in the right order:

Contract: 3 NT
Lead: ♡10

NORTH (DUMMY)
♠ 9 7 6
♡ J 6 2
◇ A K 7 4 3
♣ J 8

WEST
♠ 5 4 2
♡ **10 9 8 7**
◇ Q 10 8
♣ A 10 7

EAST
♠ K 10 8 3
♡ Q 5 4
◇ J 9
♣ K 9 3 2

SOUTH (DECLARER)
♠ A Q J
♡ A K 3
◇ 6 5 2
♣ Q 6 5 4

You have one sure trick in spades, two in hearts and two in diamonds. Four more are needed to make your contract of 3 NT. One source of extra tricks is the spade suit. If East has the ♠K, you can win a finesse. You will need two entries to dummy so you can repeat the finesse and take two extra spade tricks. The diamond suit also can be developed. If the missing diamonds divide 3-2, you can establish two extra tricks by giving up one trick. By developing both suits, you can get four extra tricks.

You must be very careful to do everything in the right order. The only entries to dummy are the ◇A and ◇K. These will be needed to take the spade finesses. One of them also will be needed as an entry to the diamond suit itself — that means you must duck an early diamond trick. Neither of the techniques is new. We already have looked at the finesse and the ducking play when developing long suits.

After winning the first heart trick, duck a diamond. Assuming the missing diamonds are divided 3-2, this play establishes the suit while leaving the ◇A and ◇K as entries. If the opponents play another heart, win and lead a diamond to dummy's king. It is not yet time to take the rest of your diamond winners since you have work to do in the spade suit.

Lead a low spade from dummy and, when East plays low, finesse the ♠J. When this wins, go back to the diamond suit. Lead a diamond to dummy's ace and, since this is the last time you will be in dummy, take your other two diamond winners. Finally, lead another low spade and finesse the ♠Q. When this wins, take your ♠A and you have nine tricks: three spade tricks, two heart tricks and four diamond tricks.

When you must promote winners in two suits, you normally should start by playing the longest combined suit first. Look at this hand:

Contract: 3 NT
Lead: ♣5

NORTH (DUMMY)
♠ 8 7 3
♡ K 8 6
◇ K J 8 3
♣ A 8 3

WEST
♠ Q 9
♡ 4 2
◇ 9 7 5 4
♣ J 9 7 5 2

EAST
♠ J 10 5 4
♡ A J 10 9 7
◇ A 6
♣ 10 4

SOUTH (DECLARER)
♠ A K 6 2
♡ Q 5 3
◇ Q 10 2
♣ K Q 6

You start with two spade tricks and three club tricks. Four more are needed to make 3 NT. Another spade trick is a possibility if the suit breaks 3-3. However, the suit is most likely divided 4-2. You can develop a trick in hearts by using one of your high cards to drive out the ♡A. You also can promote three tricks in diamonds by driving out the ◇A. Which ace should you drive out first?

Since you have more diamonds than hearts, you should drive out the ◇A first. Whatever the opponents lead back, you can win and then drive out the ♡A to establish your ninth trick.

What happens if you played the shorter suit first? Suppose you win the first trick in your hand and lead a heart to dummy's king. East wins and with such strong hearts will establish some heart tricks himself, leading the ♡J to drive out your ♡Q. When you now try to establish the diamond tricks you need, East will win the ◇A and take his three established heart winners. Together with the ♡A, these will be enough to defeat your contract.

Combining Chances

When either of two suits will give you the extra tricks you need, you sometimes can combine your chances. Look at the following hand:

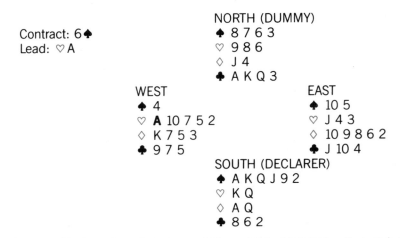

Contract: 6♠
Lead: ♡ A

NORTH (DUMMY)
♠ 8 7 6 3
♡ 9 8 6
◇ J 4
♣ A K Q 3

WEST
♠ 4
♡ **A** 10 7 5 2
◇ K 7 5 3
♣ 9 7 5

EAST
♠ 10 5
♡ J 4 3
◇ 10 9 8 6 2
♣ J 10 4

SOUTH (DECLARER)
♠ A K Q J 9 2
♡ K Q
◇ A Q
♣ 8 6 2

You can afford one loser in your small slam of 6♠. After taking their ♡ A, the opponents lead another heart, which you win with the ♡ K. You still have a potential diamond loser. When analyzing your alternatives, you see two possibilities. You could lead a diamond from dummy and, if East produces a low diamond, finesse the queen. If East has the ◇ K, you make your contract. If West has it, you are defeated.

The second alternative is to discard your ◇ Q on an extra winner in dummy. If the missing clubs break exactly 3-3, dummy's low club will become a winner. Unfortunately, the most likely division of the clubs is 4-2.

If you had to choose between the alternatives, the diamond finesse would look better. It is a 50-50 proposition while a 3-3 club break is much less than an even chance. However, you do not have to choose. Why not try both? Two chances are better than one!

After drawing trumps (you do not want the opponents to trump one of your club winners), which alternative should you try first? If you take a losing diamond finesse first, it will be too late to try the clubs. So you must play the clubs first. If they divide 3-3, you can discard your ◇ Q and you do not need to take the finesse. If the clubs do not break 3-3, you can try your second chance by taking the diamond finesse. On this hand the clubs break 3-3. If you did not give yourself this extra chance, you would be defeated, since the diamond finesse loses.

Many hands are similar to this one — you can try first one thing and then another if your first alternative does not work out. However, be careful to put your PLAN together so you can try everything in the appropriate order.

Help From Another Suit

When you cannot see how to avoid losers in one suit, take a look at the whole hand to see if another suit will help you. We already have seen how a side suit sometimes can be developed to provide extra winners for discards. Here is a different example:

Contract: 4♠
Lead: ♣Q

NORTH (DUMMY)
♠ J 9 5 4 2
♡ 6
◇ K Q 8 5
♣ A 8 4

WEST
♠ A
♡ J 7 4 3
◇ 9 6 4 2
♣ Q J 10 2

EAST
♠ K 7
♡ 10 9 8 5 2
◇ A 10 3
♣ K 7 3

SOUTH (DECLARER)
♠ Q 10 8 6 3
♡ A K Q
◇ J 7
♣ 9 6 5

You can afford three losers in your contract of 4♠. You have two trump losers, one diamond loser and two club losers. The opponents have driven out your ♣A at trick one, making all your losers quick. Since you must give up the lead, you cannot draw trumps until you have done something about your losers. You cannot do anything about the ♠A, ♠K and ◇A, so you must eliminate the two club losers. This does not look easy, since you cannot discard them on extra winners in dummy, nor does it appear that you can trump them in dummy.

If you examine the hand carefully, however, you see a way to trump your club losers! After winning the ♣A, play the ♡A, ♡K and ♡Q and discard two clubs from dummy. Now dummy has no clubs left and you can trump your two club losers. Once you have discarded dummy's clubs, it is safe to draw trumps since you no longer have too many quick losers. You will lose only two spade tricks and the ◇A.

Make sure you take the time to look at the entire hand, not just the individual suits. New possibilities will arise when you start combining the play of two or more suits.

◆ *CHOOSING AMONG ALTERNATIVES* ◆

At times, you cannot combine your options. You have more than one alternative for the extra tricks you need, but you must choose one and go with it. Let's take a look at some guidelines to help you make the right choice.

Go for the Sure Thing

Sometimes, you have one suit that may provide the tricks you need but only if the lie of the cards is favorable — you may need a successful finesse or a reasonable division of the missing cards. If you have a choice, select the suit that requires as little luck as possible.

For example, suppose declarer needs four tricks from one suit. Compare the following three layouts:

1)	DUMMY	2)	DUMMY	3)	DUMMY
	Q 5 3		Q 10 3		Q 5 3
	DECLARER		DECLARER		DECLARER
	A 7 6 4 2		K J 9 4 2		K J 6 4 2

In the first layout, declarer may be able to get four tricks. He can take a finesse by leading toward dummy's queen, hoping the king is on his left. In addition the missing cards must divide 3-2. Since declarer needs a very favorable lie of the missing cards, he would not choose this suit unless he had no alternative.

In the second layout declarer has all the missing high cards except the ace. By driving out the ace, he can promote four winners. It does not matter which opponent has the ace or how the missing cards are divided. Since this is a sure thing, declarer would definitely play this suit if he had a choice.

The third layout is closer to what declarer actually may get at the table. Declarer does not care which opponent has the missing ace but, since he does not have all the high cards, he will need the suit to divide 3-2. While this is not a sure thing, it is much preferable to the suit in the first layout.

In a trump contract you also should look for the sure thing when trying to get rid of losers. Here is an example in a complete hand:

Contract: 4♠
Lead: ♣Q

NORTH (DUMMY)
♠ 9 8 6
♡ 6 3
◇ K 7 6 2
♣ K 8 4 3

WEST
♠ Q 5 2
♡ K 9 5 2
◇ 10 3
♣ Q J 10 6

EAST
♠ 4 3
♡ A Q 10 8
◇ J 9 8 4
♣ 9 7 2

SOUTH (DECLARER)
♠ A K J 10 7
♡ J 7 4
◇ A Q 5
♣ A 5

In 4♠ you are missing the ♠Q and have three heart losers. In the spade suit you could lead from dummy and take a finesse when East plays a low card. This will work when East has the ♠Q, a 50-50 proposition. You also could try discarding one of the heart losers on an extra winner in dummy. Dummy has no sure winner, but if the missing diamonds divide 3-3, dummy's remaining diamond will become a winner. However, the most likely division of the diamonds is 4-2.

The sure way to get rid of one of your losers is by planning to trump a heart in dummy. This will work no matter who holds the ♠Q and how the diamonds break. After winning the first club trick, play a heart immediately. Suppose East wins and leads a spade. Don't be tempted to take the finesse. If it loses, West can lead another trump and you soon may find yourself with no trumps in dummy to take care of your loser. Win the spade and lead another heart. If East wins and leads another spade, again refuse to take the finesse. You have a sure thing going. Win the spade, lead your last heart and trump it in dummy. You end up losing just two heart tricks and the ♠Q.

Go for the Right Number of Tricks

If you have a choice of suits to develop, be careful to pick the one that will provide enough tricks to make the contract. For example, take a look at the following hand:

Contract: 3 NT
Lead: ♡4

NORTH (DUMMY)
♠ 8 4 2
♡ A 5
◇ Q J 9 7 3
♣ K Q 6.

WEST
♠ A 9 3
♡ Q 9 7 4 2
◇ 6 4
♣ 10 7 3

EAST
♠ 7 6 5
♡ J 10 6 3
◇ A 8
♣ 9 8 4 2

SOUTH (DECLARER)
♠ K Q J 10
♡ K 8
◇ K 10 5 2
♣ A J 5

You need nine tricks in 3 NT and start with two heart tricks and three club tricks. In the spade suit, you can drive out the opponents' ace and promote three winners. In the diamond suit you also can drive out the opponents' ace and develop four extra tricks.

Since you need four more tricks to make the contract, play the diamond suit after winning the first heart trick. That will guarantee the contract.

If you are tempted to play the spades first, look what happens. West wins the ♠A and leads another heart to drive out your remaining high card. You now have eight sure tricks but still need to develop one more. Eventually, you must play a diamond to try and get your ninth trick. East wins the ace and leads another heart. The opponents get three heart tricks and their two aces to defeat the contract. Make sure you keep an eye on your objective when trying to choose which suit to play.

Go With Your Only Chance

Suppose you have a suit that could provide the tricks you need. Unfortunately, the opponents are hard at work trying to make things tough for you — they won't always give you time to develop the suit you like best. In such cases you may have to choose another suit that, while not offering as good a chance for extra tricks, offers the only hope of making the contract. Here is an example:

Contract: 3 NT
Lead: ♠6

NORTH (DUMMY)
♠ 8 5
♡ A K J
◇ 10 8 6 2
♣ K J 6 3

WEST
♠ K J 7 6 3 2
♡ Q 6 2
◇ 7 5
♣ 10 7

EAST
♠ Q 10 4
♡ 10 9 8 3
◇ A 9 4 3
♣ 9 8

SOUTH (DECLARER)
♠ A 9
♡ 7 5 4
◇ K Q J
♣ A Q 5 4 2

You start with eight sure tricks: one spade, two hearts and five clubs. You need only one more to make your contract of 3 NT. The suit to develop appears to be diamonds. By driving out the opponents' ◇ A, you can promote more winners than you need. Unfortunately, you must watch out for the opponents. They have led a spade and are intent on driving out your ♠ A. If you let the opponents win a trick with the ◇ A, they will take enough spade tricks to defeat the contract.

Do you have an alternative? You can lead a heart toward dummy and finesse the ♡ J when West plays low. If West has the ♡ Q, the finesse will succeed and you will have your ninth trick. If East has the ♡ Q, down you go. The finesse is a 50-50 chance.

Even though the diamonds offer certain tricks, they give you no chance of making the contract. The opponents have already established their spade winners. Instead, go with the 50% chance of the heart finesse. The opponents have left you no option.

Go With the Odds

If you must choose between two suits, either of which could provide the tricks you need, select the one that gives you the best chance.

Going with the odds is definitely a good idea, but how do you know what the odds are? Given the large number of possible suit combinations, the subject can become quite complex. Even a simple finesse, which looks like a 50% chance, can be affected by such things as the bidding or the division of the cards.

For example, an opponent who opened the bidding is more likely to hold a missing king than an opponent who passed throughout the auction; an opponent who has four or five cards in a suit is more likely to hold a missing queen than an opponent who has only two or three.

It is beyond the scope of this text to delve into all the possibilities — for now, the concepts you already have seen will be a sufficient guideline. A finesse for one missing card can be viewed as a 50-50 proposition. An odd number of missing cards will tend to divide as evenly as possible, and an even number of missing cards will tend to divide slightly unevenly. Based on this, here are the key concepts that will help you *go with the odds* in the most common situations:

- The odds for a successful finesse for one missing card are approximately 50%.

- The odds of five missing cards dividing 3-2 are greater than 50% (68%).

- The odds of six missing cards dividing 3-3 are less than 50% (36% — the odds on a 4-2 division are 48%).

Let's see how this information can be applied on the following hand:

Contract: 7 NT
Lead: ♠5

NORTH (DUMMY)
♠ A Q J
♡ K Q 4
◇ A K Q 2
♣ 9 8 5

WEST
♠ ? 8 7 **5**
♡ 10 7 2
◇ J 9 7 5
♣ 6 2

EAST
♠ ? 6 4 2
♡ 9 8 6 5
◇ 10 3
♣ 7 4 3

SOUTH (DECLARER)
♠ 9 3
♡ A J 3
◇ 8 6 4
♣ A K Q J 10

You have to take all the tricks in your grand slam and the opponents have made you make a choice at trick one. You have twelve sure tricks: one spade, three hearts, three diamonds and five clubs. Do you take the spade finesse for your thirteenth trick or do you win the ♠A and hope the missing diamonds are divided 3-3 so that dummy has four diamond tricks? It's your play — the finesse is the percentage favorite.

◆ **GUIDELINES FOR DEFENSE** ◆

When you are defending, go through the same general thought process that declarer uses. Make your own plan. This is complicated by the fact that you cannot see your partner's hand, only dummy. You must use your imagination to see where the tricks for your side will come from.

The Defender's Plan

The plan for a defender involves the same four steps that declarer goes through — but keeping in mind that you are working with a partner. The first step is to determine the objective: *how many tricks do we need to defeat the contract?* Notice how *we* replaces the *you* from declarer's plan. Then you determine how far you are from the objective: *how many sure tricks do we have?* Determining the sure tricks is not as easy for a defender because you cannot see your partner's cards. Instead, you must make use of any inferences you have — from the bidding, the cards your partner plays and the way declarer plays the hand.

The third step is to determine how you can establish the additional tricks you need to defeat the contract: *where can we get extra tricks?* Again, you must imagine what the unseen hands look like, perhaps crediting partner with cards that are necessary to defeat the contract. Finally, put it into an overall plan: *how do we put it together?* In what order will you take your tricks? How can you cooperate with partner to make sure you are both working along the same lines?

The defender's plan will be discussed in more detail in the next lesson series, *The Heart Series*. For now, let's see how a defender would approach the following hand:

NORTH (DUMMY)

Contract: 4♠
Lead: ♡J

♠ Q 10 6 3
♡ K Q 4
◇ 8 5 4
♣ K Q J

EAST (YOU)

♡ J

♠ 4 2
♡ 8 6 5
◇ K 7 2
♣ A 10 7 4 3

South opens the bidding 1♠, North raises to 3♠ and South bids 4♠, which becomes the contract — you and your partner pass throughout the auction. Your partner leads the ♡J. Declarer wins the first trick with the ♡A and draws trumps with the ♠A and ♠K. He then leads a club to dummy's ♣J. What is your plan?

To defeat 4♠, you need four tricks. The ♣A is a sure trick but you need to find three more. Since declarer has drawn trumps, you will get no tricks from the spade suit. Declarer has all the high hearts, so that suit offers no possibility. Once your ♣A is driven out, declarer will have all the high clubs. That leaves diamonds as the only chance.

Although you have no tricks in diamonds yourself, remember that your partner is on the other side of the table to help you. You may not be able to visualize exactly what partner must hold, but you can see that your only hope of defeating the contract is to take three diamond tricks. If declarer has some of the missing high diamonds, don't worry. You cannot defeat every contract, but you can give it your best try.

In putting it together, you have the same considerations as declarer. For example, should you hold up the ♣A, refusing to win the first trick? That will do no good since declarer still has lots of entries to dummy. If he has only one club, this will be your last chance to win the ace.

Having gone through all this, win the ♣A and lead a diamond, hoping the complete layout is something like this:

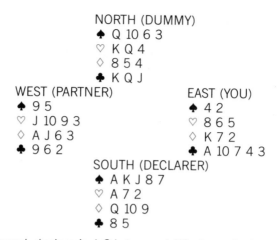

NORTH (DUMMY)
♠ Q 10 6 3
♡ K Q 4
◇ 8 5 4
♣ K Q J

WEST (PARTNER)
♠ 9 5
♡ J 10 9 3
◇ A J 6 3
♣ 9 6 2

EAST (YOU)
♠ 4 2
♡ 8 6 5
◇ K 7 2
♣ A 10 7 4 3

SOUTH (DECLARER)
♠ A K J 8 7
♡ A 7 2
◇ Q 10 9
♣ 8 5

When you lead a diamond, declarer's ◇ Q is trapped. Whatever declarer plays, you and partner can take three diamond tricks to defeat the contract. One for the defense!

◆ BIDDING ◆

Opening bids in a suit at the three level or higher show hands with a long suit (usually at least a seven-card suit) that are too weak to open the bidding at the one level (i.e., fewer than 13 points). These are called *preemptive opening bids*, or *preempts*.

The Theory Behind Preemptive Bids

Why start the bidding at the three level or higher with a hand that is too weak to open at the one level? The advantage of a preempt is that it takes up a lot of room on the Bidding Scale and makes it difficult for the other partnership to exchange information.

For example, if you were planning to open 1◇, and the opponent in front of you opened 3♡, you would be faced with a difficult problem. How do you show partner that you have an opening bid with diamonds when the auction is already at the three level? A preempt may cause the opponents to reach the wrong denomination, end up too high or too low, or be unable to get into the auction at all.

Of course, a preempt may make it difficult for your partner to bid effectively and there is also the danger that you may be doubled and defeated badly! You can minimize the risk and maximize the potential gain by preempting only with the appropriate type of hand.

Requirements for a Preemptive Opening Bid

An opening preempt at the three level or higher shows:

- A long suit — usually seven or more cards with three of the top five cards in the suit.

- A weak hand — less than the point-count values for an opening bid.

The longer and stronger your suit, the higher the level at which you can open the. bidding. Because the penalties for being defeated are greater when you are vulnerable, you should watch the vulnerability when you preempt. If you are non-vulnerable, you can open at the three level with a seven-card suit and at the four level with an eight-card suit. Here are a couple of examples, assuming your side is non-vulnerable:

♠ 9 ♡ K Q J 8 7 5 3 ◇ 9 6 3 ♣ 10 4	With a seven-card heart suit and only 6 HCPs, open **3 ♡**. This will describe your hand to partner while making it difficult for the opponents to bid to their best contract.
♠ 7 6 ♡ 5 ◇ K Q 10 8 7 5 4 2 ♣ 8 3	With only 5 HCPs and an eight-card suit, open the bidding **4 ◇**. Again, this should make the bidding very tough for the opponents. They may make the right decision but then again they may not.

One advantage of a preempt is that it is very descriptive to partner. Knowing the type of hand you have, he can respond accordingly.

The advantage of having a good long suit is that it is more difficult for the opponents to double the contract. Even if they do, the penalty is likely to be less than the value of a contract they could make.

Responding to a Preempt

If partner opens in a suit at the three level or higher, it gives you a good description of the hand — a long suit with a weak hand. Unless you have a strong hand with 16 or more points, you have little chance for game — you should pass.

With a very strong hand, you can bid game in partner's suit or in notrump, or you can bid a long suit of your own (forcing if below the game level). Since partner has at least a seven-card suit, no particular support for partner's suit is needed to raise him.

Here are some examples of responding when your partner opens 3♡:

♠ K Q 8 ♡ 2 ◇ A J 9 7 2 ♣ K 10 8 4	Even though you have enough points to open the bidding, partner is describing a weak hand. There is not enough combined strength for game, so **pass**.
♠ A K 6 ♡ J 5 ◇ K Q 9 8 ♣ A 7 6 5	With 17 HCPs you should have a chance for game even though partner has a weak hand. Knowing partner has at least a seven-card suit, raise to **4 ♡** and play in the Golden Fit.
♠ A K Q 10 8 5 ♡ 6 ◇ A J 9 6 ♣ J 3	Since you have 15 HCPs plus 2 points for your six-card suit, there should be a chance for game. Bid **3 ♠**. This is a forcing bid and gives partner an opportunity to support your suit.

Competing Against a Preempt

If your opponent opens with a preempt, you still can make use of the overcall and the takeout double to compete. Since you are starting the auction at the three level or higher, you should have a hand stronger than an opening bid. For example, suppose the opponent on your right opens 3♣.

♠ A 9 4
♡ A Q J 10 8 2
◇ K 10 3
♣ 4

With a good six-card suit and 16 points, overcall **3♡**.

♠ K J 6 3
♡ A Q 8 2
◇ K Q 7 5
♣ 4

With support for the unbid suits and 15 HCPs plus 3 dummy points for the singleton, make a takeout double.

♠ K 8 4
♡ Q J 6
◇ A J 4 3
♣ Q 10 3

Although you have enough to open the bidding, you do not have enough to enter the auction at the three level. **Pass**. The preempt has made your life difficult, as your opponent intended.

◆ **SUMMARY** ◆

When you try to establish extra tricks to make your contract, look for opportunities to combine the techniques of promoting high cards, developing long suits and finessing. In addition, the trump suit can be used in combination with the other techniques.

How you choose to handle a specific suit depends on things such as how many tricks you need or can afford to lose, and whether you can let the opponents get the lead. A useful guideline when considering a finesse for a missing queen is *eight ever, nine never*. With eight or fewer cards, take the finesse; with nine or more, play the ace and king.

When you put your PLAN together, you sometimes need to establish more than one suit. You must be careful to play the suits in the appropriate order, using your entries wisely and usually establishing the longest suit first in a notrump contract. Try to arrange your play so you can try more than one alternative.

If you must choose among two or more alternatives, use the following guidelines:

- Go for the sure thing (select the alternative that requires the least amount of luck).

- Go for the right number of tricks (select the suit that will give you enough tricks to make the contract).

- Go with your only chance (select a suit that gives you some chance of making your contract).

- Go with the odds (select the suit that offers the best chance).

When you are defending, make a plan similar to the PLAN you make as declarer. You cannot see your partner's cards, but with a little imagination you may be able to see how your side can get enough tricks to defeat the contract.

A *preemptive opening bid* at the three level or higher shows:

- Seven-card or longer suit.

- Less than the point count values for an opening bid at the one level.

If partner opens with a preempt, pass unless you have a very strong hand. If the opponents open with a preempt, you can use the overcall and the takeout double to compete.

◆ ***GROUP ACTIVITIES*** ◆

Exercise One — Combining Techniques

How would you play each of the following suits if you have plenty of entries between the two hands? How many tricks would you expect if the missing high cards lie favorably and the suit divides as you expect?

DUMMY: 1) Q J 10 5 2   2) 7 6 2   3) K Q 8 6 2 4) A Q 9 3 2 5) Q 10 3 2

DECLARER: 8 4 3   A Q J 8 3   7 5   6   K 6 5 4

Method: _____   _____   _____   _____   _____

# of Tricks: _____   _____   _____   _____   _____

Exercise Two — Choosing a Technique

How would you play each of the following suits to get the maximum number of tricks? What is the maximum number of tricks you could take?

DUMMY: 1) A J 6 3   2) A 8 4 2   3) A K J 3   4) 8 4 2   5) K 9 5 3 2

DECLARER: K 9 4 2   K J 7 5 3   8 6 2   K Q 6   8 7 4

Method: _____   _____   _____   _____   _____

Maximum
# of Tricks: _____   _____   _____   _____   _____

Exercise Three — Combining Alternatives

You are in 3 NT, and the opponents lead the ♡J. Should you play the club suit or the diamond suit first when you get the lead?

1) DUMMY	2) DUMMY	3) DUMMY
♠ 7 4 2	♠ K 4	♠ K Q 8
♡ 7 6 4 2	♡ 7 5 2	♡ 7 3
◇ K Q	◇ K Q 4	◇ 9 6 2
♣ K J 7 2	♣ J 10 8 3 2	♣ A Q 8 4 2
DECLARER	DECLARER	DECLARER
♠ A 8 6 3	♠ A 8 6 2	♠ A 4 2
♡ A 8 3	♡ A K 8	♡ A 2
◇ A 9 8 5	◇ 8 6 2	◇ A K Q 5
♣ A Q	♣ K Q 5	♣ 7 6 5 3

_____   _____   _____

Exercise Four — Choosing an Alternative

You are in 3 NT, and the opponents lead the ♠Q. Should you play the club suit or the diamond suit first when you get the lead?

1) DUMMY
♠ K 8 2
♡ 9 6 3
◇ A Q J 7
♣ Q J 4

DECLARER
♠ A 9 3
♡ A K Q
◇ 9 8 5
♣ K 10 9 5

2) DUMMY
♠ 6 4 2
♡ Q J 3
◇ K Q J
♣ Q 10 5 3

DECLARER
♠ A K 3
♡ A K 8 2
◇ 8 6 2
♣ K J 8

3) DUMMY
♠ 7 3
♡ Q 10 3
◇ A K Q 3
♣ J 10 4 3

DECLARER
♠ A 2
♡ A K J 7
◇ 6 4 2
♣ K Q 8 2

Exercise Five — Defender's Plan

You are defending a 4 ♡ contract, and your partner leads the ♠Q. Declarer wins the ♠A, draws trumps with the ♡A and ♡K and finesses dummy's ◇Q. How many tricks do you need to defeat the contract? How many tricks do you have? Where will you get the extra tricks you need? What card must partner have to defeat the contract? What should you do after winning the ◇K?

DUMMY
♠ K 5
♡ Q 10 7 3
◇ A Q J 10
♣ Q 7 3

♠Q

YOU
♠ 9 6 4 3
♡ 8 6
◇ K 8 4
♣ K J 6 2

Exercise Six — Opening Preempts

Assuming your side is not vulnerable, what is your opening bid with each of the following hands?

1) ♠ A K J 8 7 3 2
♡ 6 3
◇ 8 5
♣ 10 9

2) ♠ 8 4
♡ 8 2
◇ 3
♣ A J 10 7 6 5 3 2

3) ♠ K 4
♡ A K Q 8 4 3 2
◇ 6 4 2
♣ J

Bid: _____   _____   _____

Exercise Seven — Responding to a Preempt

Your partner opens 3 ♡. What do you respond with each of the following hands?

1) ♠ K J 8
   ♡ 8 5
   ◇ K Q J 6
   ♣ Q 9 7 3

Response: _____

2) ♠ A 8 4
   ♡ K 2
   ◇ Q 7 6 3
   ♣ A K 7 5

Response: _____

3) ♠ A Q J 10 7 4 2
   ♡ 2
   ◇ A 4 2
   ♣ K 3

Response: _____

Exercise Eight — Competing Against a Preempt

The opponent on your right opens 3♡ . What do you do with each of the following hands?

1) ♠ A K Q 8 7 3
   ♡ 7 4
   ◇ A J 4
   ♣ 5 2

Bid:_____

2) ♠ J 10 7 3
   ♡ 3
   ◇ A J 9 2
   ♣ A K J 4

Bid:_____

3) ♠ Q 8
   ♡ K 9 2
   ◇ K Q 10 4
   ♣ K 8 4 2

Bid:_____

Exercise Nine — Combining Techniques

Turn up all the cards on the first pre-dealt hand. Put each hand dummy style at the edge of the table in front of each player.

Dealer: North

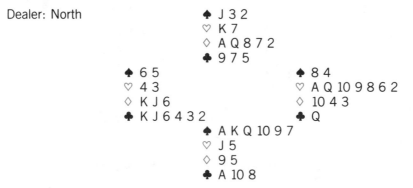

The Bidding

North passes. With a good seven-card suit and not enough strength to open at the one level, what is East's opening bid?

How can South enter the bidding?

What is East telling West about his hand? What does West do?

How many dummy points does North have in support of South's suit? Knowing that South must have more than a minimum hand to overcall at the three level, what does North bid?

How does the auction proceed? What is the contract? Who is declarer?

The Play

Which player makes the opening lead? What will be the opening lead? What is East's plan for defeating the contract? After winning the first two tricks, what does East lead next?

195

Declarer starts by making a PLAN:

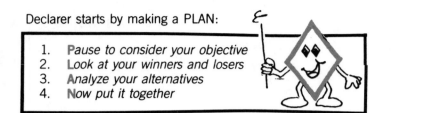

1. **P**ause to consider your objective
2. **L**ook at your winners and losers
3. **A**nalyze your alternatives
4. **N**ow put it together

How many losers does declarer have? How can declarer eliminate a diamond loser? How can declarer eliminate a club loser?

What will declarer have to do with the diamond suit? Is there a potential entry to dummy's established winner? How must the missing diamonds divide? Why must declarer be careful with the trump suit?

Exercise Ten — Eight Ever, Nine Never

Turn up all the cards on the second pre-dealt hand. Put each hand dummy style at the edge of the table in front of each player.

Dealer: East

```
              ♠ 8 4 2
              ♡ A Q 8 7
              ◇ 9 6 3
              ♣ Q 9 7
♠ K Q J 3                    ♠ A 10 9 7 5
♡ K 6 5 3                    ♡ 4 2
◇ 10                         ◇ Q 4
♣ A 8 5 4                    ♣ K J 6 3
              ♠ 6
              ♡ J 10 9
              ◇ A K J 8 7 5 2
              ♣ 10 2
```

The Bidding

East passes. With a hand not strong enough to open at the one level and a good seven-card suit, what does South bid?

How many dummy points does West have? How can West compete?

Does North have enough to bid? How many points does East have? Knowing that West must have a good hand to compete at the three level, how can East show his strength?

What will be the contract? Who will be declarer?

The Play

Which player makes the opening lead? What is the opening lead? After seeing the dummy, what will South do next?

Declarer starts by making a PLAN. How many losers does declarer have? How does declarer plan to eliminate his diamond loser? How does declarer plan to handle the club suit? What guideline is useful when considering how to play the club suit?

Exercise Eleven — Combining Alternatives

Turn up all the cards on the third pre-dealt hand. Put each hand dummy style at the edge of the table in front of each player.

Dealer: South

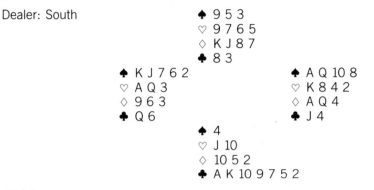

♠ 9 5 3
♡ 9 7 6 5
◇ K J 8 7
♣ 8 3

♠ K J 7 6 2
♡ A Q 3
◇ 9 6 3
♣ Q 6

♠ A Q 10 8
♡ K 8 4 2
◇ A Q 4
♣ J 4

♠ 4
♡ J 10
◇ 10 5 2
♣ A K 10 9 7 5 2

The Bidding

What is South's opening bid?

Does West have enough to enter the bidding at the three level? Does North have anything to say?

How can East compete for the contract?

South passes. How many points does West have? What does West bid?

How does the auction proceed from there? What will be the contract? Who will be declarer?

The Play

Which player makes the opening lead? What will the opening lead be?

Declarer starts by making a PLAN. How many losers can declarer afford? How many losers does declarer have? What are declarer's alternatives? Must declarer choose one of the alternatives?

Exercise Twelve — The Best Alternative

Turn up all the cards on the fourth pre-dealt hand. Put each hand dummy style at the edge of the table in front of each player.

Dealer: West

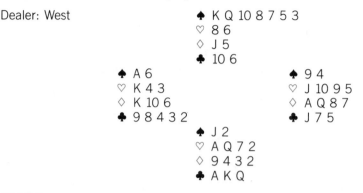

```
                    ♠ K Q 10 8 7 5 3
                    ♡ 8 6
                    ◇ J 5
                    ♣ 10 6
    ♠ A 6                           ♠ 9 4
    ♡ K 4 3                         ♡ J 10 9 5
    ◇ K 10 6                        ◇ A Q 8 7
    ♣ 9 8 4 3 2                     ♣ J 7 5
                    ♠ J 2
                    ♡ A Q 7 2
                    ◇ 9 4 3 2
                    ♣ A K Q
```

The Bidding

West passes. What is North's opening bid?

East passes. How many points does South have? Is game possible? What does South bid?

How does the auction proceed from there? What will be the contract? Who will be declarer?

The Play

Which player makes the opening lead? What will be the opening lead? If West gets to win the first trick, how would he plan to defeat the contract?

Declarer starts by making a PLAN. How many losers can declarer afford? How many losers does declarer have? What are declarer's alternatives for getting rid of a loser? Can declarer try both alternatives? Does declarer take the heart finesse? If not, why not?

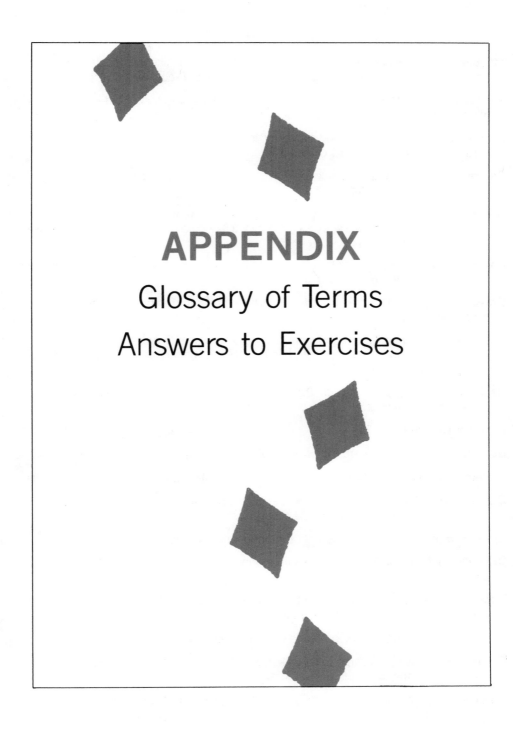

APPENDIX

Glossary of Terms

Answers to Exercises

GLOSSARY OF TERMS

Attitude — The play of a card to tell your partner whether you like a particular suit. Traditionally, a high card is encouraging and a low card is discouraging.

Blackwood Convention — Once you have agreed on a trump suit, a bid of 4 NT is artificial and asks partner how many aces he has.

Broken Sequence — Two touching high cards followed by a gap and then the next highest card. For example, ♡ K Q 10 or ♠ Q J 9.

Contract — The final bid in the auction that commits declarer's side to take the specified number of tricks in the denomination named.

Convention — A bid that conveys a meaning other than would normally be attributed to it. For example, the use of 2♣ to ask opener for a four-card major (Stayman) in response to an opening bid of 1 NT.

Cover — Playing a higher card than the one led. For example, playing the king when an opponent leads the queen or jack.

Crossruff — Trumping losers in both declarer's hand and dummy and thus using the trump cards separately.

Dangerous Opponent — The opponent that declarer wants to prevent from getting the lead, either because that opponent has established winners or can lead a card that would trap one of declarer's high cards.

Declarer — The player for the side that won the contract who first bid the denomination named in the contract.

Defense, Defenders — The side that did not win the contract.

Discard — The play of a card, other than a trump, of a different suit than the suit led.

Discarding a Loser — Playing a losing card on a potential winning card in another suit.

Distribution — The number of cards held in each suit by a particular player; the number of cards held in a particular suit by a partnership.

Draw Trumps — To lead trumps until the opponents have none left.

Drive Out (a high card) — To lead a suit and force an opponent to play a high card to win the trick.

Duck — To play a low card from both hands and surrender a trick that could have been won, usually with the object of preserving an entry.

Entry — A card that provides a means of winning a trick in a particular hand.

Equals — Cards with the same trick–taking potential. For example, the ace and king in a suit held by the same player.

Establish — To make one or more cards in a suit into winners by forcing out the opponents' higher cards.

Favorably Divided — Having the outstanding cards in a suit divided the way the declarer would like them to be — as evenly as possible.

Finesse — An attempt to win a trick with a card that is not as high as one held by an opponent by playing it after the opponent has played.

Fourth Highest — The fourth highest card of a long suit (counting down from the top). Also referred to as fourth best.

Grand Slam — A contract to take 13 tricks.

Holding — The cards one is dealt in a particular suit or in the entire hand.

Hold-up Play — Refusal to win a trick you could win in order to make it difficult for the opponents to take tricks. You break their communication and strand their winners in one hand.

Honor Sequence — Two or more honor cards in consecutive order of rank. For example, the ♡K and ♡Q.

Lead — The first card played to a trick.

Length — The number of cards held in a particular suit, often implying five or more.

Like a Suit — To have high cards in the suit and/or to want the suit led or continued.

LHO — Left-hand opponent, the player on your left.

Lose Control — Have no trumps left when the opponents get the lead and start taking their winners.

Loser — A card in declarer's hand (or dummy) that could lose a trick to the opponents.

Maintain control — Have a sufficient number of trumps to prevent the opponents from taking enough tricks in their suits to defeat your contract when they get the lead.

Overruff — To play a higher trump than one played by an opponent when you are void in the suit led.

Overtake — Play a higher card than the one already played by your side, usually for the purpose of creating an entry.

PLAN — The four basic steps that declarer goes through before starting to play a hand.

Promotion — The increase in the trick-taking potential of a card as the higher-ranking cards in the suit are played.

Quick Loser — A trick the opponents can take as soon as they get the lead.

Repeated Finesse — A finesse that can be taken more than once.

RHO — Right-hand opponent, the player on your right.

Ruff(ing) — To play a trump on a trick when you are void in the suit led.

Sacrifice — To give up a trick with the hope of getting one or more in return; to bid too high to prevent the opponents from playing in the contract of their choice.

Safe Suit — A suit that can be led without giving an opponent a trick he could not get himself.

Second Hand — The player who plays the second card to a trick.

Sequence — Two or more cards in the same suit in consecutive order of rank. For example, the king, queen and jack.

Side Suit — A suit other than the trump suit.

Slow Loser — A trick the opponents can take eventually but not immediately, since declarer has one or more winners left in the suit.

Small Slam — A contract to take 12 tricks.

Stayman Convention — An artificial response of 2♣ to an opening bid of 1 NT, asking opener to bid a four-card major suit.

Strong Two-bid — An opening bid at the two level that shows at least 22 points and is forcing to game.

Sure Tricks — Tricks that can be taken without giving up the lead.

Third Hand — The player who contributes the third card to a trick; the partner of the player leading to a trick.

Trap (a high card) — A position where a high card cannot win a trick because the opponent next to play has a higher card.

Trump — The suit named in the contract.

Two-way Finesse — The choice within a suit of which way to finesse for a missing card. For example, A-J-4 opposite K-10-3.

Unfavorably Divided — Having the outstanding cards in a suit divided the way the declarer would not like them to be — as unevenly as possible.

Winners — Sure tricks declarer can take without giving up the lead.

ANSWERS TO EXERCISES

Lesson One: Making a Plan

Exercise One
- 1) To lose no more than four tricks.
- 2) To take 12 tricks.
- 3) To lose no more than three tricks.
- 4) To take seven tricks.
- 5) To lose no more than five tricks.

Exercise Two
- 1) Three sure tricks.
- 2) Two sure tricks since there are only two cards on each side of the table.
- 3) Five sure tricks. The opponents have only four cards in the suit and even if one opponent has all four cards, your 2 still will be a winner.
- 4) Two sure tricks.
- 5) No sure tricks. You must promote a winner by giving up the lead.

Exercise Three
- 1) One loser; quick.
- 2) Three losers; quick.
- 3) One loser; slow.
- 4) Three losers; slow.
- 5) Two losers; quick.
- 6) Three losers: quick.
- 7) Two losers; one quick and one slow.
- 8) One loser; slow.
- 9) Two losers; one quick and one slow.
- 10) Two losers; slow.

Exercise Four

1) The king.	2) The ace.	3) The ace or jack.
4) The queen.	5) It doesn't matter.	

Exercise Five

1) ◇K.	2) ◇Q.	3) ♠5.

Exercise Six

1) Pass.	2) 1 NT.	3) 1 ◇.
4) 1♠.	5) 1♣.	6) 1 ◇.

Exercise Seven

1) Pass.	2) 2♠.	3) 2 NT.
4) 4♡.	5) 3♠.	6) 3 NT.

Exercise Eight

1) Pass.	2) 2♡.	3) 1♠.
4) 1 NT.	5) 2♣.	6) 3♡.

Exercise Nine
  The bidding
- South opens 1 NT.
- North responds 3 NT.
- Pass, pass, pass.
- The contract is 3 NT. South is declarer.

  The play
- West makes the opening lead of the ♠K.
- South needs nine tricks and has nine winners; he takes his tricks and runs.

Exercise Ten
  The bidding
- East opens 1◇; there are not enough points to open 1 NT.
- West does not have a suit to bid at the one level; he can't bid a new suit, clubs, at the two level with only 8 points.
- West responds 1 NT.
- Pass, pass, pass.
- The contract is 1 NT. West is declarer.

  The play
- North leads the ♡3.
- Declarer has seven winners, enough to make the contract, so he will take his tricks.
- The ♣Q must take the first club trick so the club winners in declarer's hand are not stranded.

Exercise Eleven
  The bidding
- West opens 1 NT.
- The level the partnership belongs in is game; the denomination is hearts. East responds 4♡.
- Pass, pass, pass.
- The contract is 4♡. East is declarer.

  The play
- The opening lead is the ♣Q from South.
- Declarer can afford three losers and has only three losers.
- Declarer must be careful to draw trumps so unexpected losers aren't created.

Exercise Twelve
  The bidding.
- North opens 1♠.
- South can support partner's major and bids 2♠.
- Pass, pass, pass.
- The contract is 2♠. North is declarer.

The play
- East leads the ♣K.
- Declarer has five losers and can afford five losers. Declarer does not need to look for ways to eliminate the losers.
- Declarer may not want to give up the lead.
- If declarer does not draw trumps, the opponents may trump one of his winners.

Lesson Two: Developing Tricks — Promotion and Length

Exercise One
1) Three, after giving up the lead once.
2) One, after giving up the lead three times.
3) One, after giving up the lead twice.
4) One, after giving up the lead once.
5) No tricks.

Exercise Two
1) You expect four tricks by playing the queen first.
2) You expect two tricks by playing the king first.
3) You expect three tricks by playing the jack first.
4) You expect one trick by playing the queen first.
5) You expect four tricks by playing the king first.
   In all of the examples, try to win the first trick with the high card from the short side; otherwise, your winners may be stranded even though you have one entry to dummy to go with your long suit.

Exercise Three
1) 2–1.   2) 3–1.   3) 3–2.
4) 4–2.   5) 4–3.   6) 5–3.
7) 5–4.

Exercise Four
1) Three is what to expect and what would be favorable. The opponents' cards should divide 3–2.
2) Three is what to expect, but you could take four if the opponents' cards divide 3–3.
3) Four is what to expect and what would be favorable when the opponents' cards divide 3–2.
4) Five is what to expect and what would be favorable when the opponents' cards divide 3–2.
5) Four is what to expect when the opponents' cards are divided 3–1. If they divide 2–2, you can take five tricks.

Exercise Five
1) Lose the first (or second) trick. Expect four winners when the opponents' cards divide 3–2.
2) Lose the first trick and then play the king (or vice versa). Expect four tricks when the opponents' cards divide 3–2.

3) Lose the first trick. Expect five tricks when the opponents' cards divide 3–2.
4) Lose the first two tricks. Expect three tricks when the opponents' cards divide 3–2.
5) Lose the first trick, then play the king (or vice versa). Expect only two tricks, since the most likely division of the opponents' cards is 4–2. You can take three tricks if they divide 3–3.

Exercise Six
1) ◇K.   2) ♣3.   3) ♣K.

Exercise Seven
1) 2♠.   2) 1 NT.   3) 2♣.
4) 2♡.   5) 2 NT.   6) 3♠.
7) 3♡.   8) 4♠.   9) 3♣.

Exercise Eight
1) Pass.   2) 2◇.   3) 2♡.
4) 2 NT.   5) 3♡.   6) 3◇.
7) 3 NT.   8) 4♡.   9) 3 NT.

Exercise Nine
The bidding
- North opens with 1◇.
- South responds 1♡.
- North cannot support hearts or bid a new suit at the one level and so responds 1 NT.
- South passes.
- The contract is 1 NT. North is declarer.

The play
- East leads the ♠Q.
- Declarer needs three more tricks to make the contract. The heart suit can provide them.
- Declarer plans to try to win the first heart trick with the ♡J, the high card from the short side.
- Declarer should win the first trick in his hand because the ♠K is needed as an entry to dummy's hearts.

Exercise Ten
The bidding
- There are not enough points to open 1 NT. East cannot open his longest suit, spades, because he is playing five-card majors. East opens 1♣.
- West responds 1♠, a forcing bid. West knows there is enough strength for game but does not yet know the denomination.
- East rebids 2♠.
- West places the contract in 4♠. West is declarer.

The play
- • North leads the ♡ K.
- • West has the number of losers he can afford. If West doesn't draw trumps right away, an unexpected loser could appear. After drawing trumps, West plays the diamond suit to promote two extra tricks.

Exercise Eleven
The bidding
- • South opens 1◇.
- • North responds 1♡, a suit he can bid at the one level.
- • South cannot support partner's suit or bid a new suit at the one level. With a balanced hand South rebids 1 NT.
- • North, with 12 points, knows the partnership may belong in game. North moves toward game by bidding 2 NT.
- • With 15 points South accepts the invitation and bids 3 NT.
- • The contract is 3 NT. South is declarer.

The play
- • West leads the ♣5.
- • Declarer needs two extra tricks to make the contract. Diamonds provide the opportunity.
- • Declarer wins the opening lead and then plays diamonds, even though the defenders get one trick in the suit. After declarer has lost this one trick, two extra winners are established.

Exercise Twelve
The bidding
- • East opens 1♠.
- • With support for partner's suit, West responds 2♠.
- • With a medium hand East bids 3♠.
- • With 9 points West accepts the invitation and bids 4♠.
- • The contract is 4♠. East is declarer.

The play
- • South leads the ♡ A.
- • There are four losers. Declarer has to eliminate a loser in the diamond suit if the missing diamonds are divided 3–2.
- • Declarer first draws trumps.

Lesson Three: Developing Tricks — The Finesse

Exercise One
1) One sure trick; one potential trick with the queen.
2) No sure tricks; one potential trick with the king.
3) Two sure tricks; one potential trick with the jack.
4) One sure trick; one potential trick with the queen.
5) Two sure tricks; one potential trick with the jack.

Exercise Two
1) Lead toward declarer's hand twice. If the opponent on your right holds the ace, you'll take two tricks.
2) Lead toward dummy twice, taking the finesse. If the opponent on your left holds the king, you'll take three tricks.
3) Lead toward declarer's hand twice, taking the finesse. If the opponent on your right holds the queen, you'll take four tricks.

Exercise Three
1) Lead toward the queen. If the opponent on your left has the king and the missing cards divide 3–2, you'll take four tricks.
2) Lead twice toward the king and queen. If the opponent on your left has the ace, and the missing cards divide 3–2, you'll take three tricks.
3) Lead toward the king. If the opponent on your left has the ace and the missing cards divide 3–2, you'll take three tricks.
4) Lead toward dummy twice, taking the finesse. If the opponent on your left has the king and the missing cards divide 3–2, you'll take all five tricks.
5) Lead toward the jack. If the opponent on your right has the queen and the missing cards divide 3–3, you'll take four tricks.

Exercise Four
1) Lead the queen. If it is not covered with the king, play low from dummy.
2) Lead the jack from dummy. If it is not covered, play low from your hand, taking the finesse.
3) Lead low from your hand toward the queen in dummy.
4) Lead toward dummy, hoping the opponent on your left has the king.
5) Lead the jack. If it is not covered, play low, taking the finesse.

Exercise Five
1) Lead low toward dummy and finesse the 10, hoping the opponent on your left has both the king and the jack.
2) Lead low toward the K–J–10 and finesse the 10 (or jack), hoping the opponent on your right has the queen.
3) Lead low toward the dummy, finessing the 10. You hope either the king or the queen is on your left.

Exercise Six
1) Queen.	2) Jack.	3) 4.
4) 2.	5) Ace against a suit; 3 against notrump.	

Exercise Seven
1) 1♠.	2) 1 NT.	3) Pass.
4) 1♠.	5) Pass.	6) Pass.

Exercise Eight
1) 2♡.	2) Pass.	3) 1 NT.
4) 1♠.	5) 4♡.	6) 3 NT.

Exercise Nine

The bidding

- North opens 1♠.
- East overcalls 2♡.
- The partnership belongs in a game in hearts. West bids 4♡.
- Pass, pass, pass. The contract is 4♡. East is declarer.

The play

- South leads the ♠5, partner's suit.
- Declarer loses the first three spade tricks but can trump the next spade with a high heart to avoid an overruff. Declarer must draw trumps ending up in dummy so he can take the diamond finesse.

Exercise Ten

The bidding

- East opens 1◇.
- South overcalls 1 NT.
- North can see that the partnership belongs in a game in notrump — he bids 3 NT.
- Pass, pass, pass. The contract is 3 NT. South is declarer.

The play

- West leads the ◇8, the top of a doubleton in partner's suit.
- To take nine tricks, declarer must try the spade finesse. Declarer must be careful to use dummy's high cards wisely so he can lead spades twice toward his hand.

Exercise Eleven

The bidding

- South opens 1◇.
- West overcalls 1♠.
- East responds 2♠ to West's overcall.
- East is showing 6–10 points, so West does not bid again. The contract is 2♠. West is declarer.

The play

- North leads the ◇Q, the top of touching honors in partner's suit.
- To make the contract, declarer must try the club finesse twice, using the ♠Q and ♡A as entries. The first finesse of the ♣10 loses to North's ♣Q, but the second finesse of the ♣J wins, since South has the ♣K.

Exercise Twelve

The bidding

- North opens 1♡.
- East overcalls 2◇.
- South supports North's major by bidding 2♡.
- North has a maximum hand and bids 4♡.
- Pass, pass, pass. The contract is 4♡. North is declarer.

The play
- East leads the ◇ K.
- To make the contract, declarer must try the heart finesse, being careful to lead the ♡ 10 on the first trick and playing low from his hand if West plays low. Now declarer leads another heart from dummy, and West's ♡ K is trapped.

Lesson Four: Eliminating Losers — Trumping and Discarding

Exercise One
1) With more cards in declarer's hand than dummy, declarer has the opportunity to trump two losers.
2) With only two cards in declarer's hand and more than two in dummy, there is no opportunity to trump losers.
3) With an equal number of cards in declarer's hand and dummy, there is no opportunity to trump losers.
4) Since there are three more cards in declarer's hand than dummy, declarer could trump three losers.
5) There is no opportunity to trump losers in dummy because dummy has more cards than declarer.

Exercise Two

1) One.	2) Three.	3) Two.
4) None.	5) One.	

Exercise Three

1) One.	2) One.	3) Two.
4) None.	5) None.	

Exercise Four
1) One loser can be discarded. After the ace and king have been played, declarer has no cards left and can discard a loser on the queen.
2) One loser can be discarded. After the suit is played twice, losing the first trick to the ace, declarer has no cards left in the suit.
3) Assuming the suit is divided 3–2, two losers can be discarded after the suit has been played three times, giving up a trick. Declarer can discard on dummy's two remaining winners.
4) One loser could be discarded after two winning finesses.
5) Two losers could be discarded after the suit is played twice and the opponents take the ace and the king.

Exercise Five

1) King.	2) Jack.	3) Queen.

Exercise Six

1) Double.	2) Pass.	3) 1♠.
4) Double.	5) 1 NT.	6) Pass.

Exercise Seven
    1) 1♡.   2) 1♠.   3) 2♡.
    4) 3♣.   5) 2 NT.   6) 4♡.

Exercise Eight
    1) Pass.   2) 2♠.   3) 3♠.

Exercise Nine
The bidding
- North opens 1♠.
- East doubles.
- South responds 2♠.
- West does not have to bid after South bids. West passes.
- With a medium hand of 17 points, North bids 3♠.
- South accepts the invitation and bids 4♠. The contract is 4♠. North is declarer.

The play
- East leads the ♣K.
- Declarer can eliminate a club loser by discarding a club on the diamonds but he must do this before drawing trumps. Once the opponents get the lead — which they would do if declarer tried to draw trumps — they can take four quick tricks.

Exercise Ten
The bidding
- South opens 1♡.
- West doubles.
- East shows the medium hand of 11 points by jumping to 2♠.
- With 15 dummy points West carries on to 4♠. The contract is 4♠. East is declarer.

The play
- South leads the ♡5. North plays the ♡Q, third hand high.
- Declarer can eliminate the extra heart loser, the jack, by throwing it on the extra club winner. He must do this before drawing trumps because the opponents have enough tricks to defeat the contract if they get the lead.

Exercise Eleven
The bidding
- West opens 1◇.
- North doubles.
- When East passes, South must bid and chooses 1♡.
- With a medium-strength hand North raises to 2♡.
- With only 4 points, South passes. The contract is 2♡ South is declarer.

The play
- The opening lead is the ◇A by West.
- Declarer has six losers if the missing trumps divide 3–2. He can elimiante one of the losers by trumping a diamond in dummy when the suit is led a third time. In the trump suit declarer must give up the lead twice, hoping the missing trumps divide 3–2.

Exercise Twelve

The bidding
- Playing five-card majors, North cannot bid a four-card major suit and therefore opens 1♣, lower-ranking of two three-card minor suits.
- East doubles.
- South responds 2♣.
- West bids 2♡.
- With a minimum hand East passes. West is declarer in a 2♡ contract.

The play
- North leads the ♣3, the partnership's suit. South should play the ♣J to the first trick, third hand high (only as high as necessary).
- Declarer has six losers and can eliminate a club loser by trumping a club in dummy.

Lesson Five: Watching Out for Entries

Exercise One.
1) Two: the ace and queen.
2) One, since you have only one low card in declarer's hand.
3) One: the 10, by playing the 3 from declarer's hand to dummy's 10.
4) Three: the king, 10 and 9. Play the low cards from declarer's hand and win them with the 10 and 9. The king also can be an entry by overtaking the queen or jack.
5) No entries. Declarer has no card lower than those in dummy.

Exercise Two
1) Lead toward the king and queen combination. You have two entries if the ace is on your left.
2) Lead toward the king, hoping for one entry if the ace is on your left.
3) Lead toward the queen, hoping the opponent on your left has the king.
4) Play the suit twice, driving out the ace and king. You then will have one entry to dummy.
5) Play the suit three times, giving up a trick and keeping the 9 in dummy. By that time, the opponents will have no cards left in the suit if the missing cards divided 3-2. Now you can lead your remaining low card to dummy's 9.

Exercise Three
1) Win the first trick with the king and then lead low toward the winners in declarer's hand.
2) Play the ace and then a low card from both hands (or vice versa), losing a trick. This leaves the king in dummy as an entry to the established winners.

3)   Win the first two tricks with the queen and jack. Then lead low to the ace and king in the dummy.
4)   Lose two tricks and win the third round with the ace in dummy.
5)   Win the first trick by overtaking the queen with a high card in dummy, the ace or the king.

Exercise Four
  1) One.   2) Two.   3) Two.
  4) Two.   5) None (use the ace).

Exercise Five
  1) 5.   2) 3.   3) 9.
  4) King.

Exercise Six
  1) 2♣.   2) 2♣.   3) 3 NT.
  4) 2♣.   5) 2♣.   6) Pass.

Exercise Seven
  1) 2♡.   2) 2♠.   3) 2◇.

Exercise Eight
  1) 4♡.   2) 3 NT.   3) 3♡.
  4) 2 NT.   5) 2♠.   6) 4♡.

Exercise Nine
  The bidding
  •   North opens 1 NT.
  •   The partnership belongs in game. South bids 2♣, the Stayman convention, to find out if there is a major-suit fit.
  •   North shows the four-card major suit by bidding 2♠.
  •   South now bids 4♠.
  •   The contract is 4♠. North is declarer.

  The play
  •   East leads the ◇ Q.
  •   Declarer has four losers, one too many. He can hold the trump suit to only one loser, if the suit breaks 3-2, by leading twice toward the king-queen combination. The heart suit provides the entries to dummy so declarer can lead toward his hand twice. When declarer first leads spades, West should play low rather than the ace. This is *second hand low*. Although it may not matter on this hand, it does make things more difficult for declarer.

Exercise Ten
  The bidding
  •   East opens 1 NT.
  •   West does not know what level or what denomination until he gets more information from the opener. West responds 2♣ (Stayman convention) to start to get some of the answers he needs.

213

- East rebids 2 ◇, announcing no four-card or longer major suit.
- West now bids 2 NT to invite East to game with maximum values.
- East doesn't have a maximum and passes. The contract is 2 NT. East is declarer.

The play
- The opening lead by South is the ♡Q.
- The spade suit offers the best chance to get the extra tricks declarer needs. Declarer tries to win the first trick with the high card from the short side, the queen.
- North can make things difficult by refusing to play his ♠A.
- Declarer should win the first heart trick in his hand with the ♡K and keep the ♡A in dummy so the spades won't be stranded once they are established.
- If declarer were to lead a club from either hand, the next defender would play *second hand low.* On this hand it would prevent declarer from easily establishing a club trick.

Exercise Eleven
The bidding
- South opens 1 NT.
- North does not know if the partnership belongs in a partscore or game. He is interested in finding a major-suit fit and so responds 2♣, the Stayman convention.
- South shows a four-card heart suit by bidding 2♡.
- North was not interested in hearts and so bids 2 NT inviting South to game in notrump.
- South has maximum values and carries on to 3 NT. The contract is 3 NT. South is declarer.

The play
- West leads the ◇6.
- Declarer needs to establish clubs to get the extra tricks needed to make the contract and must hope they divide 3-2.
- To make sure dummy has an entry to the established winners, South will duck the first or second club while he still has a low card left to get to the winners. He must lose a club trick sometime and makes sure it is early in the play.

Exercise Twelve
The bidding
- West opens 1 NT.
- East has enough for game and bids 2♣, the Stayman convention, to investigate a major-suit fit.
- West rebids 2♡.
- East bids 4♡.
- The contract is 4♡. West is declarer.

The play
- The opening lead by North is the ♣Q.

- Declarer has one too many losers but plans to discard a club on the ♠ Q. The problem is that there is no immediate entry to that card. An entry must be developed in diamonds. As soon as declarer gets the lead, he plays the ♠ A K and then leads a diamond to create an entry to dummy.
- Declarer cannot try to draw trumps because the opponents will get the lead in the process and will lead another club, getting rid of declarer's last club winner. If declarer then tries to create an entry in diamonds, the opponents will take the ◇ A and their club winner.

Lesson Six: Watching Out for the Opponents

Exercise One
1) The opponents have eight cards, which you expect to divide 5-3. If you take your ace on the third round, your right-hand opponent should have none left.
2) The opponents have seven cards, which you expect to divide 4-3. If you take your ace on the third round, the opponent on your right should have none left.
3) The opponents again have seven cards. When you take the ace on the second round, your right-hand opponent still will have one card left.
4) The opponents have eight cards, which you expect to divide 5–3. When you take the ace on the second round, your right-hand opponent still will have one card left.
5) The opponents have nine cards, which you expect to divide 5-4. When you take your ace on the second round, your right-hand opponent still will have two cards left.

Exercise Two
- You need nine tricks to make the contract and have nine, so there is no advantage to holding up your ace. Indeed, there may be a disadvantage — the opponents could shift to spades and defeat your contract.

Exercise Three
- In each example in Exercise One, the dangerous opponent is the one on your left — he has led the suit and presumably has the greatest length. However, when you cannot hold up enough times to exhaust your right-hand opponent of cards, then both opponents become dangerous.
- In the examples in this exercise, the opponent on your left is dangerous in the first case, and the opponent on your right in the second case. The dangerous opponent is the one who can lead a high card to trap your king.

Exercise Four
1) Play the ace and then lead the jack (or 10). If the opponent on your right plays the queen, play the king and you win all the tricks; otherwise, take the finesse. You do not mind if it loses to the opponent on your left.
2) Lead the 10 from dummy. If it is covered with the king, play the ace; otherwise, play low. You don't mind losing a trick to the opponent on your left, who is not dangerous.

3) Lead the jack from dummy and take the finesse if your right-hand opponent does not play the queen. You do not mind if your left-hand opponent wins a trick with the queen.

4) Lead low from dummy toward your hand and finesse the jack. Again, you do not mind losing a trick to the queen on your left. If the suit divides 3-2, you will take the rest of the tricks without letting the dangerous opponent win a trick.

5) If you try the finesse and it doesn't work, the dangerous opponent gets the lead. Play the ace in case your right-hand opponent has the singleton king. You do not mind if your left-hand opponent eventually wins a trick with the king, but you want to prevent your right-hand opponent from winning a trick whenever possible.

Exercise Five
1) You can see nine cards. If partner has only one (he will discard on the second round), you know declarer has three. You should wait until the third round to take your ace, leaving declarer with no low cards. If partner has two cards (following suit both times), you can win the second trick with the ace since declarer will have no low cards left.

2) Again you can see nine cards. If partner discards on the second round, you must hold up your ace until the third round since declarer started with three cards. If partner follows suit on the second round, you can safely win the trick on the second round since declarer has no low cards left.

Exercise Six
1) 2 NT.	2) 3 NT.	3) 2♠.

Exercise Seven
1) 4♡.	2) 3♠.	3) 3♣.
4) 3 NT.	5) Pass.	6) 3 NT.

Exercise Eight
1) 2 NT.	2) 3♠.	3) 3◇.

Exercise Nine
The bidding
- South opens 2 NT.
- The partnership belongs in game. With no major suit fit North responds 3 NT.
- Pass, pass, pass. 3 NT is the contract. South is declarer.

The play
- West leads the ♡K.
- Declarer can get the extra tricks he needs in the spade suit. The danger is that when the opponents get the lead they may take enough heart tricks to defeat the contract.
- South holds up the ♡A until the third round. Now East has no hearts left, and when East gets the lead with the ♠A, West's heart winners are stranded.

Exercise Ten

The bidding

- East opens 2♠.
- West cannot pass and shows a weak hand by responding 2 NT.
- East further describes his hand by bidding 3◇, knowing that the partnership is forced to a game contract.
- West cannot pass because game has not been reached. With no known Golden Fit, the best game contract looks like 3 NT.
- East has described his hand and should accept West's decision.
- The contract is 3 NT. West is declarer.

The play

- North makes the opening lead of the ♡4. South plays third hand high, the ♡A, and leads back a heart, returning his partner's suit.
- Declarer can seek extra tricks in the diamond suit by trying the finesse. If South wins a trick with the ◇K and still has a heart left to lead back to North, the opponents will take enough tricks to defeat the contract. When the heart is returned, declarer can hold up the ♡K for one round, and South then will have no hearts left if he wins a trick with the ◇K.

Exercise Eleven

The bidding

- North opens 3 NT.
- South passes. The contract is 3 NT. North is declarer.

The play

- The opening lead by East is the ♠J.
- The diamonds could provide all the tricks declarer needs. He plays the ◇K and ◇J, but West can make things difficult by refusing to take the ◇A.
- There is no sense in continuing diamonds — any established diamond winners would be stranded. Instead, declarer shifts to the club suit and establishes the remaining two tricks he needs by driving out the ♣A.

Exercise Twelve

The bidding

- West opens 2 NT.
- With enough strength for game and a six-card heart suit, East responds 4♡.
- Pass, pass, pass. The contract is 4♡. East is declarer.

The play

- The opening lead by South is the ♠J.
- Declarer has four losers and can afford only three. He could take the spade finesse, discard a loser on the diamonds or lead toward the ♣K.
- This looks like an opportunity to take a spade finesse, but declarer must beware. If the finesse loses, North can lead the ♣Q to trap East's ♣K, and declarer will lose four tricks. East should win the ♠A, draw trumps and throw a club loser on the extra diamond winner in dummy.

Lesson Seven: Managing the Trump Suit

Exercise One
1) Use the high cards; there are no losers even if the suit breaks 4–0. Expect the trumps to divide 3–1 and take three rounds to draw.
2) Use promotion, driving out the ace and king. Play three rounds, losing the first two and winning the third. Expect the trumps to divide 3–2.
3) Use the length of the suit. Draw three rounds, losing the first two. Trumps should divide 3–2.
4) Start in dummy and finesse against the king. If the finesse works, you will have no losers. Repeat the finesse and play a third round of trumps, expecting them to be 3–2.
5) Using length, there will be only one loser if the missing trumps divide 3–2. Play three rounds to draw all the trumps, losing the third round.

Exercise Two
1) There are three quick losers and no slow losers.
2) There are three quick losers and one slow loser.
3) There are four quick losers and no slow losers.

Exercise Three
1) Draw trumps right away because you do not need the trumps for any other purpose and you have only three losers, which you can afford.
2) Draw trumps because although you have to give up the lead to do so, your heart loser is slow. You then can discard your heart loser safely on the extra club winner.
3) You cannot play trumps right away because you would have to give up the lead — the opponents would take enough winners to defeat the contract. Eliminate one loser first by discarding it on the extra diamond winner and then give up the lead to draw trumps.

Exercise Four
1) With six missing cards you expect the side suit to divide 4–2. You would need two trumps to establish the suit.
2) You expect the side suit to divide 4–3 and you would need two trumps to establish the suit.
3) You expect the side suit to divide 4–2 and you would need three trumps to establish the suit.
4) You expect the side suit to divide 3–2 and you would need one trump to establish the suit.
5) You expect the side suit to divide 4–2 and you would need one trump to establish the suit.

Exercise Five
1) Play the 8 to show that you like the suit.
2) Play the 2 to show that you don't like the suit.

Exercise Six
1) Since you have 17 points, the combined total is between 33–35. Bid 6 NT.

2) You have 18 points, so the combined total is 34–36. Bid 6◇.
3) You have 22 points. The combined total is between 38 and 40. Bid 7NT.

Exercise Seven
1) You have 16 points. The combined total is between 32 and 34. Bid 4NT to invite a slam.
2) You have 16 points. The combined total is 32–34. Bid 5♣ to invite a slam.

Exercise Eight
1) You have two aces; respond 5♡.
2) You have no aces; respond 5♣.
3) You have one ace; respond 5◇.
4) You have three aces; respond 5♠.
5) You have four aces; respond 5♣.

Exercise Nine
The bidding
- East opens 1◇.
- West responds 3◇, showing 11–12 points.
- East, with a maximum hand of 21 points, bids slam in the Golden Fit, 6◇.
- Pass, pass, pass. The contract is 6◇. East is declarer.

The play
- The lead is the ♡Q by South. Dummy wins the first trick, and North encourages with the ♡8.
- Declarer cannot draw trumps first because he has too many quick losers and would have to give up the lead. Instead, he discards a heart loser on the extra spade winner in dummy by playing the ♠A and then overtaking the ♠Q with the ♠K to play the ♠J. Declarer then draws trumps.

Exercise Ten
The bidding
- South opens 1♣.
- North responds 1◇, bidding his suits up the line.
- South rebids 1♠.
- North has 18 dummy points and invites slam by bidding 5♠.
- With a minimum hand South declines the invitation by passing.
- The contract is 5♠. South is declarer.

The play
- West leads the ♡A, and East plays high, the ♡10 or ♡8, to encourage.
- Declarer can eliminate the two club losers by discarding one on the diamonds and trumping one in dummy. Declarer must be careful if the opponents play three rounds of hearts — he must trump with a high trump to avoid an overruff.

Exercise Eleven
The bidding
- West opens 1♠.
- East responds 2♠.

- West has a maximum hand and bids 4♠.
- Pass, pass, pass. The contract is 4♠. West is declarer.

The play
- North leads the ◇K. South encourages by playing the ◇9.
- Declarer can afford three losers and has only three losers as long as the missing trumps divide 3–2 and he does not lose control of the hand. Declarer should draw two rounds of trumps, leaving the last high trump outstanding, and then take his winners. If the last trump were drawn, the diamond suit would provide a source of winners for the defenders. Keeping a trump protects declarer from this.

Exercise Twelve
The bidding
- North opens 1♠.
- South has 20 points in support of partner's major suit, so there is enough combined strength for a slam. South responds 6♠.
- Pass, pass, pass. The contract is 6♠. North is declarer.

The play
- East leads the ◇A, and West discourages by playing the ◇2.
- Declarer has one loser too many. He can discard a club on a heart winner after establishing an extra trick by trumping the hearts. He needs three dummy entries to do this. Declarer can afford to draw trumps first since he doesn't have to give up the lead.

Lesson Eight: Putting it Together

Exercise One
1) Develop tricks by promotion and length. The missing cards should divide 3–2, allowing you to take three tricks after you drive out the ace and king.
2) The combination of a successful finesse against the king and a 3–2 division of the missing cards will provide five tricks.
3) By using the finesse against the ace, you can get tricks with both the king and queen. If the missing cards divide 4–2, you can set up a third trick by length. If they divide 3–3, you end up with four tricks.
4) A successful finesse followed by a 4–3 division of the missing cards will result in three tricks.
5) Leading the king to drive out the ace will promote one trick. A finesse against the missing jack will provide a second trick, and a 3–2 division of the missing cards will provide a third trick.

Exercise Two
1) Play the king and finesse the jack (eight ever). If the finesse works and the suit divides 3–2, you get all four tricks.
2) Play the ace and the king, hoping the queen will drop (nine never), giving you five tricks.
3) Try the finesse. If the suit divides very favorably, 3–3, you can take four tricks.

4) Lead toward the king and queen to try for two tricks.
5) Try the finesse by leading toward the king and then hope for a 3–2 division to give you two more tricks.

Exercise Three
   1) Clubs.   2) Clubs.   3) Diamonds.

Exercise Four
   1) Clubs.   2) Clubs.   3) Diamonds.

Exercise Five
   • You need four tricks to defeat the contract and you have only one. The extra three tricks could come from the club suit if your partner has the ♣A. Lead the ♣2.

Exercise Six
   1) 3♠.   2) 4♣ (or 3♣).   3) 1♡.

Exercise Seven
   1) Pass.   2) 4♡.   3) 3♠.

Exercise Eight
   1) 3♠.   2) Double.   3) Pass.

Exercise Nine
   The bidding
   • East opens 3♡.
   • South overcalls 3♠. West passes since East is showing a weak hand.
   • North has 11 dummy points and raises to 4♠. The contract is 4♠. South is declarer.

   The play
   • West leads the ♡4, partner's suit. After winning two heart tricks, East returns the ♣Q.
   • The key to taking enough tricks to make the contract is the diamond suit. First, declarer must try the diamond finesse and hope it works. He then wins the ◇A and trumps the next round of diamonds to establish two winners. When declarer draws trumps, he must end up in dummy with the ♠J so he can discard the club losers on the established diamonds.

Exercise Ten
   The bidding
   • South opens 3◇.
   • With 16 dummy points West doubles.
   • North doesn't have enough to bid. East has 11 points and shows his strength by jumping to 4♠. The contract is 4♠. East is declarer.

The play
- South leads the ◇ A and then shifts to the ♡ J, hoping partner has some tricks in the heart suit.
- Declarer has five losers (six if the clubs do not break 3-2). He plans to trump a diamond loser in dummy and handle the club suit by taking a finesse *(eight ever, nine never)*.

Exercise Eleven
The bidding
- South opens 3♣.
- West passes since an overcall at the three level would be dangerous with only 13 points. North passes.
- East doubles.
- West shows his 13 points by jumping to 4♠.
- Pass, pass, pass. The contract is 4♠. West is declarer.

The play
- North leads the ♣8, partner's suit.
- Declarer has two club losers and two diamond losers. One possibility is to take the diamond finesse. The other is to discard a diamond loser on dummy's last heart if the missing hearts divide 3-3. Declarer can combine both possibilities after drawing trumps. If the hearts do not break, he then can try the finesse.

Exercise Twelve
The bidding
- North opens 3♠.
- With 16 points South has enough to try a game contract and bids 4♠.
- Pass, pass, pass. The contract is 4♠. North is declarer.

The play
- East leads the ♡ J. If West wins the first trick, he would plan to defeat the contract by hoping partner had the ◇ A — then the defense could take two diamond tricks along with the ♠A.
- Declarer cannot afford to try the heart finesse. If it loses, the opponents will immediately take their two diamond tricks and defeat the contract. Instead, declarer wins the ♡ A and discards one of his losers on the extra club winner in dummy.

◆ *NOTES* ◆

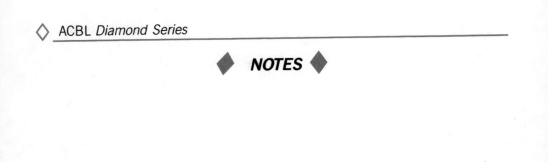

◆ *NOTES* ◆